THE WORD SET IN STONE

How Archaeology, Science, and History Back Up the Bible

DAVE ARMSTRONG

THE WORD SET IN STONE

How Archaeology, Science, and History Back Up the Bible

Published by Catholic Answers, Inc.
2020 Gillespie Way
El Cajon, California 92020
1-888-291-8000 orders
619-387-0042 fax
catholic.com

Printed in the United States of America

Cover design by ebooklaunch.com
Interior design by Russell Graphic Design

978-1-68357-319-7
978-1-68357-320-3 Kindle
978-1-68357-321-0 ePub

To my three grandchildren: Cecilia Joy, Estelle Marie, and Joseph Charles. May you always love and serve our wonderful Lord, who blessed Judy and me with you, and we pray that you will always attain your desires and dreams. Tons of love to you from "Papa" and "G'ma."

CONTENTS

ACKNOWLEDGMENTS

I'd like to express my admiration and appreciation for all the good folks at Catholic Answers—in particular, Jimmy Akin and Tim Staples. God bless *all* of you at "CA," and thanks for your dedication and service.

I would like especially to thank the editors of Catholic Answers. I've repeatedly worked with Todd Aglialoro since 2003, when he accepted (after a seven-year wait for me!) and edited my first published book, *A Biblical Defense of Catholicism*. I owe him a great debt of gratitude as an author and apologist. Drew Belsky, the content editor at Catholic Answers, with whom I worked directly on this volume, immeasurably improved it with his suggestions and insight. Editors are the unsung heroes who lie behind good books. I could never do all the hard work that they do (a labor of love), which makes me admire it all the more.

Lastly, I sincerely thank the atheists—particularly Jonathan M.S. Pearce—with whom I engaged in dialogue on archaeological matters for well over a year. This book would not exist were it not for them. My hope and prayer is that some of them will be *persuaded* (with the necessary aid of God's grace) by the evidence herein that they invariably demand to see.

INTRODUCTION

What we may call *biblical archaeology* flourished from the 1930s to the 1950s, under the leadership of the great Methodist archaeologist and polymath William Foxwell Albright (1891–1971) and Jewish archaeologist and rabbi Nelson Glueck (1900–1971). In his 1959 book, *Rivers in the Desert*, Glueck summed up his and Albright's high view of the Bible and their belief that archaeology strongly supports it:

> It may be stated categorically that no archaeological discovery has ever controverted a biblical reference. Scores of archaeological findings have been made that confirm, in clear outline or exact detail, historical statements in the Bible. By the same token, proper evaluation of biblical descriptions has often led to amazing discoveries.[1]

This is roughly what is now called a *biblical maximalist* position within archaeology. Arguably, today's most prominent maximalists are Scottish evangelical Protestant Egyptologist and archaeologist Kenneth A. Kitchen (b. 1932) and American archaeologist James K. Hoffmeier (b. 1951). Kitchen, though a firm defender of the historicity of the biblical accounts (and in that sense a "traditionalist"), doesn't, however, uncritically accept the overall outlook or (especially) the methodology of Albright and his cohorts, like G. Ernest Wright (1909–1974) and Cyrus Gordon (1908–2001). He rather bluntly made this clear:

> The treatments given here by me are not based on Albright, Gordon, or the vagaries of the little local (and

very parochial) United States problem of the long-deceased American Biblical Archaeology/Theology school.[2]

Biblical minimalism, on the other hand, has dominated the archaeology of Israel and the Near East since the 1970s. Prominent minimalist Thomas L. Thompson, professor of theology at the University of Copenhagen from 1993 to 2009, made this grandiose proclamation:

> The results of my own investigations, if they are for the most part acceptable, seem sufficient to require a complete reappraisal of the current position on the historical character of the patriarchal narratives.[3]

I want to deal with specific objective matters in relation to the text of the Bible that can be addressed by archaeology or other forms of science, starting with premises (for the most part) that Christians and non-Christians accept in common. I'm *not* trying to *prove biblical inspiration*. That's a much more involved and complex argument. What I'm doing is "defeating the defeaters" offered up by biblical skeptics, anti-theist atheists (who specialize in and constantly focus on criticizing the Bible, Christians, Christianity), and archaeological minimalists.

If they argue, for example, that a particular city *wasn't in existence* when the Bible says it was, then, in response, I seek archaeological data to prove or at least offer strong evidential support for the biblical view. This approach defends the Bible's accuracy.

Skeptical arguments against biblical accuracy are often incorrect and fallacious. In other words, if a skeptic contends, "The Bible is inaccurate history and therefore clearly not inspired because of errors a, b, c, d, e, and f," I will argue via secular science—most often, but not exclusively, archaeology—that supposed errors a, b, c, d, e, and f are actually *not* errors and can almost always be resolved in a way that is *consistent* with belief in biblical inspiration. If the Bible is inspired, then it should be historically accurate and not self-contradictory. It becomes, to put it another way, a strong *cumulative* argument.

This book deals with objective, historical issues that we can analyze through the means of scientific (mostly archaeological) analysis. It's what Christians are often asked to do: give solid evidence for what we believe.

The format throughout the chapters is simple:

1) Present the material to be considered.
2) Summarize how Bible skeptics, archaeological minimalists, or anti-theist atheists question and cast doubt upon this material.
3) Refute the skeptical concerns and give a positive case for the biblical data from secular research.

Lastly, I must add a clarifying note regarding miracles and the supernatural, a common theme in the Bible and in this book. In many of my chapters, I speculate about possible natural causes for events that Christians usually regard as purely miraculous. In doing so, I'm not being "theologically liberal" or hostile to the possibility of miracles. I fully believe in them—that they happened and that they still happen today.

God can and does do whatever he wants, and the process of salvation is supernatural. Moreover, many biblical events can hardly *not* be miraculous, such as the killing of the Egyptian firstborn, the raising of the dead, walking on water and through walls, and Balaam's talking donkey, not to mention transubstantiation, the Incarnation, the Virgin Birth, the atonement, Jesus' resurrection and ascension, and other directly "theological" miracles.

On the other hand, as a clear example of God's using non-miraculous means to accomplish his ends, we see that when he decided to judge his chosen people, he used the Assyrians to conquer the northern kingdom of Israel, in about 722–720 B.C. (Ezek. 23:1–10), and the Babylonians, led by Nebuchadnezzar, to conquer the southern kingdom of Judah (including the destruction of the Temple) in 586 B.C. (vv. 11–34). Then, not long afterward, God used the Persian king Cyrus to help the exiled Jews return to Jerusalem and rebuild their temple (2 Chron. 36:23; Ezra 6:3–5; Isa. 45:1–6,13). None of this was miraculous, but it was all in the "service" of God's expressly stated will.

Standard Christian understanding of God's sovereignty holds that God's providence is large and complex enough to include natural events and extraordinary timing (as a function of his omniscience and being outside time) for the accomplishment of his purposes.

For example, a meteor—that God utilized for judgment—may have destroyed Sodom. If that was indeed the case, God knew that a meteor would be approaching soon and used the natural event in conjunction with his warning about the judgment. It was still his will to judge for sin. How he did it is a separate question.

Other times, it may be a *mixture* of the natural and miraculous. In these cases, I throw out interesting possibilities or theories, not necessarily taking a position. I never claim that things *must* have been the way I suggest.

As another example, let's consider the incident of God providing quails for the wandering Hebrews to eat in the desert. As always, God could have worked through outright miracles if he so chose (he could have created a million quails on the spot and sent them down to the complaining Hebrews), or he could have marvelously arranged in his providence for lots of quails to appear right at the time when he said they would appear. Both are entirely in his capability, and each is an extraordinary event, showing his power (omnipotence) and his omniscience and sovereignty over nature. He knew from all eternity that the ancient Israelites would complain in the wilderness about not having meat (longing for their wonderful time of slavery in Egypt), and he knew (if the natural explanation is what actually happened) that quail would migrate across their path at precisely the time this murmuring came about.

I'm not opting for any of these scenarios. I'm simply saying that it is entirely possible (and no less glorying to God) that a natural explanation (that can be explored through our knowledge of bird migration) could account for the abundance of quail. If that is the case, the inspired, infallible Bible would again be accurate in reporting what happened (as it always is).

A theologically liberal or skeptical mentality does exist, whereby every miracle in the Bible is "explained away" by natural processes because of disbelief in *all* miracles from the outset. I detest that, and it's not at all my own position.

Rather, mine is a view that fully accepts the possibility and factuality of actual divine, supernatural miracles, while at the same time recognizing that God's omniscience and omnipotence, providence and sovereignty are such that he can and does *also* incorporate natural events into his divine plans for the human race and the accomplishment of his will.

CHRONOLOGY

Near-Eastern Archaeological Periods

Bronze Age	(3300 B.C.–1200 B.C.):
Early Bronze Age I	3300 B.C.–3000 B.C.
Early Bronze Age II	3000 B.C.–2700 B.C.
Early Bronze Age III	2700 B.C.–2200 B.C.
Early Bronze Age IV	2200 B.C.–2000 B.C.
Middle Bronze Age I	2000 B.C.–1750 B.C.
Middle Bronze Age II	1750 B.C.–1650 B.C.
Middle Bronze Age III	1650 B.C.–1550 B.C.
Late Bronze Age I	1550 B.C.–1400 B.C.
Late Bronze Age IIA	1400 B.C.–1300 B.C.
Late Bronze Age IIB	1300 B.C.–1200 B.C.
Iron Age	(1200 B.C.–586 B.C.):
Iron Age I A	1200 B.C.–1150 B.C.
Iron Age I B	1150 B.C.–1000 B.C.
Iron Age II A	1000 B.C.–900 B.C.
Iron Age II B	900 B.C.–700 B.C.
Iron Age II C	700 B.C.–586 B.C.

Timeline of the Patriarchs

Following the scholarly maximalist timeline of Kenneth Kitchen and others (none "fundamentalists") who regard the Bible as historically accurate, here are the approximate dates of early biblical figures and patriarchs and events. I will be provisionally utilizing these dates in my treatment of these figures and events in this book.[4]

Noah and the Flood—c. 2900 B.C.

Patriarchs—c. 1900–1600 B.C.
("2000–1500 at the outermost limits")

Abraham—born c. 1880–1860 B.C.

Isaac—born c. 1850–1820 B.C.

Jacob—born c. 1775 B.C.

Joseph—born c. 1737–1717 B.C. The Bible states that he was seventeen when sold into slavery (Gen. 37:2).

Moses—c. 1340 or 1330–c. 1220 or 1210 B.C., extrapolating from Kitchen's date for the Exodus

Exodus from Egypt—c. 1260–1250 B.C.

Israeli "Conquest" of Canaan—c. 1220 or 1210–c. 1170 or 1160 B.C.

1

SEARCH FOR THE GARDEN OF EDEN

And the Lord God planted a garden in Eden, in the east.

—GENESIS 2:8

The Christian apologist's task with regard to the Garden of Eden is to determine whether the story goes beyond *mere mythology* and can be verified archaeologically or by other scientific criteria. Genesis—even in its earliest chapters about Eden—does undeniably contain several verifiable elements, which can be remarkably confirmed in various ways.

We'll be analyzing, for example, evidence for the four rivers mentioned in Genesis 2:10–14. The Tigris and Euphrates are well known and have been identified by those names since ancient times, so what primarily remains to be examined are the *Pishon* and *Gihon* rivers.

Additionally, two places and three minerals allegedly found in one of them are mentioned in the story of the Garden of Eden: *Havilah*, in which can be found gold and "bdellium and onyx stone," and also the region of *Cush*.

True or pure mythology usually doesn't reference verifiable historical events or places, or if it does, it's only in a cursory or superficial manner. Historical accounts, on the other hand, make statements that can be objectively confirmed or disconfirmed by science. I contend that several aspects in the account of the Garden of Eden in the book of Genesis are indeed historically verifiable to a significant extent.

Carol A. Hill is a Presbyterian geologist, who addressed the question of whether Eden, as described in the Bible, was an actual place that can be located through an analysis of the story in Genesis and its connection to geography and geology. She ponders the topic in her article, "The Garden of Eden: A Modern Landscape."[5]

Genesis 2:10–14 reads,

> A river flowed out of *Eden* to water the garden, and there it divided and became *four rivers*. The name of the first is *Pishon*; it is the one which flows around the whole land of *Havilah*, where there is *gold*; and the *gold* of that land is good; *bdellium* and *onyx stone* are there. The name of the second river is *Gihon*; it is the one which flows around the whole land of *Cush*. And the name of the third river is *Tigris*, which flows east of Assyria. And the fourth river is the *Euphrates*.

Hill's study of this fascinating topic upholds the notion that the Bible is trustworthy and accurate, insofar as it can be tested by secular fields of knowledge—even as early as Genesis 2. Adam and Eve were real people, referred to as such in the New Testament. The Fall and original sin are also real, even if the Bible may have used symbolic language (the trees and the forbidden fruit) to represent these acts that happened in history. Hill stated in summary, before providing various scientific reasons for her views,

> The Garden of Eden was a historical place. One reason for this belief is because the Bible gives its geographic location: two of the names of the four rivers mentioned in Genesis 2:10–14 have been preserved from biblical times. According to the Bible, the Garden of Eden was located somewhere in southern Iraq where the Euphrates and Hiddekel (Tigris) Rivers flowed into the head of the Persian Gulf—that is, they flowed on a modern landscape that is still recognizable today.

1. All four rivers were historical rivers, not mythical rivers made up in the mind of the Genesis writer.
2. All four rivers flowed into the Persian Gulf in the land of Mesopotamia. They were not rivers that flowed in other parts of the world as has been suggested by various authors.
3. All four rivers (or now-dry riverbeds) of Genesis are *still there*; that is, the Genesis writer identified a modern landscape, one which is almost identical to that which still exists in the Iraq-Arabia-Iran area today.

Havilah is mentioned twice elsewhere in Genesis, referring to two different people: a son of Cush (10:7) and a son of Joktan (v. 29). Often in the Old Testament, lands are named after persons. Havilah is often regarded by biblical scholars as referring broadly to Arabia, rather than particular places, and Joktan as a sort of chief of Arabian tribes.

The *International Standard Bible Encyclopedia* notes that the Greek geographer and historian Strabo (c. 64 B.C.–c. A.D. 24) suggested "a district on the Arabian shore of the Persian Gulf" but that no "exact identification" has been made.[6]

Hill describes what we can find out about the Pishon River, according to scientific analysis:

There is no river flowing from the western mountains of Saudi Arabia down to the head of the Persian Gulf . . . but there is evidence that such a river did flow there sometime in the past. . . . It was . . . at about 2000 B.C., that the climate turned hyper-arid and the rivers of Arabia dried up.

In his article, "The River Runs Dry,"[7] James Sauer describes how satellite images have detected an underground riverbed along the Wadi al Batin (wadi means the same thing as arroyo, a dry riverbed). Sauer identified this river as the Pishon River of the Bible, a river which flowed at a time when the climate was wetter than it is today.

The Wadi al Batin/Wadi Rimah system drains some 43,400 square miles of Saudi Arabia and Kuwait. The now-dry Wadi al Batin enters the Persian Gulf at Umm Qasr in Kuwait, but in the past the Pishon entered the Gulf north of Umm Qasr, in the Euphrates-Tigris river basin. The evidence for this is a triangular, fan-shaped, delta plain of cobbles and pebbles in the Dibdibah area, which has its apex near Al Qaysumah and which extends northward toward the Euphrates. . . .

This is where the satellite photos come in. These photos indicate that the Wadi al Batin continues to the southwest, beneath the sand, and emerges as the Wadi Rimah (that is, both wadis were part of the same river system in the past, before being covered by sand dunes). About eighty miles further in the upstream direction, the Wadi Rimah bifurcates into the Wadi Qahd on the northwest, and the Wadi al Jarir on the southwest. The Wadi al Jarir continues up gradient to the area of the Mahd adh Dhahab gold mine exactly as the Bible says: "The River Pishon encompasses the whole land of Havilah, where there is gold" (Gen. 2:11). Sauer remarked in his article: "This implies extraordinary memory on the part of the biblical

> authors, since the river dried up between about 3500 and 2000 B.C."

The Evangelical Protestant flagship magazine *Christianity Today* took note of this theory in its article, "Do Photos Evidence Lost Edenic River?"

> Former NASA scientist Farouk El-Baz was assessing environmental damage to the Kuwaiti desert after the Persian Gulf War when he first noticed smooth pebbles of basalt and granite that looked out of place amid the local limestone.
>
> "We can find these rocks in abundance only in the western part of the Arabian Peninsula," he said, "right on the east side of the Red Sea." El-Baz is now director of the Boston University Center for Remote Sensing. His satellite photo analysis revealed a dry channel connecting the western mountains with Kuwait, partially covered by sand dunes. . . .
>
> The Hijaz Mountains, from which spring this "Arabian River," do produce gold, and the river passes a city called Hadiyah. . . .
>
> El-Baz says the climate in the Arabian Desert and other nearby areas was much wetter about 5,000 years ago. He believes some of the river's flow may still be in an underground aquifer and available for irrigation.[8]

Hill closely scrutinizes the minerals mentioned in Genesis 2:10–14. First of all, we know quite a bit about the presence of gold and gold mines in Arabia, in conjunction with the Pishon River:

> Mahd adh Dhahab (literally meaning "cradle of gold")[9]

> was the largest and one of the richest gold mines of the ancient world. It is believed to be the fabled "Ophir" of the Bible, the source of King Solomon's gold. (Ophir was another one of Joktan's sons; Gen. 10:29.) . . . Based on the number of ancient mine tailings (refuse left over after the ore is treated), geologists have estimated that the Mahd adh Dhahab mine produced more than 950,000 ounces (about 30 metric tons) of gold in antiquity. . . .
>
> Gold suddenly appears in the archaeological record of Mesopotamia in the Uruk Period (about 3500 B.C.). . . . A small variety of gold artifacts have been recovered in southern Iraq that date to about 3500 B.C.; for example, in Uruk those found in the layers underlying the White Temple. . . .
>
> Where did these ancient Mesopotamian peoples get all of the gold and silver that they used for their jewelry and temples? They must have had established trade relations with places where these metals were being mined, since Mesopotamia itself is devoid of metal deposits. The nearest gold-silver mine to Ur and Uruk is Mahd adh Dhahab.

As to the other minerals mentioned in the text, Hill speculates in a fascinating way for many paragraphs about the "onyx stone" (Gen. 2:12) but comes to no firm conclusions. Still, there is no compelling reason to believe that the Bible is inaccurate regarding this reference. She details several plausible possibilities.

In the case of bdellium, however, she thinks the evidence is much more clear cut:

> Bdellium species known from Arabia are *Commiphora mukul* and *Commiphora schimperi.*

> All of these kinds of gum-resins (frankincense, myrrh, and bdellium) were used in the ancient Middle East for religious (incense), cosmetic (perfume), and medicinal purposes. . . .
>
> The trees from which myrrh and bdellium are extracted grew during ancient times only in southern Arabia and northern Somaliland.

Thus, the Bible is accurate in Genesis 2. Bdellium grew in ancient times *only* in the place associated with it in the Bible (Havilah, in Arabia) and one other place not far away (Somalia, only about 150 miles across the Gulf of Aden). Even if it *were* found in many other places, the Bible is still correct in associating it with Arabia. It simply states that it was there (in Havilah). Things like this, having to do with scientifically or historically and archaeologically verifiable data, multiplied scores and scores of times, tend to give those familiar with them a strong sense that the Bible is historically trustworthy.

What remains is to ponder Cush and the Gihon River. Hill wrote about the former,

> The Kassites (or *kaöšû*) people lived to the east of Mesopotamia in the Old Babylonian Period (1800–1600 B.C.). Before then, however, this area was known as the land of Elam or Susiana, where the inhabitants of the Plain of Susa lived. If the Cush intended by the Hebrew word *kush* is the territory of the Kassites, then the river referred to in Gen. 10:13 must have come from the east of Mesopotamia, or what today is western Iran.

The notes for the New American Bible state, "*The land of Cush* here and in 10,8 is not Ethiopia (Nubia) as elsewhere, but the region of the Kassites, east of Mesopotamia."[10] The *International Standard Bible Encyclopedia* holds that Cush was "probably a province East of the Tigris." [11]

Kevin Burrell, assistant professor of Old Testament at Burman University, Canada, stated in his book about the Cushites,

> Whereas outside the book of Genesis Cush comes to be identified almost exclusively with Nubia, it will be demonstrated here that for the Genesis author, Cush as a reference to a geographical region denotes not African Cush, but rather a primordial land far to the east. [12]

Burrell, however, "fundamentally" departs from the view of "identifying the Genesis primeval Cush with the Kassites." He equates it, rather, with ancient Meluhha, "also known as the 'eastern' Ethiopia in classical sources, which this study maintains holds the key to understanding the Cush of the Genesis primordial account." He in turn defines Meluhha, in present-day terms, as "Iran, Pakistan (especially along the Baluchistan), the Persian Gulf and the Indus civilization as the most probable geography of the 'black land' of Meluhha."

The McClintock and Strong Biblical Cyclopedia provides more valuable insight about the confusing use of "Ethiopia": "The ancients, in short, with the usual looseness of their geographical definitions, understood by Ethiopia the extreme south in all the earth's longitude."[13]

Hill continues,

> The major rivers that run through western Iran (formerly Susiana) are the Karkheh and the Karun. The Karun is by far the longer of the two, and Iran's only navigable river.

> These two rivers provided a route of communication between the heart of Susiana and southernmost Mesopotamia. In the third millennium B.C., caravan routes along both rivers went through Susiana to Sumer and Akkad. . . .
>
> Following this reasoning, the most likely candidate for the biblical Gihon River is the Karun. The word "compasseth" in Hebrew means "to revolve, surround, or border, or to pursue a roundabout course, to twist and turn." That is exactly what the Karun River does. It is a meandering river with great bends. Its course is 510 miles long, but its distance (in a bird's-eye view) is only 175 miles long.

Our bottom-line task with regard to the Gihon River is to first identify it and then to better understand why Genesis describes it as flowing "around the whole land of Cush." We have to find a river that flows to the area of the confluence of the Tigris and Euphrates rivers. The Karun River seems to fit that bill but is confined to present-day Iran. There are still mysteries and disagreements in this area of inquiry (to be expected), but the above proposals may provide serious food for thought.

Hill summarizes her argument and evidence concerning the location of the Garden of Eden:

> The Bible locates the Garden of Eden at the confluence of the four rivers of ancient Mesopotamia. The Bible correctly identifies the Pishon River as draining the land of Havilah (Arabia), from whence came gold, bdellium, and onyx stone. The Bible also correctly identifies the Euphrates and Tigris, both of which are modern rivers which drain approximately the same area of Mesopotamia as they did in ancient times. The Gihon, while not positively identified, is probably the Karun (and/or Karkheh),

> which "encompasses" (winds around) the whole land of Cush (western Iran). Thus, the Bible locates the Garden of Eden as somewhere near where the head of the Persian Gulf may have existed some 6,000 years ago—that is, on a modern landscape similar to that which exists in southern Iraq today.

I found a map[14] that shows the confluence of the four rivers (one now dry) that Carol Hill proposes. The Persian Gulf expanded and receded in size and depth several times throughout history, as a geological article on that topic[15] indicates. It may be that the Garden of Eden was in a location now under the waters of the northern Persian Gulf,[16] or not far north of the present shore. In any event, the landscape and environment—probably of *any* location we might select—have vastly changed, as have many regions, particularly in the Near East.

I'm not as interested in *pinpointing* Eden as I am in showing that the biblical indicators of location are of a sort that can be scientifically analyzed. That's the exciting aspect of all this. These place names and descriptions of things associated with them, like gold and onyx, are not mere myth. We get the general idea of location from two known named rivers (that no one disputes)—the Tigris and Euphrates—and the other two candidates presented above have plausible cases to be made for them.

The Garden of Eden was, therefore—for those who regard the Bible as historically trustworthy and inspired by God—corroborated by scientific backing, clearly in the general region near where the Tigris and Euphrates rivers meet.

2

NOAH'S FLOOD: HOW IT COULD HAVE HAPPENED

And God saw the earth, and behold, it was corrupt;
for all flesh had corrupted their way upon the earth. And God
said to Noah, "I have determined to make an end of all flesh;
for the earth is filled with violence through them; behold,
I will destroy them with the earth."

—GENESIS 6:12–13

In this chapter, I attempt to gather up many sorts of scientific evidences and corresponding data from historiography, archaeology, and the Bible in favor of one particular hypothesis of a local Flood in ancient Mesopotamia (present-day Iraq), which occurred around 2900 B.C.

Many Christians (and biblical skeptics and atheists alike) assume that the biblical account of Noah's Flood, or the Deluge, can be interpreted *only* as referring to a global catastrophic event in which the entire world was literally covered with an amount of water so deep that every mountain was covered—including Mt. Everest, at an elevation of 29,032 feet, or 5.5 miles above sea level.

It's beyond my purview to survey the universal Deluge view. It's held (and has been historically held) by many sincere and pious and educated Christians, for many reasons that they can and do provide, and we shouldn't deride them. Suffice it to say, with all due respect to those who disagree, that the consensus of Catholic and Protestant biblical scholars for well over a century has been in favor of a local Flood. You don't need to be a biblical skeptic or theological liberal to take this tack.

Frankly, I have no patience at all for theological liberalism and (from my perspective) heterodoxy, and my own position flows from a strong adherence to the inspiration and infallibility of the Bible as divine revelation, and from a constant desire to employ traditional exegetical and hermeneutical analysis, backed up by believing Christian scholars who (largely) hold the same positions regarding the nature of the Bible.

The *Catholic Encyclopedia* article "Deluge" was written in 1908, so it's not a *recent* development in scholarly biblical thinking. And it states,

> There are . . . certain scientific considerations which oppose the view that the Flood was geographically universal. Not that science opposes any difficulty insuperable to the power of God; but it draws attention to a number of most extraordinary, if not miraculous phenomena involved in the admission of a geographically universal Deluge. . . .
>
> The water required by the biblical Flood, if it be universal, amounts to about 4,600,000,000 cubic kilometers. Now, a forty days' rain, ten times more copious than the most violent rainfall known to us, will raise the level of the sea only about 800 meters; since the height to be attained is about 9,000 meters, there is still a gap to be filled

> by unknown sources amounting to a height of more than 8,000 meters, in order to raise the water to the level of the greatest mountains.[17]

Baptist theologian Bernard Ramm discussed the question of frequent biblical non-literal, hyperbolic (exaggerated) language:

> Fifteen minutes with a Bible concordance will reveal many instances in which universality of language is used but only a partial quantity is meant. All does not mean every last one in all of its usages. Psalm 22:17 reads: "I may tell all my bones," and hardly means that every single bone of the skeleton stood out prominently. John 4:39 cannot mean that Jesus completely recited the woman's biography. Matthew 3:5 cannot mean that every single individual from Judea and Jordan came to John the Baptist. There are cases where all means all, and every means every, but the context tells us where this is intended. Thus, special reference may be made to Paul's statement in Romans about the universality of sin, yet even that "all" excludes Jesus Christ.
>
> The universality of the Flood simply means the universality of the experience of the man who reported it. When God tells the Israelites he will put the fear of them upon the people under the whole heaven, it refers to all the peoples known to the Israelites (Deut. 2:25). When Genesis 41:57 states that all countries came to Egypt to buy grain, it can only mean all peoples known to the Egyptians. Ahab certainly did not look for Elijah in every country of the earth even though the text says he looked for Elijah so thoroughly that he skipped no nation or kingdom (1 Kings 18:10). From the vantage point of

> the observer of the Flood all mountains were covered, and all flesh died.[18]

But what about Noah himself? Is there any evidence that he was a real person? If so, where and when did he live, and how much can we find out about him and his surrounding culture?

Carol Hill has done wonderful and fascinating work in this respect, in her article "A Time and a Place for Noah."[19] She makes her case based on many aspects that can be deduced from historical and archaeological evidence, including

> Sumerian cuneiform texts known as the "Gilgamesh Epic" and "King List." Both documents attest to a great flood survived by Ziusudra (or Utnapiötim or Atra-hasis, alternate Babylonian names for Noah), who was the "king" of the ancient city of Shuruppak in Mesopotamia. Gilgamesh was the fifth king of the first dynasty of Uruk following the great Flood, and is known to have been a real person who reigned in Mesopotamia around 2650 B.C. . . .
>
> The Sumerian King List mentions ten antediluvian kings, with Ziusudra being the "king" who lived in Shuruppak just before the flood. The mention of Shuruppak is important because the ancient ruins of this city still exist today as the archaeological mound of Fara (also sometimes spelled Farah), which has been partially excavated in modern times. On the basis of pottery types, cylinder seals, and proto-cuneiform tablets found at Fara, it is known that this city was founded in the Jemdet Nasr Period, and that it was a significant urban center during this time. The Jemdet (also sometimes spelled "Jamdat" or "-amdat") Nasr Period dates from ca. 3100–2900 B.C.

> At Shuruppak (and also at Uruk), the last Jemdet Nasr remains are separated from the subsequent Early Dynastic I Period by clean, water-lain clay deposited by a flood. This flood clay is nearly five feet thick at Uruk, and two feet thick at Fara. If these deposits do represent Noah's Flood and the division between antediluvian and postdiluvian societies, then a date (the end of Jemdet Nasr time) is established for this historical event. . . .
>
> From the above archaeological evidence, it can be deduced that the Old Testament Genesis Flood most likely happened ca. 2900 B.C. ± 100 years.

The Bible states that Noah's ark was built of gopher wood, covered with pitch (that is, bitumen, asphalt, or tar). Neither was available in the region of Shuruppak and so had to be imported. How did Noah obtain them? Hill explains:

> The bitumen would not have been that difficult to obtain. The center of bitumen production in Mesopotamia was (and still is) at Hit, located along the Euphrates River about eighty miles west of Baghdad. Bitumen at Hit occurs in "lakes" where lines of hot springs are welling up along deep faults. Even today, bitumen is packaged into reed baskets at Hit and floated down the Euphrates in boats. Bitumen has been used in southern Mesopotamia since the Ubaid Period, but the bitumen industry only became well established by ca. 3000 B.C.—or by the time that Noah lived.
>
> Obtaining high-quality wood would have been a far more difficult task, as timber would have had to have been imported from a great distance. Precious wood is known to have come into Mesopotamia from three main sources—from Elam (now western Iran), from

> the Amanus-Lebanon Mountains (now Syria), and from Anatolia (now western Turkey, near Carchemish). Sumerian trade was based mostly on shipping along the Euphrates River, and large numbers and types of boats are mentioned in Sumerian texts. Exactly what kind of timber was used for building the ark is not known, as "gopher wood" is an "old," pre-Hebraic word that has not been successfully translated by scholars, so that its botanical identification is uncertain. Probably the "gopher wood" of Genesis 6:14 was either cedar or cypress, with cedar perhaps being the best candidate, since cedar is a straight wood, ideal in the making of large boats.
>
> It is known that trade had already become established with the Amanus Mountains by Jemdet Nasr time, and the transportation of cedar trunks up to 100 feet long from that area has been documented. The Lebanon-Amanus region was a rich source of timber to Mesopotamia in ancient times, and many Mesopotamian kings sent expeditions to fetch its famous cedars.

Hill does, however, acknowledge a "major difficulty" based on archaeology and other considerations: "the stated size of the ark in Genesis 6:15." Difficulties of wooden boats of about 300 feet in length or more are well known to those familiar with large ships and their engineering. Anthony Slaven, professor of business history at the University of Glasgow, wrote about this, maintaining that "size . . . presented problems for wooden ships. Once the keel exceeded 300 feet there was a loss of rigidity."[20]

One major reason for this difficulty is that the longest practical single beam of wood is about 263 feet long. Thus, a boat longer than that necessarily requires seams between beams. But in the water (especially large bodies of water with waves), such a boat would be subject to "hogging and sagging,"[21] meaning an upward or downward curving, respectively, in the middle of a beam, which in turn causes a loss of watertight characteristics. Wooden boats over 300 feet have *not* been successful at all, which is why, historically, we don't observe any that are longer than that.

Perhaps for this reason, none of the three existing ark replicas (Grant Co., Kentucky: 510 feet long; Hong Kong: 450 feet; Dordrecht, Netherlands: 450 long) actually floats on water (with or without a load of animals, and pitch to keep the water out). The last mentioned is technically in the water but isn't free-floating. It's upheld by twenty-one steel barges.

In short, as Hill explains in agreement with such analysis, "the size of wooden ships is limited to about 300 feet due to their inherent-strength instability above this size." So how, assuming an 18-inch cubit (interpreting the biblical account literally), can we reconcile the seaworthiness of a wooden boat with dimensions of about 450 feet long, 75 feet wide, and 45 feet deep? Hill proposes two "possible explanations":

> First, it may be that the dimensions of the ark given in Genesis 6 are of symbolic nature, the symbolism of which is now lost in antiquity. Second, it may be that the dimensions of the ark were never converted from a sexagesimal system into a decimal-based numbering system. If one arbitrarily divides the ark dimensions by either ten or six, one comes up with a size more compatible with boats known to have existed in Jemdet Nasr time. This is not to say that the Bible is wrong. It is to suggest that the *autograph* (original) documents were correct, but that the original numbers of Genesis 6 are not part of a numerical system that we recognize today.

This is not mere idle speculation or special pleading. Hill examines the complex and still not fully understood numbering system of the ancient Sumerians:

> Proto-Sumerian inscriptions, such as those found at Uruk, used a sexagesimal numbering system. Along with the numbers 60 and 10 on which the sexagesimal system is based, the number 6 was also used in a special "bi-sexagesimal" system. Examples of the Mesopotamian sexagesimal system are still with us in the form of the 60-minute hour, the 60-second minute, and the 360° circle, with 60-minute degrees and 60-second minutes. The Sumerian sexagesimal numbering system (counting in 10s or 60s) is also a precursor of our own decimal system (counting only in 10s).
>
> It has recently (in the 1970s and 1980s) been discovered that the Mesopotamian numbering system is not as straightforward as previously supposed. It is now known that the arithmetic values of the numeral cuneiform signs were changeable depending on the context involved. For example, even in a single text, the same Sumerian cuneiform number sign can be read either as ten or six, depending on the context. This discovery warrants the utmost caution in interpreting the true arithmetic value of numbers presented in the early chapters of Genesis, which were probably ultimately derived from the Mesopotamian cuneiform.
>
> The ancient Semitic scribes who first wrote down the story of Genesis probably computed in sexagesimal units, since this was the system used at that time.

We mustn't succumb to what the famous Anglican apologist C.S. Lewis described as "chronological snobbery." Just because events purported to have happened some 5,000 years ago may seem, *prima facie*, implausible or even impossible to us, that doesn't preclude rational analysis and possible explanations (some of which I am presently proposing).

In short, experience and science strongly suggest the almost certain unseaworthiness of a 450-foot-long wooden boat built in c. 2900 B.C. But if we have a plausible explanation for a non-literal biblical reading of the ark's actual dimensions (i.e., "literal" meaning our current numbering system), it seems—all things considered—that we should incorporate that factor into our analysis.

I move on now to various scientific considerations having to do with a proposed Flood in the Mesopotamian floodplain—how it could endure over the time mentioned in the Bible, considerations of draining, and other aspects able to be scrutinized in light of modern science and historical parallels.

Basically, the largest task in this scenario is to get to a Flood as described in the Bible in its duration and scope—even if construed as a local phenomenon—that can sustain itself for some eleven to twelve months without, in this instance, draining into the Persian Gulf, the one direction in relation to the Mesopotamian floodplain (unlike the other three) with no barriers or elevation gain.

Carol Hill hits a home run in this respect in her article "Qualitative Hydrology of Noah's Flood."[22] She discusses local weather patterns, including what are called "100-year" or "1,000-year" precipitation events:

> An example of this happening was in 1969 over the Jordan basin, when cyclonic circulation patterns persisted for 24 days, and rain and snow fell for almost two months. The stalling of this front, over a period of 80 hours, brought an average of 75 inches (300 mm) of rain to the

> basin—the highest amount in 150 years—and caused considerable flooding.

She alludes to large Mississippi River floods in 1927 (15 inches of rain in 18 hours and waters starting to recede only after two months) and 1973 (over three months of flooding in some areas). Then she compares known weather patterns with the biblical account of the Flood:

> If the "second month, seventeenth day of the month" of Genesis 7:11 is interpreted as denoting the season of the year when the Flood started . . . then the Bible is in remarkable accordance with the weather patterns that actually exist (and have existed) in the Mesopotamian area. If one compares the tropical calendar of today with the sidereal calendar of the Mesopotamians for the years around 2900 B.C., then this would place the "second month, seventeenth day" in about the middle of March when meteorological conditions bring the most abundant rain to the Mesopotamian region. Genesis 7:12 says that it was a "heavy" rain which fell upon the earth (land) for forty days and forty nights, and this is the type of rainfall (continuous downpour) that can result from the activity of maritime air masses characteristic of this season. . . .
>
> The Bible (Gen. 8:1) also records that sometime before the 150 days of Genesis 7:24 (five months or about in the middle of August, assuming a middle-of-March start date for the Flood), a wind passed over the earth causing the waters to subside. This wind could correspond with the northwest shamal wind that blows almost continuously during the summer months. . . . Thus, the Genesis account accurately records the actual meteorological situation that exists (and has existed) in Iraq (Mesopotamia). . . .

> The Mesopotamian alluvial plain is one of the flattest places on earth. The surface of the plain 240 miles (400 km) inland from the head of the Gulf is less than 60 feet (20 m) above sea level, and at An Nasiriyah, the water level of the Euphrates is only eight feet (<3 m) above sea level, even though the river still has to cover a distance of more than 95 miles to Basra. . . . Before any dams were built (before ~1920), about two thirds of the whole area of southern Mesopotamia (Babylonia) could be underwater in the flood season from March to August.

She mentions snow melt as a factor in prolonged floods as well and the similarity between the Tigris and the Mississippi in this regard: with large floods often occurring in spring, with melting snow. Springs played a role as well, according to the text (Gen. 7:11, 8:2):

> Springs exist all over Mesopotamia and surrounding highlands . . . near ancient Sippar, Babylon, and Kish; those in the vicinity of Hit; and those in the Jezira desert region between Baghdad and Mosul.

The entire article is fascinating and should be read by anyone interested in Noah's Flood, and particularly this hypothesis as to its location and extent.

Carol's husband is physicist Alan E. Hill, distinguished scientist of the Quantum Physics Institute at Texas A&M University. He has spent some forty years inventing and developing lasers of the *Star Wars* variety. In the early 1960s, while at the University of Michigan, Alan was the first person to discover nonlinear optics. In his article, "Quantitative Hydrology of Noah's Flood," Alan rhetorically asks,

> (1) How could the flood waters, if constrained to a local region, have stayed backed up for 150 days, and (2) How could the ark have traveled against the current, landing in the mountains of Ararat, instead of floating with the current down to the Persian Gulf?[23]

He maintains that, using the data on rain and duration in the Bible, a local Flood in the Mesopotamian plain of about a forty-foot depth is not only possible, but plausible.

The region of Mesopotamia is essentially a huge bowl, 600 miles long from the Persian Gulf to the northwest. Steep escarpments that rise dramatically up to about 3,300 feet set the boundaries of the bowl to the north and the east. More gradually rising terrain to the south and west attains 1,300 feet.

But why wouldn't the water simply quickly drain out to the Persian Gulf? This is what atheists and universal Flood adherents alike find puzzling.

The rate at which floodwaters including those caused by storm surges off the Persian Gulf would empty back into the same Gulf is dependent upon the slope of the surrounding land. Over 400 miles northwest of Ur (which was on the Persian Gulf shore in Noah's time), the Tigris and Euphrates rivers drop only 300 feet in elevation—a grade of only about 0.01 percent. These conditions would have caused a very slow runoff, especially considering the receding flood water being partially replaced by snow melt and springs.

I found several peer-reviewed scientific articles that analyzed floods in coastal areas, rate of drainage, and what is possible. One such article stated,

> Designers of coastal drainage systems recognize the unique characteristics of coastal flooding, particularly the

> impacts of tides, low elevations, and high groundwater tables. . . . The rate at which gravity can drain an area depends in part on the difference in elevation between the area being drained and the place to which the water flows. The greater the difference in elevation, the greater the slope of the "hydraulic head" and the faster the water can drain.
>
> Coastal areas generally are low-lying and thus vulnerable to flooding. High tides can decrease the elevational difference and further slow gravity drainage. Moreover, storm surges in coastal areas frequently occur during rainstorms, and can completely stop natural drainage.[24]

Note that this is from scientific study that has *nothing to do* with Noah's Flood. It's simply describing hydrology. Since southern Mesopotamia is one of the flattest places on earth (the only raised areas being mounds of the archaeological remains of cities like Shuruppak and Uruk), it is one of the places where we would most expect a slow drainage of flood waters—precisely what the Genesis text requires. This aspect suggests a remarkable harmony between the Bible and actual topography in present-day Iraq.

Another article, specifically about the Persian Gulf, notes a "period of the flooding of the Gulf and the subsequent flooding of the low-lying delta region when sea levels rose perhaps a few meters above its present level between about 6000 and 3000 yr BP." This time period is 4000–1000 B.C. (My model has the Flood occurring around 2900 B.C.) The article (again, not one specifically about Noah's Flood) also tosses out this tidbit:

> During-Caspers[25] notes evidence for ancient civilizations on the bottom of the now northern part of the Persian Gulf.

> Excavations at Ur and elsewhere have led to evidence of a flooding event at about 4000–3000 B.C.[26]

As an example of a storm surge in the area, peak winds of up to 150 miles per hour were in fact recorded in Super Cyclonic Storm Gonu[27] in June 2007, in Oman, the United Arab Emirates, and Iran, not far from southern Iraq. It was the most powerful tropical cyclone known to have hit the Arabian Peninsula and attained peak one-minute winds of 170 miles per hour and gusts of 195 miles per hour, with a 17-foot storm surge on the coast of Oman, in the Gulf of Oman, which is connected to and southeast of the Persian Gulf. Waves along the coast of the United Arab Emirates on the southern end of the Persian Gulf were 32 feet high.

Now for the next point of controversy: the ark's destination. Does Mt. Ararat—16,854 feet high in elevation, located in the extreme east of current-day Turkey on the border with Armenia—present a problem with the scenario I have laid out? It could be claimed that it does, since it lies far from my proposed location for the Flood. I submit that it does *not* once we scrutinize the matter more closely. Carol Hill observes,[28]

> The Bible does not actually pinpoint the exact place where the ark landed, it merely alludes to a region or range of mountains where the ark came to rest: *the mountains of Ararat* (Gen. 8:4). . . . "Mountain" in Genesis 8:4 is plural; therefore, the Bible does not specify that the ark landed on the highest peak of the region (Mt. Ararat), only that the ark landed somewhere on the mountains or highlands of Armenia (both "Ararat" and "Urartu" can be translated as "highlands"). In biblical times, "Ararat" was actually the name of a province (not a mountain),

> as can be seen from its usage in 2 Kings 19:37: "Some escaped into the land of Ararat" and Jer. 51:27: "Call together against her (Israel) the kingdoms of Ararat, Minni, and Askkenaz." . . .
>
> Only in the eleventh and twelfth centuries A.D. did the focus of investigators begin to shift toward Mount Ararat as the ark's final resting place, and only by the end of the fourteenth century A.D. does it seem to have become a fairly well established tradition. Before this, both Islamic and Christian tradition held that the landing place of the ark was on Jabel Judi, a mountain located about 30 miles (48 km) northeast of the Tigris River near Cizre, Turkey.[29]

Jabel Judi is 6,854 feet in elevation. Alan Hill shows (with all kinds of scientific and mathematical calculations) that the ark could have been blown by strong winds to its landing place near Cizre (elevation: 1,237 feet), where the plain starts transforming into foothills and mountains (the "mountains of Ararat"), and the traditional landing site, Jabel Judi.[30]

The biblical text doesn't require the ark resting on *top* of a mountain. It says "came to rest upon the mountains of Ararat." Ararat was a *region*, and it's where the ark's traditional resting place (according to Christian thinking prior to the eleventh century) was located: just north of the Mesopotamian floodplain, where the hills and mountains begin.

The science and math are technical, but for those who can understand it, Alan Hill's article should be a compelling read. Jabel Judi or Mt. Judi is in a location (37°22'10"N 42°20'39"E) where the hills and mountains abruptly arise from the Mesopotamian floodplain. Thus, it makes perfect sense for a boat that came from southern Mesopotamia, floating on massive floodwaters, to land at the first higher elevation landforms that it ran into.

Carol Hill offers more great information in her book, *A Worldview Approach to Science and Scripture: Making Genesis Real*, in chapter six: "Noah's Flood: Global or Local?" She supports a landing place for the ark on Jabel Judi by noting that it wasn't "far from a region of vineyards and olive trees."[31] The Bible states that a dove came back with an olive leaf (Gen. 8:11) and that Noah planted a vineyard after the Flood (9:20). She noted that we know that wine was made in northern Mesopotamia from before 3000 B.C. This requires a hot climate, but not *too* hot or dry, with mild winters.

North of this area (present-day Mt. Ararat) and the southern floodplain, we don't find vineyards. But northern Iraq—or ancient Assyria, or northern Mesopotamia—does have them, along with moderate rainfall and lots of streams. The Bible refers to the area in this regard (2 Kings 18:32), mentioning both vineyards and olive trees. Olive trees also need particular conditions to survive—conditions met by this area.

Then there is the question of the absolute uniqueness of a flood the likes of which we're examining or proposing. Has something like this happened at any other time in history?

The answer is a well documented "yes." Take for example the 1926–1927 Mississippi River Flood, an event that spawned many musical accounts in the folk and blues genre and was, no doubt, the subject of many old-timers' fireside stories for years afterward. Here we find striking analogies to Noah's Flood. It was the worst flood in the history of the United States, covering 27,000 square miles with depths as much as 30 feet, for several months, with the floodwaters in some areas reaching 56 feet. In May 1927, the waters of the Mississippi River near Memphis, Tennessee, were 80 miles wide.

The rainfall began in August 1926 and lasted until April 1927. That's eight months, or more than 240 days—six times the length of the forty-day rains in Noah's Flood (Gen.

7:4,12). The entire Genesis Flood, up until the waters dried up, lasted ten and a half months (see Gen. 7:11, 8:13). The waters in the Great Mississippi Flood took even *longer* to dry up: *an entire year.*

Moreover, both areas are similar and analogous insofar as

- both are in very flat areas;
- both lie near large bodies of water (the Gulf of Mexico and the Persian Gulf);
- both have a large river or rivers running through them (the Tigris and Euphrates and the Mississippi);
- both floodplains are located at virtually the same latitude[32]; and
- both have "rings" of mountains or much higher elevations around the flat basin and flood plain on three sides: in the U.S. South, there are mountains in Arkansas, Tennessee, and northern Alabama and Georgia.

This one Mississippi flood covered an area larger than my proposed local Mesopotamian Flood (likely twice as large or more). And that's just *one* flood. Certainly, we can extrapolate from these data and deduce that there have been many more such floods in the entire history of the world. This one was within the previous hundred years. Both of my parents were alive when it happened.

We don't even have to do much guesswork. On January 7–8, 1966, 71.8 inches of rain fell in twenty-four hours on Reunion Island,[33] approximately 670 kilometers east of Madagascar in the Indian Ocean, during Tropical Cyclone Denise. Therefore, we know from our own scientific observation that it's *possible* to rain that much in a day.

Cherrapunji, Meghalaya, India holds the record for the amount of rainfall in a year: 86 feet 10 inches, from August 1860 to July 1861.[34] We can get close enough to render it at least *thinkable* or *possible* to conceive of the ultimate superstorm: Noah's Flood. Accurate records of global weather have been available only since 1880.[35] Much larger storms during all of history before that can't be ruled out.

We do know of huge meteorological and climatological catastrophic events, such as the Altai floods in Siberia, from 12–15,000 years ago[36]; the Black Sea Deluge[37] (about 5600 B.C.); the Missoula floods[38] in the northwest United States, from 12–15,000 years ago; the Zanclean flood[39] that refilled the Mediterranean Sea 5.33 million years ago; and the Bonneville flood[40] in Utah and Idaho (14,500 years ago). One article on prehistoric "monster hurricanes" states,

> A new record of sediment deposits from Cape Cod, Mass., show evidence that twenty-three severe hurricanes hit New England between the years 250 and 1150, the equivalent of a severe storm about once every forty years on average. Many of these hurricanes were likely more intense than any that have hit the area in recorded history.[41]

There is a field of study called *paleotempestology*: the study of past cyclones, hurricanes, and other catastrophic meteorological events. It stands to reason that in all of planet earth's history, something like Noah's Flood is entirely possible and, I submit, *did indeed happen*.

Another topic that advocates of a local Flood have to grapple with is the question of *anthropological universality*: the notion that all the human beings in the world were in the Mesopotamian floodplain in c. 2900 B.C. and were wiped out, save for those in the ark. The *Catholic Encyclopedia* in its 1908 article "Deluge" espouses this view. But (helpful as it always is) this source is not authoritative or magisterial—that is, it's not binding on Catholics.

There's not sufficient space here to explore in depth the anthropological universality of the Flood, and to do so would force us well outside the realm of secular science and into theology and exegesis. But our concern here is the Flood itself, not its consequences. And this much is certain: given the abundant scientific evidence, it is gravely unreasonable to dismiss Noah's Flood as scientifically impossible.

3

WALKING THE JOURNEY OF ABRAHAM

Then the Lord appeared to Abram and said,
"To your descendants I will give this land."

—GENESIS 12:7

We can't find out *much* (if *anything*) specifically about the patriarch Abraham, revered in Christianity, Judaism, and Islam alike as "the father of faith." Archaeologists have not yet found physical, or "hard," evidence that he existed.

Nevertheless, if the purported accounts of Abraham in Genesis are verified as accurate, according to what we know from history and archaeology, then we have an objective and rational basis for believing that Abraham *did* exist *in history*, as opposed to being merely fictional or mythological (like Heracles of Greek mythology).

Particularly—as I will primarily contend in this chapter—we can offer strong archaeological evidence that cities and regions mentioned in the Bible as having been visited or lived in by Abraham did indeed *exist* before and during the time period involved. If they *didn't* exist then, it would clearly present a problem.

Such verifications don't *prove* the Bible's inspiration, but they do support its *historical accuracy* and highly suggest that many biblical skeptics have gone too far in their negative or agnostic opinions.

According to the Bible, Abraham was a man who took many journeys. Joshua 24:2–3 states,

> Thus says the Lord, the God of Israel . . . "I took your father Abraham from beyond the River and led him through all the land of Canaan, and made his offspring many."

The usual or "standard" view is that Abraham came from Ur of the Chaldeans (see Gen. 11:27–28,31), which is close to the Persian Gulf, west of the Euphrates, in southern Mesopotamia (current-day Iraq). Some biblical evidences regarding Abraham's journey to Canaan, however, suggest another city: Urfa (also known as Sanliurfa and, in ancient times, Edessa) in present-day Turkey (southeastern Anatolian region).

Gary Rendsburg, professor of Jewish history in the Department of Jewish Studies at Rutgers University, makes the case for Urfa being the biblical Ur of the Chaldeans or Chaldees:

> A serious geographical problem plagues the story: a journey from Ur to Canaan would not pass through Harran. . . .
>
> A more attractive suggestion is that Abraham's hometown is the city of Ur in northern Mesopotamia = modern-day Urfa in southeastern Turkey, 44 km [27 miles] north of Harran. Most likely, this city is the one mentioned as Ura in cuneiform tablets from Ugarit (fourteenth-thirteenth centuries BCE), where it is associated with the Hittite realm. A journey from Urfa to Canaan would indeed pass directly through Harran.

> Local (Turkish) Jewish, Christian, and Muslim tradition identifies this city as biblical Ur, the birthplace of Abraham. In fact, this notion was commonly accepted in nineteenth-century biblical scholarship.[42]

Cyrus H. Gordon, professor of Hebraic studies at New York University, adds,

> The biblical evidence is by itself conclusive in placing Ur of the Chaldees in the Urfa-Haran region of south central Turkey, near the Syrian border, rather than in southern Mesopotamia . . .
>
> Genesis 24:4, Genesis 24:7, Genesis 24:10, and Genesis 24:29 tells us that Abraham's birthplace was in Aram-Naharayim where Laban lived.[43]

The journey from Ur to Haran (also spelled "Harran"—see Gen. 12:4–5; Acts 7:3–4), undertaken by Abraham, was 27 miles. M. Bözdeniza et al. noted that "the known written documents about Harran indicate that its history goes as far back as 2500 B.C."[44] Tamara M. Green placed the city's origin at around 2000 B.C. and observed that it was "founded as a merchant outpost by Ur."[45] She noted that "the abundance of goods that passed through the area must have proved a temptation, for raids upon the caravan were frequent." Either date is earlier than the estimated time of Abraham's birth: around 1880–1860 B.C., according to the copiously researched scholarly determinations of Egyptologist Kenneth A. Kitchen.[46] Haran was ideally located on a trade route between the Mediterranean and the plains of the Tigris River.

> **Genesis 12:6** Abram passed through the land to the place at Shechem, to the oak of Moreh. At that time

the Canaanites were in the land (see also 33:18).

Archaeology informs us that Shechem was settled (or resettled) before Abraham was born—"in around 1900" B.C.—and that it had "a two-hundred-year period of prominence as a city-state, covering the centuries from 1750 to 1540" B.C.[47] David G. Hansen observed,

> Archaeological investigations have corroborated much of what the Bible has to say about Shechem's physical and cultural aspects. Archaeology has confirmed Shechem's location, its history, and many biblical details. . . .
>
> In the original Hebrew, the word translated in our English Bible as "city" meant a permanent, walled settlement. . . . Genesis 34:20 and 24 report that Shechem had a city gate; therefore it was fortified.[48]

The Bible refers to Abraham dwelling "by the oaks of Mamre . . . at Hebron" (Gen. 13:18; see also 14:13, 18:1, 35:27), and also to the burial of his wife Sarah there (23:2,19). Archaeologists Avraham Negev and Shimon Gibson provide the evidence for Hebron's existence during Abraham's lifetime:

> The earliest ancient settlement was established . . . during Early Bronze III [2700–2200 B.C.]. . . . This city was destroyed in a substantial conflagration. Not long afterwards and the same period the city was built anew. . . .
>
> Following a period of abandonment, settlement of the site was renewed in Middle Bronze IIB [1750–1650 B.C.].[49]

A 2018 article on the city[50] at Hebron.org (including a video) notes the discovery in that year of stairs (recently opened to the public) from the time of Abraham:

> Dr. Emmanual Eisenberg of the Israel Antiquities Authority led the dig in Tel Hevron. . . . In what is today's Admot Yishai neighborhood, near the Tomb of Jesse and Ruth is a flight of stairs, over 4,000 years old, leading from the valley below into the ancient city of Hebron.

Another location that the Bible claims Abraham visited and lived in is Beersheba (Gen. 21:14,29–33; 22:19). Biblical scholar John J. Bimson noted about it:

> Sarna has argued . . . "The biblical passages refer only to a well and a cultic site. . . . No king or ruler is mentioned, and no patriarch ever has dealings with the inhabitants of Beersheba." . . . In 1967, Aharoni held the view that the absence of early archaeological evidence does not contradict the patriarchal narratives, which, he then suggested, have only the *area* of Beersheba in mind, not a town.[51]

The biblical data appear perfectly consistent with this scenario. Beersheba is mentioned eleven times in Genesis in the RSV. None of the passages requires the interpretation of even a *town*, let alone a city. The first mention, in Abraham's time (Gen. 21:14), refers to "the wilderness of Beersheba."

> **Genesis 14:17–18** After his return from the defeat of Ched-or-laomer and the kings who were with him, the king of Sodom went out to meet him at the Valley of Shaveh (that is, the King's Valley). And Melchizedek king of Salem brought out bread and wine; he was priest of God Most High.

These two things have to do with Jerusalem. Most scholars think Salem was a name for ancient Jerusalem (one of several). Mt. Moriah is the spot in Jerusalem (currently the Temple Mount) where Solomon's temple was built some 600–700 years after Abraham was willing to sacrifice his son there. The traditional spot is currently covered by the Islamic Dome of the Rock.

Many seem to think that Jerusalem began, or first became a significant city, at the time David became king (c. 1000 B.C.). This is untrue. It was already very old by that time. Archaeological evidence exists for a settlement in the area as early as 4500–3500 B.C. The first mention of the city that we know of occurred around 2000 B.C. in the Egyptian Execration Texts[52] from the Middle Kingdom (2040 to 1782 B.C.). Massive walls (with four- and five-ton boulders) 26 feet high were built in Jerusalem by the seventeenth century B.C.—some 600 years before King David. The famous Ebla discoveries (including 1,800 complete clay tablets), discovered in Syria in 1974–1975, date to between approximately 2500–2250 B.C. They refer to the name of ancient Jerusalem as *Ye-ru-sa-lu-um*.[53]

Thus, an abundance of undeniable evidence exists showing that Abraham's meeting with Melchizedek is a plausible event, given the known chronology of ancient Jerusalem. Nothing that we know would make such a meeting at that time and place impossible. In other words, the biblical account can't be casually ruled out as historically inaccurate or "mythical," as not a few biblical skeptics or archaeological minimalists would claim.

4

SODOM OBLITERATED

Then the Lord rained on Sodom and Gomorrah brimstone and fire from the Lord out of heaven . . . and lo, the smoke of the land went up like the smoke of a furnace.

—GENESIS 19:24, 28

Prior to the last fifteen years or so, the leading archaeological theory, for those who believe that Sodom and Gomorrah existed, placed the location of these cities on the south end of the Dead Sea, on the eastern shore—although there were several prominent advocates among archaeologists as far back as the nineteenth century for a northeastern shore location, and this was, in fact, the consensus location from the fourth century until the early 1900s.

The buzz and fun discussion currently taking place is largely the result of the Tall el-Hammam excavations in Jordan, led (beginning in 2006) by archaeologist Steven Collins, dean and professor at Trinity Southwest University. He has written voluminously and passionately about his positions.

Brian Nixon, of *Assist News Service*, quotes Collins in covering the "northern" theory:

> The traditional "Southern Theory" site of Sodom does not have the geographical parallels described in the [biblical] text. Namely: 1. One can see the whole area from the hills above Jericho (Bethel/Ai), 2. It must be a well-watered place (described "like Egypt"), 3. It has a river running through it (the Jordan), and 4. It must follow the travel route of Lot [who, Nixon elaborates, went to the other side of the Jordan, eastward, away from Jericho].

"What does all this mean?" Nixon concludes. "Simple: the traditional sites attributed as Sodom may be incorrect."[54]

He again cites Collins, summarizing some of the findings of the dig in the year 2010:

> To start with, the Tall el-Hammam site has twenty-five geographical indicators that align with the description in Genesis. Compare this with something well known—like Jerusalem—that has only sixteen. Other sites have only five or six. So this site has a greater number of indicators than any other Old Testament site. That is truly amazing.
>
> Second, our findings—pottery, architecture, and destruction layers—fit the timeframe profile. Meaning we should expect to find items like what we are finding from the Middle Bronze Age. This is exactly what we are uncovering.
>
> Though . . . much research still needs to be conducted, I feel that the evidence for this being the ancient city of Sodom is increasing by the day.

Collins has provided extensive argumentation for a chronology of the Tall el-Hammam/Sodom archaeological site.[55] His analysis nicely lines up with our proposed dates of

Abraham, and he estimated that Sodom was destroyed "between 1750 and 1650" B.C. Based on various archaeological evidences, Collins concluded that

> the patriarchs—from Terah through Joseph—belong entirely to the Middle Bronze Age, with most of that sequence occurring during MB2 (1800–1540 BCE).

These dates correspond with the work of Kenneth Kitchen—so Collins noted, citing Kitchen's exhaustive examination of, for example, "treaties and covenants; family customs; religion; geopolitics in Canaan; personal names; the price of slaves, and more." Collins concludes at length,

> Interestingly, if Tall el-Hammam *is* Sodom as I think the geographical and archaeological evidence categorically confirms, then it constitutes a most remarkable confirmation of the historical veracity of the patriarchal narratives.

Amanda Borschel-Dan, in a *Times of Israel* article on this topic, sums up the evidence for some sort of massive explosion in Sodom and its surrounding area:

> As reported in *Science News*, at the recently concluded Denver-based ASOR Annual Meeting, director of scientific analysis at Jordan's Tall el-Hammam Excavation Project Phillip J. Silvia presented a paper, "The 3.7kaBP Middle Ghor Event: Catastrophic Termination of a Bronze Age Civilization." . . .
>
> According to the paper's abstract, the scientists discovered evidence of a "high-heat" explosive event north of the Dead Sea that instantaneously "devastated approximately 500 square kilometers." . . . Silvia told

Science News that the blast would have instantly killed the estimated 40,000 to 65,000 people who inhabited Middle Ghor, a 25-kilometer-wide circular plain in Jordan.

Radiocarbon dating of the site yielded a date of about 1700 B.C. The article continues:

> Contemporary potsherds' glazes apparently experienced temperatures high enough to transform them to glass, "perhaps as hot as the surface of the sun," Silvia told the news source. . . .
>
> "The destruction not only of Tall el-Hammam (Sodom), but also its neighbors (Gomorrah and the other cities of the plain) was most likely caused by a meteoritic airburst event," the authors conclude.[56]

In summary, Steven Collins and Phillip Silvia further elaborate in a technical conference paper,[57]

> A pottery sherd found in a sealed MB2 context on the Upper Tall shows evidence of exposure to extreme temperature in that one surface has been melted into glass. Examination of this "vitrified" sherd at New Mexico Tech (NMT), Northern Arizona University (NAU), and North Carolina State University (NCSU) found bubbles inside melted zirconium crystals in the glass that indicate boiling of the crystal at over 4,000° C. The glass (melted clay) layer is less than 1mm thick, and thermal discoloration of the clay penetrated only halfway through the 5mm thickness of the sherd. This led the research team to conclude that the temperature profile to which the sherd was exposed was between 8,000° C and 12,000° C for less than a few milliseconds.

What does all this mean in layman's terms? It's quite simple: *something* caused an almost unimaginably hot burst of heat at this time and place in history. The best explanation that scientists from many varying fields came up with was "a meteoritic airburst." That's a plausible explanation for the remarkable melting phenomenon at the site, which created glass-like rocks.

Many skeptics would note the natural and historic event and simply move on. But it does precisely verify the accuracy of the *biblical text*. Christians believe that there is such a thing as judgment and that God exercises it at times when human beings become irreparably wicked. The Flood was another such instance—so we believe in faith, but not without reason.

The Bible—especially an early book like Genesis—was written in pre-scientific, pre-philosophical, and phenomenological language (that is, using descriptions of *appearances*). Hence, the author of Genesis (whom many Christians and Jews believe to be Moses) chose to describe the ostensible explosion of a meteor as "brimstone and fire" that "rained" down upon Sodom and Gomorrah.

This makes perfect sense once it is understood that "brimstone" was an ancient term for *sulfur*, one of the most reactive elements, which is still found in abundance on the shores of the Dead Sea today. The "smoke" alluded to in Genesis 19:28 may have also referred to this, among other things (perhaps more specifically to what we now know as sulfuric acid), and "fire," at least partially or possibly, described "burning pitch," since bitumen is also prevalent in the same area.

God utilizes natural forces or supernatural ones, or a mixture of the two, as he decrees. In this instance, we believe—based on hard science—that he judged Sodom and

Gomorrah through the use of a meteor, which he indirectly caused to come into existence through natural processes and laws that he initially set into motion, just as with all the rest of his creation. And he knew exactly when and where it would strike.

5

JOSEPH IN EGYPT

Now Joseph had a dream, and when he told it to his brothers they only hated him the more.

—GENESIS 37:5

The state of scientific evidence regarding Joseph the patriarch is similar to that for Abraham: we don't have, as of yet, any hard evidence. But archaeological corroboration for many details of the account of Joseph's life, recorded in Genesis—including details about Egypt, where he became a high official—can be verified in various ways.

A mythical or fictional account simply couldn't be substantiated in this fashion and would often exhibit anachronism. On the other hand, if we can back up so many details *about* or *associated with* Joseph's life, as the Bible presents it, it stands to reason that Scripture is accurate regarding his historical existence, too.

One of the best-known events in Joseph's life is his being sold into slavery by his brothers, which is recorded in Genesis 37:25 and 28, along with several particular details that we will examine.

Genesis 37:28 informs us that Joseph was sold to "Midianite traders" for "twenty shekels" and that they took him to Egypt. Verse 25 adds the details that they were "a caravan of Ishmaelites coming from Gilead" on camels, and that they carried "gum, balm, and myrrh." Verse 36 notes that he was sold to Potiphar, who was "an officer of Pharaoh, the captain of the guard." We shall examine these details to see if they stand up to scientific scrutiny.

The people in this "caravan" are called "Ishmaelites" in Genesis 37:25 and 27, yet they are also called "Midianites" in two later verses. So we know they are people called by both these names, and they were from (or at least were coming from) Gilead. This was in an area that is currently northwestern Jordan.

The *Encyclopedia Britannica* states that the Midianites were

> of a group of nomadic tribes related to the Israelites and most likely living east of the Gulf of Aqaba in the northwestern regions of the Arabian Desert. They engaged in pastoral pursuits, caravan trading, and banditry. . . .
>
> The Midianites traditionally have been identified as Ishmaelites, in part because of an unclear passage in Genesis (37:28) that refers to the traders to whom Joseph was sold by his brothers as both Midianites and Ishmaelites. In addition, the story of Gideon in Judges contains a verse (8:24) that includes an apparent interpolation identifying the Midianites as Ishmaelites.

Ellicott's Commentary for English Readers[58] observed that "gum" was "probably gum tragacanth, though some think that it was storax, the gum of the styrax tree (see Gen. 30:37)." Tragacanth was obtained from astragalus root, a type of bean or legume that flourishes in about twenty species in Israel.[59] This commentary continues,

> "Balm," that is, balsam, was probably the resin of the *balsamodendron Gileadense*, a tree which grows abundantly in Gilead, and of which the gum was greatly in use for healing wounds. "Myrrh" was certainly ladanum, the gum of the cistus rose (*cistus riticus*). As all these were products of Palestine valued in Egypt, Jacob included them in his present to the governor there (Gen. 43:11).

The *Cambridge Bible for Schools and Colleges* comments upon a number of fascinating details, noting that "balm" (or "mastic"), a famous product of Gilead (see Gen. 43:11; Jer. 8:22), was used for incense, and to soothe and heal wounds, and that "myrrh" was used by "priests" (as incense) and by "physicians" as well as "embalmers."[60]

In the New Testament, myrrh was mentioned as one of the three gifts of the three wise men (Matt. 2:11), and with regard to anointing Jesus' body (John 19:39). But it had been around for a long time before that—a time that preceded Joseph's era. Thus, the Bible is not guilty of historical anachronism (things being mentioned in the wrong historical period) in these passages.

Thus, I would point out that the "gum" (tragacanth) and "the balm of Gilead" are acknowledged in secular science today as substances from ancient Israel or Palestine, including Gilead (modern-day Jordan), precisely as the Bible accurately states.

Shimshon Ben-Yehoshua and Lumir Hanus, in a wonderful article on spices in the ancient Near East, note that "balm of Gilead, known also as the Judaean balsam, grew only around the Dead Sea Basin in antiquity." Myrrh, however, seems not to have been an indigenous Palestinian or Judean product. They write,

> The connection between the source of ancient spices, mainly the Arabian Peninsula and India to Mesopotamia and Europe, is known as the Incense Road. Archaeologists placed the date of the beginning of the incense trade sometime around 1800 BCE, but it is more than likely that trade commenced earlier.[61]

Biblical skeptics argue that the text exhibits anachronism. But archaeological and historiographical evidence massively shows that trade routes for at least myrrh (and likely also balm of Gilead and tragacanth) were long established by the time of Joseph.

In interpreting Genesis 37:25, skeptics such as Adam Lee[62] contend that the verse refers to the trade route called the "King's Highway," which ran through Gilead—and for which, Lee insists, "there is no evidence . . . in the second millennium BCE." If in fact the text presented supposed historical facts that don't match the dates involved, this would be a problem. But the text doesn't mention the King's Highway, although the road is mentioned in Numbers 20:17 and 21:22. Nevertheless, the King's Highway is not directly relevant to Genesis 37:25, because it was too far east (in Jordan), so that, ironically, the critic in this case has *his* basic geographical facts wrong.

Genesis 37:17 informs us that the incident where Joseph was traded into slavery occurred at Dothan, located in the present West Bank, at what is now the archaeological site Tel Dothan, roughly in the middle on a line between the Sea of Galilee and Tel Aviv. Dothan was located on a different trade route, later called the Via Maris, and it was a large walled town by the time of the Early Bronze Age (3300–2000 B.C.).[63] The two Bible commentaries already cited (in their analyses of Genesis

37:25) expand our knowledge of the ancient Via Maris route and Dothan:

> Dothan lay on the trade route that led from Gilead through the valley of Jezreel towards Egypt. . . . The trade route followed by caravans passed (1) from Gilead on the east of the Jordan, (2) by a ford, across the Jordan, (3) by Beth-Shean or Beisan, down the plain of Jezreel, and so (4) by Lydda and the coast, to Egypt.[64]

> Dothan was situated on the great caravan line by which the products of India and Western Asia were brought to Egypt. As the eastern side of Canaan is covered by the great Arabian Desert, the caravans had to travel in a north-westernly direction until, having forded the Euphrates, they could strike across from Tadmor to Gilead. The route thence led them over the Jordan at Beisan, and so southward to Egypt.[65]

The Via Maris also dates from the Early Bronze Age.[66] Both Dothan and the Via Maris were already quite ancient by the time Joseph ran into a caravan following the Via Maris through Dothan and was sold by his brothers into slavery.

Another indication that the biblical texts about Joseph are historically accurate comes from Egyptologist Kenneth Kitchen's discussion, exhaustive and amazing in its detail, of the price of slaves in the ancient Near East. He contends that we know from "ancient Near Eastern sources" the price of slaves in that region in significant detail, from 2400 B.C. to 400 B.C., and that we know "from the Laws of Hammurabi and documents from Mari and elsewhere" that the price was twenty shekels—precisely as the Bible states.[67]

I maintain, based on Kitchen's extraordinary multifaceted scholarship, that Joseph lived in the eighteenth century B.C., so these sources perfectly corroborate the biblical view, since they derive from the nineteenth and eighteenth centuries B.C.

Kitchen goes on to note that Exodus 21:32 (in the Mosaic Law) required a payment of "thirty shekels" to a slave owner "if someone else's ox gores the slave to death." Sure enough, this was the price of slaves in the fourteenth and thirteenth centuries, when Moses lived. Kitchen concludes by asking a pointed question, in effect toward biblical skeptics:

> If all these figures were invented during the Exile (sixth century B.C.) or in the Persian period by some fiction writer, why isn't the price for Joseph 90 to 100 shekels, the cost of a slave at the time when that story was supposedly written? And why isn't the price in Exodus also 90 to 100 shekels? It's more reasonable to assume that the biblical data reflect reality in these cases.

Another aspect of the story of Joseph that can be verified or questioned by means of archaeology and historical research is the alleged famine in Israel during the times of both Abraham and Joseph (Gen. 12:10; 26:1–2; 42:5; 43:1) and the contrasting abundance of food in Egypt (12:10; 41:57; 42:1–2; 47:12)—though, Egypt, too, suffered to a lesser degree (47:13).

Archaeologist James Hoffmeier noted that this lines up with what we know regarding Egypt, Canaan, and famine, as well as migratory patterns:

> For a period roughly from 1800 to 1540 B.C., Egypt was an attractive place for the Semitic-speaking people of

> western Asia to migrate. . . . This span of time coincides with the traditional "Patriarchal Period" and therefore fits the period and circumstances described in Genesis when Abraham, Isaac (almost), and Jacob went to Egypt in search of food, water, and green pastures.[68]

Genesis 39:4 informs us that Joseph was an "overseer" of the house of Potiphar (39:1), a high-ranking official under Pharaoh. Hoffmeier backs up the existence of such an office at that time:

> Papyrus Brooklyn 35.1446 [dated 1809–1743 B.C.] lists the Semitic names of dozens of male and female servants attached to a particular estate. The third column from the right on the papyrus contains their trade or occupation. Interestingly, a number of these servants are identified as *hry-pr*, literally, "he who is over the house," which is translated "domestic servant."[69]

This is a good place to clearly state what I claim to be establishing or substantiating, both here and throughout this book. Hoffmeier doesn't prove that *Joseph* held this office. That would be very strong evidence. But that doesn't leave us with *no* evidence at all. The point of this argument and many related ones in this chapter and others, is to show that what we know from secular history and archaeology is quite *consistent* with the biblical account. It doesn't absolutely prove the complete historical trustworthiness of the Bible, let alone its inspiration. But it *does* provide striking evidence that the Bible has an extraordinarily accurate "historical sense."

Events and descriptions in the Bible nicely "fit in" with what we have been able to determine from secular science and studies. That's what accurate historical accounts do.

They're not anachronistic, and they are able to be verified in particulars by outside sources. The more we verify these instances of correspondence, the more the overall case is strengthened.

I submit that I have demonstrated this characteristic of the Bible, and will continue to, again and again in this book. It's the *cumulative impact* of so many evidences, all in one direction, that gives the overall argument its force and strength.

Correspondence of biblical Egyptian names in the Joseph narrative with archaeological and linguistic data provides another line of argumentation for the accuracy of the biblical text. The names in question are Potiphar, Joseph's master (Gen. 39:1); his wife Asenath and father-in-law Potipherah; and Zaphenath-paneah, Joseph's Egyptian name, given to him by Pharaoh (41:45).

Hoffmeier stated about these four names: "All agree that they are undeniably Egyptian."[70] Kitchen believes that the dating of *Zaphenath* is "Middle Kingdom to early New Kingdom (early to mid-second millennium)" and *Asenath* also to the Middle Kingdom.[71] This scheme fits nicely into the known time frame for the life of Joseph.

The *Jewish Encyclopedia* observes,

> The form "Potiphar" is probably an abbreviation of "Potiphera"; the two are treated as identical in the Septuagint. . . . "Poti-phera" is the Hebrew rendering of the Egyptian "P-di-p-R" = "He whom Ra [*i.e.*, the sun-god] gave." This name has not been found in Egyptian inscriptions; but names of similar form occur as early as the twenty-second dynasty.[72]

The title *Pharaoh* and the later usage of "Pharaoh [Name]" are also aspects that can be analyzed to see if the biblical accounts are accurate, based on what we know from secular history and archaeology. *Pharaoh* is used by itself many times in Genesis and Exodus.[73] Hoffmeier noted a change in this practice:

> In subsequent periods [after 1100 B.C.], the name of the monarch was generally added on. This precise practice is found in the Old Testament. . . . After Sheshak (ca. 925 B.C.), the title and name appear together (e.g., Pharaoh Neco, Pharaoh Hophra).[74]

The first appearance of "Pharaoh" in the Bible (RSV) with a name attached is "Pharaoh Neco" in 2 Kings 23:29 and 33–35. The dates of the Bible and Egyptian history line up again. Pharaoh Neco killed King Josiah (2 Kings 23:29). The *Encyclopedia Britannica* reckons Josiah's dates as c. 648–609 B.C. and Pharaoh Neco II's dates of reign as 610–595 B.C. Thus, in the second year of his reign, he killed King Josiah of Judah.

The only other instance of a pharaoh (with that particular title) being named in the Old Testament is "Pharaoh Hophra," in Jeremiah 44:30. Jeremiah lived from c. 650–c. 570 B.C. Hophra (or Greek, Apries) reigned from 589 to 570 B.C. His reign was completely within Jeremiah's lifetime, so that the latter could refer to him as a contemporary historical figure.

Moreover, the Bible refers to "Shishak king of Egypt" during the lifetime of King Solomon, who reigned from c. 971–931 B.C. (1 Kings 11:40) and also at the time of his successor Rehoboam (r. c. 931–913 B.C.), when Shishak attacked Jerusalem and despoiled the newly built Temple of Solomon (2 Chron. 12:2, 9). Shishak is generally identified with Pharaoh Shoshenq (AKA Sheshonk) I (r. 945–924 B.C.). Once again, then, the historical timelines are in perfect harmony. Shoshenq's reign overlaps that of both Solomon and Rehoboam. The bottom line (as we've seen countless times) is that the Old Testament habitually recounts verifiable history.

> **Genesis 41:41–42** And Pharaoh said to Joseph, "Behold, I have set you over all the land of Egypt." Then Pharaoh took his signet ring from his hand and put it on Joseph's hand, and arrayed him in garments of fine linen, and put a gold chain about his neck.

This event is known as Joseph's investiture. Over forty Egyptian depictions of this sort of investiture ceremony have been discovered, from 1479 to 950 B.C., showing a pharaoh on a throne, with a prince figure wearing a gold necklace and white linen, and some sort of insignia (seal, staff, ring, etc.). Hoffmeier noted,

> Huy, Viceroy of Cush under Tutankhamun [r. 1333–1323 B.C.] . . . [is shown] receiving a rolled-up linen object along with a gold signet ring.[75]

Kitchen added:

> Of the Egyptian nature of the trappings for royal appointments to high office—linen robe, gold collar, state seal, etc.—there can be no doubt whatever.[76]

It all lines up with the biblical account, in striking detail. The account of Jacob's and Joseph's burials does, too. Egyptian physicians "embalmed" Jacob (Gen. 50:1–3), and Joseph was "embalmed" and "put in a coffin in Egypt" (v. 26). Neither practice was known in the land of Canaan during this time or the entire Bronze Age.[77]

Is it plausible to believe that a Semite or Israelite or Hebrew could have attained such a high office in Egypt as Joseph (and later Moses) did? Isn't that stretching credulity too far? No—the evidence again corroborates the biblical narrative about Joseph in Egypt. A tomb was discovered in Saqqara (or Sakkara) in the 1980s that included a Semitic man, Aper-el. His titles included "vizier," "mayor of the city," and "judge," and he served Pharaoh Amenhotep III (r. c. 1387–c. 1350 B.C.) and Pharaoh Akhenaten (r. c. 1350–c. 1335 B.C.) as overseer of Lower Egypt.

If it took all the way until the 1980s to discover this, we ought not be surprised or "scandalized" that we lack direct evidence for Joseph in this regard, as Hoffmeier observed, while noting additionally that "his provenance in Genesis is the Delta, still an underexcavated area."

Lastly, we have the question of how long Joseph lived. Genesis 50:22 states that he "lived a hundred and ten years." This is known (from thirty discovered occurrences in Egyptian texts over the last 2,000 years) to be an Egyptian symbolic or "ideal" age, whereas seventy and eighty are the *biblical* ideals (2 Sam. 19:32,35; Ps. 90:10). The Bible states that Joseph died in Egypt as a high official.[78]

No one is claiming that archaeology provides *direct proof* of Joseph in Egypt. We won't ever find a plaque that says: "I, Joseph, the Israelite with the coat of many colors, was sold into slavery by my brothers, and am now a big shot in the Egyptian government."

Instead, the nature of the argument is that if the narratives about Joseph appear *prima facie* to be historical, and the events described are not such that they seem to be fanciful fairy tales, and line up favorably with what we have been able to learn about ancient Egypt from scholarly non-biblical research, then they should be considered by fair-minded, reasonable people as accurate history, short of directly contrary evidence.

Furthermore, the fact that the Bible is a *religious* document has no relevance to the question of the nature and degree of its historical accuracy (which, I have consistently maintained, is extraordinary and well-nigh unquestionable). The two different aspects can be independently scrutinized.

6

THE CURIOUS CASE OF CAMELS

So Jacob arose, and set his sons and his wives on camels.

—GENESIS 31:17

Many biblical skeptics have claimed that camels in the Bible are anachronistic and portrayed in ways that are historically inaccurate. For example, a transcript of a National Public Radio show proclaims:

> Camels as a means of transportation abound in the Old Testament. When Abraham sends a servant to look for a bride for his son Isaac, that servant chooses Rebecca. And why? Because of her kindness in offering to water the camels. That's just one of dozens of camel cameos in the Bible, mostly in the book of Genesis, but scholars have long suspected that those camel caravans are a literary anachronism.[79]

Time Magazine joins in:

> The Bible says that Abraham, along with other patriarchs of Judaism and Christianity, used domesticated camels—

> as well as donkeys, sheep, oxen, and slaves—in his various travels and trade agreements. Or did he? . . .
>
> The phantom camel is just one of many historically jumbled references in the Bible.[80]

Can the integrity of the Bible survive this onslaught? The answer is a resounding "yes."

Let's look at how Christians and Jews have responded to these rather serious charges of inaccuracy. Dewayne Bryant surveys the record of use of camels in the ancient Near East:

> The camel was well known in Egypt from earliest times, as early as the Fourth Dynasty [c. 2613–2494 B.C.]. . . . Although the domestication of the camel may have come much later, it nevertheless preceded the age of the patriarchs. . . . A cylinder seal from Syria (c. 1800 B.C.) depicts two short figures riding a camel.[81]

He outlines the mention of camels in the Bible:

> The Bible records the existence of domesticated camels in the patriarchal narratives, but their footprint is actually quite small. They are listed among the very last items in the total wealth of both Abraham (Gen. 12:16) and Jacob (30:43; 32:7,15). They are mentioned as being used for travel by the patriarchs (24:10–64; 31:17,34) and by the Midianites (37:25). The Egyptians used them for transport as well (Exod. 9:3). Despite their use for transportation, however, the donkey appears as the favored mode of transportation for the patriarchs. In the ancient Near East as a whole, the same might be said during the early second millennium B.C.—the camel was known and domesticated, but not widely used until later.

Archaeologist Joseph P. Free makes the crucial distinctions:

> Many who have rejected this reference to Abraham's camels seem to have assumed something which the text does not state. It should be carefully noted that the biblical reference does not necessarily indicate that the camel was common in Egypt at the time, nor does it evidence that the Egyptians had made any great progress in the breeding and domestication of the camel. It merely says that Abraham had camels.[82]

Kenneth Kitchen sums up the matter similarly: "The camel was for long a *marginal* beast in most of the historic ancient Near East (including Egypt), but it was *not* wholly unknown or anachronistic before or during 2000–1100."[83]

Orthodox rabbi and Bible scholar Joshua Berman offers fascinating related insights:

> Camels in Genesis are right where they belong. It is true that camels were not domesticated in Israel until the time of Solomon. But read Genesis carefully and you see that all its camels come from outside of Israel, from Syria, Mesopotamia, and Egypt, where there is ample evidence of domestication of the camel during the period of the patriarchs. . . .
>
> But what about the camels that carried Joseph off to Egypt (Gen. 37:25)? Here, too, Scripture tells us that the camels arrived from outside of Canaan. And just as the spices they bore surely came from the east, so, too, we may surmise, did the camels. And while Jacob rode camels on his trek back from Mesopotamia (31:17; cf. 30:43), nowhere in Genesis does anyone ride a camel originating in Canaan. In the Joseph story, the brothers descend to Egypt exclusively

on donkeys (42:26–27; 43:24; 44:3, 13); that's what people rode in Canaan. And thus when Joseph sends them to fetch Jacob, he provides them with donkeys and she-asses (45:23); those were the animals they knew how to handle.[84]

There are many articles about camels in the ancient Near East and in relation to the biblical accounts (see Appendix A).

Below you will find a synopsis of the Old Testament references to camels, to back up the points made. The word *camel* in the RSV-CE appears fifty-five times in the thirty-nine Old Testament books that Catholics, Protestants, and Orthodox agree are canonical:

1) Genesis 12:16. The first mention of camels in the Bible describes them as being possessed by the pharaoh of Egypt. Translations differ a bit, but some (NASB, CEV, TEV) clearly state that Pharaoh "gave" camels and the other things mentioned to Abraham. Other versions (Confraternity, NAB) state that Abraham "received" camels, or that Pharaoh was "presenting him" with them (Moffatt) or that Abraham was the "recipient" of camels, and also "sheep, oxen, he-asses, menservants, maidservants, she-asses" (RSV-CE). A pharaoh would obviously have the power and resources to procure all of this, including camels. None of this has any bearing as to whether camels were domesticated (widely or at all) in Israel during Abraham's time.

2) Genesis 24:10–64 (sixteen times). These all refer to Abraham's camels, which (it appears) he originally received from Pharaoh. How do we know that? Apart from the above data, it's a reasonable deduction from what one of his servants said: "The Lord has greatly blessed my master, and

he has become great; he has given him flocks and herds, silver and gold, menservants and maidservants, camels and asses" (v. 35).

This strongly reflects Pharaoh's possessions as listed in Genesis 12:16.

Horses are *not* mentioned. Why? Well, it's because the earliest known date for them in Egypt is "about 1700–1550 B.C."[85] Thus, the Bible is proven to be historically accurate yet again.

3) Genesis 30:43, 31:17, 34, 32:7, 15. Jacob has camels (and "large flocks, maidservants and menservants," and "asses"). These obviously were in his possession as the son of Isaac, who had inherited them from his father Abraham. It would be like someone bringing koala bears and kangaroos from Australia to the United States, which then reproduce. This doesn't prove that there is large-scale domestication of these animals in America. It proves that a select few were present in America after having been brought from somewhere else.

4) Genesis 37:25. In this instance, the camels are possessed by "Ishmaelites coming from Gilead." Gilead is in present-day Jordan—close to Israel, but not *in* it. So once again, the Bible is *not* saying that camels were indigenous to or domesticated in Israel. Archaeological proof of domestication *in Gilead* applies to the time period of the tenth century B.C. (more on that below).

5) Exodus 9:3. This refers to camels—not necessarily domesticated—in Egypt, many proofs of which I presented above.

6) Leviticus 11:4; Deuteronomy 14:7. Moses mentions camels as one of the unclean animals, not to be eaten, as part of the Law that he delivered to Israel. This occurs in

the Sinai Peninsula—not part of Israel or Canaan at the time. But the instructions refer to "all the beasts that are on the earth" (11:2), not just specifically in Israel. So this proves little with regard to widespread use of camels in Israel. There's no evidence (archaeological or from the Bible) that they *were* until the tenth and ninth centuries B.C.

Thus far, in our survey, nothing proves that the Bible is dead wrong or anachronistic about camels.

That is the entire biblical mention of camels up through the life of Moses. As we see, it is never stated that Moses was riding a camel, etc. It simply says that Egyptians had them and that they shouldn't be eaten as part of the dietary prohibitions in the Jewish Law.

7) Judges 6:5, 7:12. This time, the camels are described—so many that they "could not be counted"—as in the possession of "the Midianites and the Amalekites and the people of the East" (6:3). Midian was in the northwest Arabian Peninsula. The Amalekites are from the Negev, the southern part of Israel now, but "historically part of a separate region (known in Roman times as Arabia Petraea)." Thus, again, it wasn't part of either Judah or Israel, neither prior to the ninth century B.C. nor until much later (1922, in fact). When Judges 6:4 refers to these enemies killing animals of Israel, no camels are mentioned. Rather, they leave "no sheep or ox or ass."

8) Judges 8:21, 26. The camels referred to are owned by Zebah and Zalmunna, who are "kings of Midian" (8:5).

9) 1 Samuel 15:3. The camels (to be slain) are owned by the Amalekites.

10) 1 Samuel 27:9. The camels are owned by the "Geshurites, the Girzites, and the Amalekites" (v. 8). David took

away camels and other animals. This would explain the origin of his having camels. Once again, they don't originate from Israel itself, though this is almost the time that even the minimalist biblical archaeologists say the camel was domesticated in Israel. The Geshurites "dwelt in the desert between Arabia and Philistia." The Girzites dwelt "between the south of Palestine and Egypt."

11) 1 Samuel 30:17. Refers to camels owned by the Amalekites (see also vv. 1,13).

12) 1 Kings 10:2 (see also 2 Chron. 9:1). These are owned by the Queen of Sheba (v. 1). Scholars differ as to whether Sheba was in South Arabia or modern-day Sudan. In any event, it wasn't ancient Israel. But this is about the time where all agree that archaeology gives evidence of camel domestication in Israel.

13) 2 Kings 8:9. The camels in this instance are from Damascus, Syria.

14) 1 Chronicles 5:21. The camels are owned by the Hagrites (v. 19), who lived east of Gilead in present-day Jordan. Note that the Israelites "carried off fifty thousand of their camels." That's certainly enough to start widespread domestication in Israel. This was "in the days of Jeroboam king of Israel" (v. 17). Jeroboam was the first king of the northern kingdom of Israel (as opposed to Judah). He reigned for twenty-two years, sometime in the last third of the tenth century B.C. In other words, this was *right before* the first archaeological evidence of widespread camel use in Israel, in the ninth century B.C.

15) 1 Chronicles 12:40. This describes Israelites using camels to carry food, just before David becomes king

(c. 1000 B.C.). But it's not evidence of *widespread* use or domestication.

16) 1 Chronicles 27:30. "Over the camels was Obil the Ishmaelite." In other words, even when David has many camels, a non-Jew takes care of them, because he is familiar with how to do it, whereas the Jews are not.

17) 2 Chronicles 14:15. Camels are obtained after a successful battle with the Ethiopians, during the reign of King Asa of Judah (v. 1), who reigned between 913–910 and 873–869 B.C., during the time that all agree camels were present in large numbers in Israel.

18) Ezra 2:67 (see also Neh. 7:69). Describes the Israelites having 435 camels at the time of their return to Israel from Babylon, which occurred in 539 B.C., some 300 or more years after the time everyone agrees many camels were in domestic use in Israel.

19) Job 1:3, 17; 42:12. Virtually no Christian scholars believe that the book of Job can be dated earlier than King Solomon's reign (about 970 to 931 B.C.), and many think it was written several hundred years after that. For example, Bible scholar John E. Hartley states:

> The interplay between this book and other OT books, especially Isaiah, can best be accounted for by placing this work in the seventh century B.C.[86]

Another commentary on Job places the date of the book even later:

> It is between 500 (date suggested by the influence of Zechariah on Job) and 450 (date suggested by the influence of

Job on Malachi) that the book was probably composed.[87]

In other words, almost all of the estimates are after the time (tenth century) that the "skeptical" (and even Bible-believing) archaeologists agree about evidence for wide-spread (and domesticated) camels in Israel.

20) The remaining references (Isa. 21:7, 30:6, 60:6; Jer. 2:23, 49:29,32; Ezek. 25:5; Zech. 14:15) occur after this same period and are, therefore, utterly uncontroversial. Isaiah lived in the eighth century B.C., Jeremiah in the seventh and sixth, Ezekiel in the sixth, and Zechariah in the sixth and maybe into the fifth.

Once again, then, the Bible is absolutely right—and those who are inexplicably hostile to it dead wrong.

7

OUT OF EGYPT WITH MOSES

And when she could hide him no longer she took for him a basket made of bulrushes, and daubed it with bitumen and pitch; and she put the child in it and placed it among the reeds at the river's brink.

—EXODUS 2:3

I entered into a controversy with a prominent anti-theist when he flat-out denied that pitch was available in Egypt during the time of Moses (whether locally or through trade). This stimulated my curiosity and indeed became the back-and-forth exchange that kick-started a series of discussions that evolved into this book. The issue of pitch is a relatively insignificant detail in the overall scheme of things, yet it provides a good opportunity to archaeologically verify the Bible's accuracy—as far back as some thirty-four centuries ago.

My atheist friend claimed that bitumen was available *only* in Sumeria (which is also untrue). The *Encyclopedia Britannica* defines bitumen as

> dense, highly viscous, petroleum-based hydrocarbon that is found in deposits such as oil sands and pitch lakes (natural bitumen). . . . In some areas, particularly in the United States, bitumen is often called asphalt. . . . Bitumen is also frequently called tar or pitch.

One scientific article documents the use of pitch or bitumen in ancient Egypt before the time of Moses, "during the earlier Chalcolithic and Early Bronze Age periods (3900–2200 B.C.)."[88]

A second article cited in this one documents "the first evidence of the trade and export of raw bitumens from the Dead Sea area within Canaan and to Egyptian trading centers on the mainland route to Egypt between 3900 and 2200 B.C."[89] It even notes that "their earliest use was in making reed baskets impermeable to liquids."

Was pitch present in Egypt at the time of Moses? It *was*, according to archaeological research, long before, by trade, and it was also available near Cairo, probably relatively close to where Moses was born.

Archaeology can't prove every minute particular. It operates in generalities. But for what it *has* shown us in this regard, everything fits perfectly with the biblical account of a basket of bulrushes (which held baby Moses) being waterproofed by pitch and bitumen in the fourteenth century B.C. in Egypt, on the Nile Delta.

More evidence for bitumen use in Egypt (and for caulking reed baskets) during the time of Moses might be found in the *shaduf*: an early crane-like tool used in irrigation. This useful machine was "invented in Mesopotamia and Egypt around 2000 B.C."[90] It had a long pole with (usually) a bitumen-covered reed basket at the end. It "appeared in Upper Egypt sometime after 2000

B.C., during the Eighteenth Dynasty (ca. 1570 B.C.)."[91]

Now let's get to Moses himself. First of all, could he read and write?

In Exodus 24:4, we read that "Moses wrote all the words of the Lord." (See also Lev. 26:46; Deut. 31:9; Josh. 8:32, 23:6; Mark 12:26.) And in Acts 7:21–22: "Pharaoh's daughter adopted him and brought him up as her own son. And Moses was instructed in all the wisdom of the Egyptians, and he was mighty in his words and deeds." (See also Exod. 2:10.)

The well-known atheist Bart Ehrman wrote an article on his blog concerning the question of whether Moses (who he denies even existed, but places in the thirteenth century B.C. *if* he did exist) could have written the Hebrew in the first five books of the Bible (called the *Torah* or *Pentateuch*) that has been passed down to us in manuscripts.[92]

He wrote a letter regarding this question to an academic colleague of his, Joseph Lam.[93] Lam answered Ehrman as follows:

> If there was a Moses, raised in the Egyptian court, he probably would have learned to write in Egyptian! The texts of the Pentateuch, whoever wrote them, are *not* in the thirteenth-century language; they are in classical first-millennium Hebrew. Whatever a hypothetical thirteenth-century Moses wrote, whether in Egyptian or Canaanite or something else, that's *not* what we have preserved in the Pentateuch.

The key concepts that we need to consider and understand, in pondering the above, are the notions of 1) *appropriation of existing cultural forms* and 2) *the inherently evolving nature of language*. Many scholars inclined to be skeptical toward the Bible will say things like, "Hebrew didn't exist until the tenth century B.C.; therefore, neither Moses nor anyone else prior to the tenth century could have written the Pentateuch." Lam (whatever his own views of the Bible may be) essentially states just that.

But I submit that such a statement and the premises behind it involve a sort of sleight-of-hand. It disregards or minimizes ever-evolving language and also the universally accepted later editing and slight modifications (grammar, spelling, changing geographical names, etc.) of the Bible.

Kenneth Kitchen, who more or less defends the "traditional" view of Moses, takes all of this into account in his summary of the evidence for an early form of Hebrew or proto-Hebrew prior to Moses, and a plausible written Pentateuch by his time (possibly written by Moses):

> The recently invented West Semitic alphabet [was] a vehicle deigned by and for Semitic speakers (and writers). The oldest known examples have been the Lachish dagger epigraph from a seventeenth-century tomb and the Tell Nagila sherd (Middle/Late Bronze, ca. 1600); we now have also the Wadi Hol graffiti in Egypt from northwest of Thebes, about the seventeenth century. . . . To these must be added the proto-Sinaitic inscriptions of disputed date—circa 1800 or circa 1500. This system of not more than thirty simple, semipictographic letters would have been very easy to use in writing up (on papyrus) a "first written edition" of the patriarchal traditions from Abraham to Jacob, to which a Joseph account could be added. This set of basic narratives could then be recopied from circa 1600 to the thirteenth century, then given a "late Canaanite" editing in that phase of the script, eventuating into early standard Hebrew language and script from the united monarchy [c. 1000 B.C.] onward. . . . This straightforward

> view is at least consistent with all the *factual* data that we currently possess, and keeps theorizing to a minimum.[94]

Kitchen in his book addresses the topic of the plausibility of Moses, or someone like him, writing much of the Pentateuch. It would have required someone who had "experience of life at the Egyptian court" and "knowledge of treaty-type documents":

> Exodus 2:10 . . . implies his becoming a member of the ruling body of courtiers, officials, and attendants that served the pharaoh as his government leaders under the viziers, treasury chiefs, etc. Such a youth would need to be fully fluent in Egyptian (not just his own West Semitic tongue); so he would be subjected to the Egyptian educational system.[95]

Kitchen notes how Pharaohs Sethos I (r. c. 1294–1279 B.C.) and Ramesses II (r. 1279–1213 B.C.) signed treaties with Hittite kings and that "scribes at *both* courts produced drafts to be exchanged for mutual approval or amendment"—which would in turn "explain how a Hebrew leader might later come to use this convenient and appropriate framework for the Sinai covenant."

In another article, Kitchen highlights the striking similarities between the Pentateuch and other ancient Near Eastern treaties from the same time period:

> At the heart of Exodus and Leviticus (and almost all of Deuteronomy) we have two exposés of a treaty-type covenant between Israel and its heavenly King, echoed also in Joshua 24. The format and content of these three presentations is basically consistent (with minor

> variations). From the ancient biblical world, between c. 2800 B.C. and Julius Caesar (46 B.C.), we have from the Near East *over 100 examples* of such documents. Importantly, the format *varies* from age to age—and that of Ex-Lev., Deut. & Jos. 24 is consistent in all three cases *exclusively* with the forms current within c. 1350 to c. 1180 B.C., *and with no other period, earlier or later.* . . .
>
> As a foreigner at court, he [Moses] surely was put to serve in the Egyptian "foreign office." . . . There, he would be involved with treaties, laws, etc.[96]

Kitchen describes a plausible scenario for the early parts of the Bible having been originally written by Moses and later revised or modified into later versions of Hebrew:

> From the fourteenth/thirteenth century onward, the [Canaanite] alphabet could be freely used for any form of communication. The contemporary north Semitic texts found at Ugarit in north Phoenicia illustrate this to perfection. . . . The Amarna evidence [c. 1360–1332 B.C.] and handful of pottery finds prove clearly that Canaanite was the dominant local tongue and could be readily expressed in alphabetic writing. . . . During the two centuries that followed, circa 1200–1000, standard Hebrew evolved out of this form of Canaanite, probably being fully formed by David's time. Copies of older works such as Deuteronomy or Joshua would be recopied, modernizing outdated grammatical forms and spellings.[97]

Various archaeological evidences of proto-Hebrew or paleo-Hebrew, proto-Sinaic or proto-Canaanite writing, and use of the alphabet before the time of Moses exist. One object, dated to 1450 B.C., was discovered in 1995:

> Newly deciphered Egyptian symbols on a 3,400-year-old limestone ostracon from Luxor's Tomb of Senneferi appear to be the first written evidence of the ABC letter order of the early Semitic alphabet.[98]

Further exciting discoveries in Egypt related to the Semitic/Hebrew origins of the alphabet have pushed back the previously accepted time period:

> Egyptologists have found limestone inscriptions that they say are the earliest known examples of alphabetic writing. Their discovery is expected to help fix the time and place for the origin of the alphabet. . . .
>
> Carved in the cliffs of soft stone, the writing, in a Semitic script with Egyptian influences, has been dated to somewhere between 1900 and 1800 B.C., two or three centuries earlier than previously recognized uses of a nascent alphabet.[99]

In March 2022, a ground-breaking discovery was announced with regard to ancient Hebrew: "The earliest proto-alphabetic Hebrew text—including the name of God, 'YHWH'—ever discovered in ancient Israel." The lead "curse tablet" is dated at circa 1200 B.C. and is purported to be "the first attested use of the name of God in the Land of Israel and would set the clock back on proven Israelite literacy by several centuries—showing that the Israelites were literate when they entered the Holy Land, and therefore could have written the Bible as some of the events it documents took place." This would be "500 years older than the previously attested use of the tetragrammaton YHWH."[100]

This "curse tablet" was discovered at Mount Ebal, the site of what appears to be an altar built by Joshua (Josh.

8:31; see also Deut. 27:15–26), discussed in chapter ten. The ceremony was held there in accordance with Deuteronomy, once Joshua and the Israelites entered Canaan:

> And afterward he read all the words of the law [to the people], the blessing and the curse, according to all that is written in the book of the law (Josh. 8:33–34).

Gershon Galil, professor of biblical studies and ancient history at the University of Haifa, cited in a *Times of Israel* article, commented further on the find,

> We know that from the moment they came to Israel, the Israelites knew how to write, including the name of God, clearly. . . . It's not too surprising; people already knew how to write in other places.[101]

The article continues:

> Galil told *The Times of Israel* that the text is largely written in an archaic proto-Canaanite script, with some letters coming from hieroglyphs. The latest date of the epigraphic analysis would put it circa the twelfth century, while some elements are dated to even earlier. . . .
>
> "The person who wrote this text had the ability to write every text in the Bible," Galil stated.

The tablet was probably inscribed with an iron pin, a practice mentioned in Job (19:24). In fact, an iron stylus was also found at the same site. It's known that the lead came from mines in Greece, active in the Late Bronze Age.

Now let's discuss some geography.

> **Exodus 1:11** Therefore they set taskmasters over them to afflict them with heavy burdens; and they built for Pharaoh store-cities, Pithom and Ra-amses. (See also Gen. 47:11; Exod. 12:37; Num. 33:3,5.)

Pi-Ramesses was the new capital of Egypt, built by Pharaoh Ramesses II (r. 1279–1213 B.C.), on the Pelusiac branch of the Nile. It had a population of more than 300,000. We know that the Pelusiac branch eventually silted up, creating water supply problems. Thus, around 1075 B.C., the capital was moved to Tanis on the new Tanitic branch of the Nile, 62 miles northwest of Pi-Ramesses.

James Hoffmeier writes:

> Locating Rameses of the exodus narratives occupied early Egyptologists for a century before its identification was finally established. In the 1950s the Coptic Christian Egyptologist, Labib Habachi, began investigating a little-known site in the NE Delta called Qantir. He believed that he had identified Pi-Ramesses. . . . There is no more doubt that this is ancient Pi-Ramesses, the city built by and named for Ramesses the Great.[102]

Kenneth Kitchen, from whom we've heard much already, specializes in the ancient Egyptian Ramesside Period (i.e., Dynasties 19–20) and the Third Intermediate Period of Egypt, as well as ancient Egyptian chronology, having written more than 250 books and journal articles on these and other subjects since the mid-1950s. He adds, regarding what skeptics refer to as the utter lack of Egyptian evidence regarding the Exodus:

> Warrior-pharaohs always report victories, but *never* defeats. . . . A "draw" is glossed over as a victory; so, Ramesses II's

> battle of Qadesh with the Hittites. Thus, the successful escape of a good-sized body of rebellious slaves—such as our Hebrews under Moses—will *not* be found celebrated in any Egyptian official text! . . . There will *never* be found any official Egyptian record of the Exodus. . . . The old adage applies with a vengeance: "Absence of evidence does *not* prove to be evidence of absence."[103]

Thus, the Bible is minutely accurate again, about place names at precisely the right period of history, and in relation to the known history of Egyptian pharaohs.

As for Pithom, though opinions are mixed, some archaeologists believe that Tell el-Retaba is the site of ancient Pithom. If so, the distance between Pi-Ramesses (Qantir) and Pithom (Tell el-Retaba)—the two biblical "store-cities"—is about 29 miles. They are both located in the eastern Nile Delta region. Exodus 11:1 informs us that the Hebrew slaves "built" Pithom. This would be during the reign of Pharaoh Ramesses II (1279–1213 B.C.). Recent extensive Polish-Slovakian excavations confirmed this. Here is what the researchers concluded as to the date:

> In the Second Intermediate Period (eighteenth-sixteenth century B.C.), the first settlers—the Hyksos from Syria-Palestine—appeared in the area. With the beginning of the New Kingdom (sixteenth century B.C.), an Egyptian settlement was established on the site. In the thirteenth century B.C., during the reign of Ramesses II, a fortress surrounded by "Wall 1" was established. During the reign of Ramesses III in the first half of the twelfth century B.C., a new, larger fortress was constructed and surrounded by a much more massive "Wall 2."[104]

In other words, there was a "settlement" 500 years before this time, but apparently no large-scale structures, let alone a "fortress." Thus, when the Bible says the city was "built," it referred to the fortress walls and other large structures being built, or the city being significantly *fortified*. We might say, similarly, that "the *modern* city of San Francisco was built after the earthquake of 1906" when, in fact, the city was *re*-built then.

On the same page, the researchers note that in the fourteenth century B.C., there was a "settlement hiatus for 100 years." Then, at the "beginning of thirteenth century B.C." (i.e., precisely the time of Pharaoh Ramesses II), there was "construction of fortress with 'Wall 1' (core and enlargement); several decades of fortress usage." As for the biblical reference to "store-cities" the researchers described various structures on the site that would be consistent with that notion: "defense walls, housings, stables for animals, granaries, and burial chambers" along with "small houses, extensions and small silos."

And what were the primary building materials? Exodus 5 refers six times to "bricks" (5:7–8, 14, 16, 18–19). Likewise, the article states, "All structures in Tell el-Retaba were constructed of material commonly referred to as 'mud brick.'"

> Defense walls were among the most massive constructions that were built of mud bricks in ancient Egypt.[105]

So *that* obviously lines up with the biblical description. These mud brick walls were about 20 feet thick, and the site included "granaries," according to the Polish Center of Mediterranean Archaeology, University of Warsaw.[106] This was no small-scale building task.

For more on building materials in ancient Egypt, we can look to Exodus 5.

> The same day Pharaoh commanded the taskmasters of the people and their foremen, "You shall no longer give the people straw to make bricks, as heretofore; let them go and gather straw for themselves. But the number of bricks which they made heretofore you shall lay upon them, you shall by no means lessen it." . . .
>
> So the taskmasters and the foremen of the people went out and said to the people, "Thus says Pharaoh, `I will not give you straw. Go yourselves, get your straw wherever you can find it; but your work will not be lessened in the least." So the people were scattered abroad throughout all the land of Egypt, to gather stubble for straw. . . . The foremen of the people of Israel saw that they were in evil plight, when they said, "You shall by no means lessen your daily number of bricks" (vv. 6–8, 10–12, 19).

Robert J. Littman, chair of the Classics Department at the University of Hawaii; Jay Silverstein, adjunct professor of archaeology at the University of Hawaii; and Marta Lorenzon, archaeologist at the University of Helsinki, address precisely this topic. They state,

> Egyptians collected top-soil because it had the right composition of clay, silt, and sand and formed the hardest and most durable brick. . . . To create bricks capable of bearing the weight of large structures and surviving the elements, straw temper is added. . . .
>
> Two New Kingdom Egyptian sources—a leather scroll from the fifth year of Ramesses II's reign and Papyrus Anastasi III from the third year of Merneptah's reign, both from the thirteenth century—refer to brick making. According to the former, the daily quota was 2,000 mudbricks. . . .

> An Egyptian leather scroll in the Louvre, dated to year 5 of the reign of Ramesses II (1275 BCE), relates that 40 stable masters (junior officers) were each responsible for a quota of 2,000 bricks produced by men under them. . . .
>
> This daily quota, documented from the time of Pharaoh Ramesses II, is reflected in the biblical texts Exodus 5:8: "number of bricks" and 5:19: "your daily number of bricks."[107]

How important was the straw in the process, and how difficult to find it in this place in Egypt? The researchers further comment:

> We made some bricks without straw. We used the same process to manufacture the mudbricks but left out the straw chaff. The bricks without straw were fragile and broke easily. . . .
>
> If Pharaoh did not supply the Israelites with straw, presumably from his storage units, then the search for the right chaff would have been almost impossible, which is perhaps the point of the story.

A similar scholarly article describes some of the advantages of using straw in brickmaking:

> Tempers, sometimes referred to as degreasers or additives, include both vegetal (especially straw or chaff) and nonvegetal inclusions (e.g., potsherds, grog, ashes). They are added to the matrix to make the mixture more pliable, to increase tensile strength, and to improve thermal behavior.[108]

Virginia L. Emery, postdoctoral fellow in Western heritage at Carthage College, informs her readers, in harmony with the above observations,

> Chopped straw is then added to the earth mixture in a ratio of roughly one part straw to five parts earth.[109]

Yet another scholarly source adds to the evidence:

> P. Anastasi III (verso) 1.2–3.3, dated to the reign of Merneptah (r. 1224–1214 BCE), includes a ledger of sorts recording various building works, including the making of bricks. P. Anastasi IV 12.6 = P. Anastasi V 3.1, dated to the time of Seti II (r. 1214–1208 BCE), includes the complaint, "there are no men to mold bricks, and there is no straw in the district," calling to mind Exodus 5:16.[110]

Specifically regarding Pithom (Tell el-Retaba) and the straw and bricks issue, Slovakian researchers Miroslav Černy and Jozef Hudec, both from the Institute of Oriental Studies, Slovak Academy of Sciences (Bratislava), state,

> Production of mudbricks was recorded on the paintings in the tomb of Rekhmire (Eighteenth Dynasty). Men moisturized dug-out soil, kneaded it with minced straw, and transported it to a place where they molded it into rectangular forms into bricks, which were then placed in the sun to dry. . . .
>
> Chopped straw and animal dung increase the strength and plasticity. . . . Bricks were connected together by a mortar made from mud blended with sand, straw, and chaff.[111]

We now see that the Bible's accuracy regarding the two

store-cities Pi-Ramesses and Pithom is rather spectacularly verified in at least eleven distinct ways:

1) the specific time frame of the city of Ramesses (or Ra'amses);

2) the specific time frame of the city of Pithom;

3) the *name* of the city of Pithom;

4) the *name* of the city of Ramesses;

5) Pithom being made (solely) of (mud) *bricks*;

6) the function of Pithom as a *store-city*;

7) the function of Ramesses as a *store-city*;

8) Pithom being built (or, technically, rebuilt or fortified) *at the same time as Ramesses*, during the time of Pharaoh Ramesses II;

9) *straw* (or chaff) being an important cohesive ingredient in the bricks (bricks without straw were far inferior);

10) a *daily quota of brickmaking* for workers to meet; and

11) the *extreme difficulty of finding enough straw* without the Egyptians providing it.

8

THE TEN PLAGUES AND THEIR AFTERMATH

"I will lay my hand upon Egypt and bring forth my hosts, my people the sons of Israel, out of the land of Egypt by great acts of judgment."

—EXODUS 7:4

In the biblical, Christian worldview—among those who accept biblical inspiration—extraordinary recorded events may be purely natural phenomena, wholly supernatural, or a combination. That's the question to be pondered with regard to the plagues of Egypt.

Sometimes in the Bible God is described as having caused a natural event. In these cases, the meaning would be that God "upholds" creation and caused the origin of natural laws, which now govern natural events, short of the rare miraculous divine intervention with a miracle. In God's providence, these natural events occur at just the right time, so that it can be said that God caused them. Other times, they are purely miraculous.

As to the exact nature of the plagues in particular, I'm not averse to any of these three possible scenarios. I have no ironclad opinion, no "agenda" to uphold. As stated previously, I fully believe that God can and does perform miracles, in both the past and the present. I'm only submitting possible natural explanations for consideration. That said, I shall explore the notion that nine of the ten plagues of Egypt *may* have a plausible natural explanation or cause.

Greta Hort (1903–1967), a brilliant Danish scholar, wrote an influential article about this, called "The Plagues of Egypt."[112] I don't read German, so I will rely on the descriptions of archaeologist James Hoffmeier[113] and scientific articles dealing with similar subject matter.

1) Plague of Blood

> **Exodus 7:20–21** Moses and Aaron . . . lifted up the rod and struck the water that was in the Nile, and all the water that was in the Nile turned to blood. And the fish in the Nile died; and the Nile became foul, so that the Egyptians could not drink water from the Nile; and there was blood throughout all the land of Egypt.

Hort tied this "plague" to the Nile's annual rise in July through September, where it is usually reddish in appearance owing to the presence of *Roterde*, particles of soil, suspended in the water. Hort posits a scenario that could result in the four conditions of red color, death of fish, foul smell, and undrinkability: millions of organisms called *flagellates* (*Euglena sanguinea* and *Haematoccus pluvalius*), probably originating from Ethiopia, in the floodwaters. At night, flagellates require more oxygen, which would cause the death of fish.

An article in *Live Science*, entitled "The Science of the 10 Plagues," opines similarly:

> The sudden appearance of red-hued waters in the Nile could have been caused by a red algae bloom, which appears when certain conditions enable a type of microscopic algae to reproduce in such great numbers that the waters they live in appear to be stained a bloody red. . . . These algae blooms can certainly be harmful to wildlife, as the algae contain a toxin that can accumulate in shellfish and poison the animals that feed on them.[114]

Now, a suspicious reader could fairly object that these explanations deny a literal turning to blood of the Nile, which the text, *prima facie*, seems to assert. But it's a question of whether the text *must* be taken *literally*, or whether it can be properly interpreted as phenomenological language, or the language of appearances. We know that the Bible often expresses that sort of language, and also that it does so specifically regarding "blood," like in Joel 2:31 ("the sun shall be turned to darkness, and the moon to blood") and Revelation 6:12 "the full moon became like blood").

Joel 2:31 seems at first glance to read literally, whereas Revelation 6:12 uses the comparative and analogical term "like." I daresay that no serious commentators would interpret either passage literally. They both clearly employ a metaphor for "red color." *Perhaps* Exodus 7:20–21 is an instance of the same thing.

2) *Plague of Frogs*

> **Exodus 8:6** So Aaron stretched out his hand over the waters of Egypt; and the frogs came up and covered the land of Egypt.

Hort argued that the next five plagues were caused by the

first. Frogs typically show up at the end of the Nile's flooding in September and October. Exodus 7:25 states that "seven days passed" between the first and second plagues. The death of the frogs (Exod. 8:13) was—so Hort surmised—due to *bacillus anthracis* from the dying and decomposing fish. The *Live Science* article provides more examples of this strange phenomenon:

> As it happens, the phenomenon of "raining frogs"[115] has been reported multiple times throughout history and in a range of locations around the world. A report published July 12, 1873 in *Scientific American* described "a shower of frogs which darkened the air and covered the ground for a long distance," following a recent rainstorm. . . .
>
> And in May 2010 in Greece, thousands of frogs emerged from a lake in the northern part of the country.[116]

3) *Plague of Gnats*

> **Exodus 8:16** Then the Lord said to Moses, "Say to Aaron, 'Stretch out your rod and strike the dust of the earth, that it may become gnats throughout all the land of Egypt.'"

The *Live Science* article on the plagues makes the rather obvious point that a "pile of dead frogs" would naturally lead to "a swarm of insects of some sort." This is perhaps the most plausible natural explanation of any of the plagues, and it would apply to the next one as well.

4) *Plague of Flies*

> **Exodus 8:21** Else, if you will not let my people go, behold, I will send swarms of flies on you and your servants and your people.

Flies are, of course, always present when dying and dead organic matter is to be found. A study from the journal *Caduceus* notes that fly bites might have led to the plague of boils later on.[117]

5) *Plague of Pestilence*

> **Exodus 9:2–3** For if you refuse to let them go and still hold them, behold, the hand of the Lord will fall with a very severe plague upon your cattle which are in the field, the horses, the asses, the camels, the herds, and the flocks.

Hort maintains that this was a result of anthrax spread by the frogs of the second plague. *Live Science* offers a plausible theory of what may have caused this:

> Rinderpest, an infectious and lethal viral disease . . . is thought to have originated in Asia, and traveled to Egypt 5,000 years ago . . . the New York Times reported in 2010.[118] Its mortality rate was exceptionally high, often exceeding 80 percent. It killed an estimated 200 million cattle in the eighteenth century, according to a study published in the journal *Medical History* in 1997,[119] and when rinderpest emerged in Africa in the nineteenth century, it killed 5.2 million cattle, causing one third of the population of Ethiopia to die of starvation, a study published in the journal *Science* reported in 2008. [120]

6) *Plague of Boils*

> **Exodus 9:9** And it shall become fine dust over all the land of Egypt, and become boils breaking out in sores on man and beast throughout all the land of Egypt.

Based on Deuteronomy 28:35 (knees, legs, foot), Hort deduced that this was caused by a fly from the fourth plague: *Stomoxys calcitrans*, which carried anthrax. The infection would have been spread as a result of these flies coming in contact with rotting animals after the fifth plague. *Stomoxys calcitrans*, also known as the stable fly, is indeed able to transmit disease, including boils. A scholarly article devoted to this topic states,

> Anthrax . . . affects animals and humans, inducing pulmonary, gastro-intestinal, or cutaneous symptoms, including a boil-like skin lesion. . . . Outbreaks are most common in areas characterized by alkaline, calcareous soil, and in warm environments with periodic episodes of flooding. . . .
>
> *B. anthracis* infections can also be mechanically transmitted by stable flies.[121]

Another similar article noted that "most of the soils in Egypt are alkaline, with pH values from 7 to 9"[122]

7) *Plague of Hail and Thunderstorms*

> **Exodus 9:23–24** Then Moses stretched forth his rod toward heaven; and the Lord sent thunder and hail, and fire ran down to the earth. And the Lord rained hail upon the land of Egypt; there was hail, and fire flashing continually in the midst of the hail, very heavy hail, such as had never been in all the land of Egypt since it became a nation.

The *Egypt Independent* newspaper reported in 2010 about a notable hailstorm:

> A heavy downpour of hail shocked residents of Cairo,

> Giza, and Helwan . . . turning streets and lawns into white, sparkly terrain.[123]

A severe thunderstorm happened in Egypt again in March 2020. CGTN Africa reported:

> Three people have lost their lives and 37 [were] injured in Egypt after severe thunderstorms and flooding in the country. The government has declared a state of emergency and advised citizens to stay home as the North African country braces for more rain until this weekend.[124]

8) *Plague of Locusts*

> **Exodus 10:12**, 15 Then the Lord said to Moses, "Stretch out your hand over the land of Egypt for the locusts, that they may come upon the land of Egypt, and eat every plant in the land, all that the hail has left."

Locust swarms have been common throughout the Near East and Africa both in ancient times and now. An Israeli article about locusts explains:

> Throughout history, locusts have been symbolic of major devastation. As depicted in legends and ancient texts all over the world, plagues of locusts were said to [have] caused famines, human migrations and untold destruction.[125]

2020 was a very bad year for locusts in various countries of Africa, according to an NPR report:

> The swarms are gargantuan masses of tens of billions of flying bugs. They range anywhere from a square third

> of a mile to 100 square miles or more, with 40 million to 80 million locusts packed in half a square mile. They bulldoze pasturelands in dark clouds the size of football fields and small cities. In northern Kenya . . . one swarm was reported to be 25 miles long by 37 miles wide—it would blanket the city of Paris twenty-four times over.[126]

A cited expert noted the extreme amount of damage locusts can cause:

> When they do descend, they can have almost total devastation. They can cause 50 to 80 percent of crops to be destroyed, depending on the time [of year].

So many locust swarms have been documented throughout history that it's entirely plausible that the plague of locusts was a purely natural event.

9) *Plague of Darkness*

> **Exodus 10:22–23** So Moses stretched out his hand toward heaven, and there was thick darkness in all the land of Egypt three days; they did not see one another, nor did any rise from his place.

This plague has traditionally been associated with desert sandstorms, or *khamsins*, which frequently occur in Egypt in March. Hort noted that conditions would be even worse after the aftermath damage to crops from the earlier plagues, causing even more dust to be swept up in the storms, and yet more darkness.

These sorts of sandstorms, which regularly occur in Egypt between March and May, are likely similar to what happened during the famous "Dust Bowl" period in the Great Plains of the United States in the 1930s. One particularly frightening storm took place on what was called "Black Sunday," April 14, 1935, in Oklahoma and Texas. A National Weather Service article describes it:

> A mountain of blackness swept across the High Plains and instantly turned a warm, sunny afternoon into a horrible blackness that was darker than the darkest night . . . a massive wall of blowing dust that resembled a land-based tsunami. Winds in the panhandle reached upwards of 60 mph, and for at least a brief time, the blackness was so complete that one could not see their own hand in front of their face.[127]

10) *Plague of the Death of Egyptian Firstborn*

> **Exodus 11:4–5** And Moses said, "Thus says the Lord: About midnight I will go forth in the midst of Egypt; and all the firstborn in the land of Egypt shall die, from the firstborn of Pharaoh who sits upon his throne, even to the firstborn of the maidservant who is behind the mill; and all the firstborn of the cattle."

It's difficult to conceive of a purely natural explanation for this plague. Some of the previous nine plagues, however, were also of a "selective" nature, which suggests direct divine, miraculous, or supernatural intervention. In the (fourth) plague of flies, only the Egyptians were affected, not the Hebrews (Exod. 8:21–22), though geographical separation may explain that. In the (fifth) plague of pestilence, God distinguished between Egyptian and Hebrew cattle (9:4–7). The (seventh) plague of hail, again, did not affect the Hebrews in Goshen (v. 26).

All of this suggests that it was usually a *mixture* of natural and supernatural occurrences, and not (or at least not *always*) purely one or the other. A purely natural explanation is not possible, or so it seems, in the cases of four out of the ten plagues.

Having examined the devastation wrought upon Egypt to free Moses' people, let's now look at some contentions regarding what became of those people once they were freed.

> **Exodus 12:37** And the people of Israel journeyed from Rameses to Succoth, about six hundred thousand men on foot, besides women and children. (See also Num. 1:45–46.)

If taken literally and including women and children, the number is about two million. Biblical skeptics and atheists have had a field day with these numbers for hundreds of years, with words like "ridiculous" and "mythical" and "fictional" freely slung about. They say (plausibly!) that such large numbers stagger the imagination—that the logistics of that many people traveling for forty years in a desert would simply be impossible. And they could also point out (as I do myself) that this is far more than the estimated population of the city they left (Pi-Ramesses).

Anti-theist atheist polemicist Jonathan M.S. Pearce provides an example of this scoffing skepticism:

> The probability that this actually happened as described, or even at all, is so remotely small as to be laughable. But more than anything, the story looks incredibly mythological or fictional in nature. These claims are ridiculous. Don't be precious and reactive because this is your precious Bible. These claims are ridiculous.[128]

Colin J. Humphreys, a renowned physicist who has also been published in leading biblical journals, takes up the challenge and addresses this topic:

> It is shown that if there were "273 firstborn Israelites who exceed the number of Levites" (Num. 3:43), then the total number of Israelite men aged over twenty in the census following the Exodus was about 5,000, not 603,550, as apparently recorded in Numbers. The apparent error in Numbers arises because the ancient Hebrew word *lp* can mean "thousand," "troop," or "leader," according to the context. . . .
>
> The total number of men, women, and children at the Exodus was about 20,000 rather than the figure of over 2 million apparently suggested by the book of Numbers.[129]

Jewish writer Ben-Zion Katz deals with the same question in a similar manner:

> Another modern suggestion—first suggested by Flinders Petrie (1853–1942), is that ףלא, usually translated "thousand," should be translated like ףולא (troop or contingent). Examples of this use of ףולא include Exodus 15:15, "clans of Edom (יפולא םודא)," and Gen. 36:15–30 (also in regard to Edom).
>
> Aside from the fact that ףולא means contingent, in several instances in the Bible, the word ףלא itself may not literally mean "thousand":
>
> They were every one of them heads of ancestral houses of the *contingents* of Israel (Josh. 22:14).
>
> Why, my *clan* is the humblest in Manasseh, and I am the youngest in my father's household (Judg. 6:15).
>
> And you, O Bethlehem of Ephrath, least among the *clans* of Judah (Micah 5:1). . . .
>
> Recognizing the military nature of the census, I

> believe it is still possible to translate אלף as "contingents" by understanding the two phrases—the one that precedes the word אלף and the one that follows it—as two different kinds of measurement. Thus, to take Numbers 1:21 (the fighting men of Reuben) for example:
>
> Instead of translating 46 אלף and 5 hundred as "46,500," it could be translated as "46 contingents, or [i.e., equaling] 500 [men]." Standard concordances list "or" as one of the meanings for a connecting *vav*, as in Exodus 21:17: "He who curses his mother *or* his father shall surely be put to death."[130]

We can also inquire as to how many Hebrew slaves might have been in the larger capitol city, Pi-Ramesses, built in the time of Pharaoh Ramesses II (r. 1279–1213 B.C.), in order to see if the Bible and archaeology and historiography line up. The *World History Encyclopedia* asserts that "over 300,000 people" lived in Pi-Ramesses at the time of Ramesses II and the Exodus, as held by most maximalist biblical archaeologists (thirteenth century B.C.).[131]

John Madden, in his article "Slavery in the Roman Empire: Numbers and Origins," states: "The evidence from papyri suggests that in all likelihood slaves in Egypt never rose much above 10 percent of the population and in poorer areas there dropped to as low as 2 percent."[132] That gets us to a figure of 30,000 or less (possibly 80 percent less), which lines up with Humphrey's educated estimate of "about 20,000."

Various mass migrations throughout history can more than match these numbers by percentage. My own native Detroit, Michigan lost 49 percent of its population between 1950 and 2000 (755,729 people), and another 29 percent between 2000 and 2019 (275,266 people).[133] Twenty or thirty thousand people on the move is "nothing" compared to these numbers (which are about 14 and 38 times higher than 20,000).

None of this is *proof* of anything, but my intent is to show that the numbers of slaves in Egypt are roughly *consistent* across the analyses of Bible commentators, historians, and archaeologists, which congruence lends itself to the Bible being accurate.

In this proposed explanation that I have offered, "600,000" and "603,550" are essentially translation errors that crept into the biblical manuscripts, based on a misunderstanding of the terms, per the above explanations.

The pressing question (and it's a difficult one, I freely concede) at this point of the discussion becomes: "If the numbers of Hebrews in the Exodus in virtually all Bibles are indeed wrong, why haven't translators *corrected* them?"

The task of the translator is to render as accurately as he knows how the *received text* before him. The biblical text as it stands undeniably has these large numbers. Manuscript errors, by definition—we need to understand—*are not actually part of the Bible*, but rather later emendations. Therefore, if we can reasonably, plausibly establish that they are indeed manuscript errors, then the accuracy of the Bible itself is not affected.

The best we can do about this difficulty is what scholars like the ones I cited above have done: enter into serious analysis of what caused these large numbers that seem logistically and even historically impossible (given what we know) to enter into the sacred text, and explain how and why the actual numbers involved were considerably smaller.

What's far *more* difficult to believe is that about two million men, women, and children—close to the entire population of Paris, and roughly 6.67 times the entire estimated population of ancient Pi-Ramesses—departed Egypt all at once. That appears to be, on many levels, historically, demographically, and even logically impossible.

9

THE RED SEA, AND MIRACLES IN THE DESERT

The Egyptians said, "Let us flee from before Israel; for the Lord fights for them against the Egyptians."

—EXODUS 14:25

In the biblical, Christian worldview, extraordinary recorded events (ostensibly miraculous at first glance) may be partly natural and not wholly supernatural. That's the question to be pondered with regard to Moses' (and God's!) famous parting of the Red Sea. Was it a purely natural phenomenon, wholly supernatural, or a combination? Any of those scenarios is possible in the biblical worldview.

I don't have a firm position on the parting of the Red Sea (i.e., as to the scientific explanation I shall present). Nor am I trying to explain away or dismiss any miracle (which more theologically liberal commentators or those who deny biblical inspiration are often prone to doing). I fully believe in miracles and the omnipotent, omniscient God's capability of bringing them about. I believe that this happened, in history. I also believe that various possible explanations for it can be set forth (including the view that it was purely a supernatural act of God).

Biblical skeptics often assert one or more of the following things regarding an event like the parting of the Red Sea:

1) that it's impossible, because *miracles* are impossible;

2) that its seemingly "mythical" or fantastic character proves that the Old Testament is historically unreliable; and

3) that a natural explanation is not to be had, either.

Along these lines, Egyptian archaeologist Zahi Hawass gives his opinion of the entire Exodus story as presented in the Bible: "Really, it's a myth. . . . Sometimes as archaeologists we have to say that never happened because there is no historical evidence."[134]

I believe that whatever occurred in this instance, with Moses, Pharaoh, and a body of water, about 3,250 years ago, God was behind it, for his purposes, and that it was extraordinary. I'm providing readers with this particular natural explanation of the parting of the Red Sea for the sake of pondering and consideration—as food for thought. If nothing else, it's certainly fascinating.

Carl Drews is a software engineer who has a Master of Science degree in atmospheric and oceanic sciences from the University of Colorado at Boulder and a Graduate Certificate in oceanography. His Master's thesis was "Application of Storm Surge Modeling to Moses' Crossing of the Red Sea; and to Manila Bay, the Philippines."[135] He works for the National Center for Atmospheric Research, a top U.S. institution. His article, which made quite a splash, is "Dynamics of Wind Setdown at Suez and the Eastern Nile Delta."[136] It has been discussed and analyzed in many well-known venues, including *New Scientist*, *The Atlantic*, *The Guardian*, *Smithsonian Magazine*, *The Washington Post*, and a host of other news and information outlets.[137]

NPR provides an overview:

> "This is something that is known in meteorological science as wind setdown," Drews tells NPR's Guy Raz. . . .
>
> After modeling a body of water that resembled the waters trapping Moses and the Israelites, Drews enforced the laws of physics and applied a wind stress to the water body. . . .
>
> "The place I picked is not at the Red Sea proper, it's at the north end of the Suez Canal in one of the shallow lagoons along the Mediterranean Sea." . . . This is the same area where a British general named Alexander Tulloch witnessed a similar wind setdown event in 1882.
>
> "He observed a strong east wind blow all night long, and in the morning the water had completely disappeared," says Drews. "The lake was blown seven kilometers to the west."[138]

The Guardian cites Drews:

> The simulations match fairly closely with the account in Exodus. . . . The parting of the waters can be understood through fluid dynamics. The wind moves the water in a way that's in accordance with physical laws, creating a safe passage with water on two sides and then abruptly allowing the water to rush back in.[139]

Drews explains his scientific research and speculations in his article published by *Plos One*. The phenomenon of the *wind setdown* "occurs in shallow coastal areas when strong winds blow offshore." His experiment simulated "a wind setdown event at the eastern end of the Lake of Tanis, which extended from Damietta to Pelusium during the Egyptian New Kingdom Period (approximately 1250 B.C.)."

The model demonstrated that a gap could have opened up "where the Pelusiac branch of the Nile flowed into the Lake of Tanis." This would result in a land bridge about 3 miles wide and 2 to 2.5 miles in length, which would remain open for four hours under a wind of 64 miles per hour.

In chapter eight, I provided evidence suggesting that there were about 20,000 people involved in the Exodus. Keeping in mind Drews's numbers above, the average width of a man (shoulder-to-shoulder) is about 1.5 feet. If we use that figure for each person (knowing that women and children are smaller), it could, I submit, account for space *between* people.

Now, in an area that is 3.1 miles wide (16,368 feet), approximately 10,912 people could fit side by side (using the width of males). This means that only two rows would be required to add up to 20,000 people (or ten rows of 2,000 each, which would take up one fifth of the width available). A slow walk is about two miles an hour, a fast walk three miles an hour. If we use the slower rate of walking, the distance could be covered in an hour and fifteen minutes, and the model allows four hours.

It is thus seen that the passage (assuming the possibility of Drews's model) is *entirely possible*—not a "logistical" problem at all for this number of people. If the Egyptian army was far enough behind the Hebrews so that the soldiers couldn't shoot arrows at them, then they could all get across before the Egyptians started pursuing them across the dry bed of the area formerly occupied by water.

Exodus 14:21 states, "The Lord drove the sea back by a strong east wind all night." In Drews's higher time estimate (with a higher wind), the land was dry for 7.4 hours. That could easily be construed as "all night" (say, 11 P.M. to 6:24 A.M.). Once the Egyptians were on the dry bed, the waters rushed back due to the wind ceasing, by God's providence—just at the right time.

The whole thing is altogether plausible, *provided* that Drews's figures and calculations are correct. Of course, they can be questioned in a number of areas, particularly regarding details of the topography and layout of the Nile Delta, with all its various ever-evolving waterways, 3,250 years ago.

Three years after his groundbreaking article, Drews published "Using Wind Setdown and Storm Surge on Lake Erie to Calibrate the Air-Sea Drag Coefficient" in the same journal.[140] He stated,

> On December 1–2, 2006 and January 30–31, 2008 there were strong windstorms over the Great Lakes that caused extreme surge events on Lake Erie. In both cases the wind came from the west, producing displacements between the water levels at the western and eastern ends of the lake of 4.2 m [13.8 feet] in 2006 and 5.1 m [16.7 feet] in 2008.

This is noteworthy because Lake Erie, one of the Great Lakes (about 30 miles from my home in Michigan) is a shallow body of water, as far as lakes go, with an average depth of 62 feet. Thus, the differential in water level between western and eastern ends of the lake (it's about 241 miles long) amounted to 22 percent of the average depth in the 2006 storm and 27 percent in 2008.

To provide a mental image of what this means, I have a small pool in my backyard that is 4 feet deep and 15 feet in diameter. The equivalent difference in water level, compared to these storms on Lake Erie, would be a difference of depth of 10.6 inches higher on one side of the pool compared to the other (analogy to the 2006 storm), or 13 inches (analogy to 2008). We can readily observe, then, that such wind events could cause dry land to appear in shallower bodies of water, especially if the winds are significantly stronger.

There is a second requirement to match up with Exodus 14: the water has to part, leaving navigable dry (or muddy!) land for a long enough time for 20,000 people to cross it, *and* it has to be deep enough when it returns to normal depths to drown the Egyptians (14:26–28). Drews set his model (for various scientific reasons) at 3 meters' depth (or 9.8 feet) for "the Pelusiac branch of the Nile from Bubastis to Daphnae," where he believes that the "parting" may have occurred. If this calculation is correct, it's more than enough to drown the Egyptian army.

Now we move on to the Israelites' wanderings in the wilderness.

We read in Numbers, "And the Lord's anger was kindled against Israel, and he made them wander in the wilderness forty years." (See also Exod. 16:35; Num. 14:33–34; Deut. 2:7, 8:2, 4, 29:5; Josh. 5:6; Acts 7:36, 13:18; Heb. 3:9, 17.)

Could 20,000 people survive as traveling nomads in the Sinai Peninsula? Sure! We have an analogous group of people *today*: the portion of Bedouins who are still nomadic. According to a story in the *Irish Times*, there are still some 115,000 who live a nomadic life in the Negev Desert—the southern portion of Israel that is similar in topography and arid climate to the neighboring Sinai Peninsula (now controlled by Egypt), where the Israelites (according to the Bible) wandered for forty years.[141] Too bad Moses didn't have Google Maps!

The Negev is 4,700 square miles in area, whereas the Sinai Peninsula is 23,166 square miles, or 4.93 times larger. So let's make a demographic comparison:

- 20,000 Hebrews in an area of 23,166 miles = 1.16 square miles per person average
- 115,000 Israeli Bedouins in an area of 4,700 square miles = 0.04 square miles per person

The ancient Hebrews had twenty-nine times more area to live in than the current-day Bedouins, in similar conditions.

We see that it is entirely possible, then, even if the wandering Hebrews were *not* fed manna (the supernatural food that fell from the sky—see Exod. 16:1–36) and quail (Num. 11:31–32) from God, as the Bible says. If the nomadic Bedouins can survive today—almost five times as many, in a similar desert area almost five times smaller—so could the ancient Hebrews.

This is a non-issue. Those who make an issue out of it invariably assume the number of two million people wandering around. That issue was dealt with in the previous chapter.

Jewish Bible scholar Richard Elliott Friedman was interviewed regarding this issue. His interviewer asked, "Following publication of *Reform Judaism*'s Spring 2013 edition in which Professor David Sperling and Rabbi David Wolpe asserted that the biblical Exodus is a fiction, you wrote expressing concern to the magazine editors. Why?" Here is his reply:

> Those archaeologists' claims that the Exodus never happened are not based on evidence, but largely on its absence. They assert that we've combed the Sinai and not

> found any evidence of the mass of millions of people who the Bible says were there for forty years. That assertion is just not true. There have not been many major excavations in the Sinai, and we most certainly have not combed it. Moreover, uncovering objects buried 3,200 years ago is a daunting endeavor. An Israeli colleague laughingly told me that a vehicle that had been lost in the 1973 Yom Kippur War was recently uncovered under 16 meters—that's 52 feet—of sand. Fifty-two feet in forty years! . . .
>
> There is no archaeological evidence against the historicity of an exodus if it was a smaller group who left Egypt. Indeed, significantly, the first biblical mention of the Exodus, the Song of Miriam, which is the oldest text in the Bible, never mentions how many people were involved in the Exodus, and it never speaks of the whole nation of Israel. It just refers to a people, an *am*, leaving Egypt.[142]

Egyptologist Kenneth Kitchen also takes on this common skeptical complaint—that there is "no evidence whatsoever" of the presence of wandering Hebrews for forty years in the Sinai Peninsula after the Exodus.

> Beware of the spin "we've found no evidence, so [no one] was there" attitude. We have at present almost no "on the ground" camps left by Egyptian, Hittite, Assyrian, or Babylonian invasion-forces in the Levant. No camps in transit, any more than for our Hebrews going from Egypt to Moab to Canaan.[143]

What about the miraculous food the Israelis received as they wandered in the desert? We read about it in Exodus and Numbers:

> And the Lord said to Moses, "At twilight you shall eat flesh." . . . In the evening quails came up and covered the camp (Exod. 16:11–13).

> "You shall not eat one day, or two days, or five days, or ten days, or twenty days, but a whole month, until it comes out at your nostrils and becomes loathsome to you, because you have rejected the Lord who is among you" (Num. 11:19). (See also vv. 4-18, 20–33; Ps. 78:26–31.)

Kenneth Kitchen states,

> Twice on their travels (down to, and up from, Mount Sinai), the Israelites got involved with migrating quail. . . . It is a fact that quails do migrate via Sinai twice a year. They fly from farther south up to Europe in the spring, going through the Suez and Aqaba gulfs in the evenings (hence their presence on the Sinai Peninsula's west and east flanks then).[144]

Thus, the Bible informs us that (again, positing a natural event),

1) quails migrate through the *Sinai Peninsula*,

2) particularly along the *coastlines* (Exod. 16:1), and

3) they do so *in the spring* (Exod. 16:1; Num. 10:11, 11:31,34).

The season (down to the day) and the specific place are recorded. An article on quails in the journal *Ornis Fennica* observed,

> Eilat, Israel, is located at the northern edge of the combined Sahel, Sahara, and Sinai deserts. During spring

> migration, the quails reach this region after a long and arduous journey. . . . Eilat is situated at the northern edge of over 2,000 kilometers of continuous Sahel, Sahara and Sinai deserts. . . .
>
> Along the Red Sea coast quail was distinctly more common in spring than in autumn.[145]

Experts on quail migration confirm that one such area is the west coast of the Sinai Peninsula—precisely where the biblical accounts locate the appearance of them. Medical missionary John Wilkinson describes their spring migration journey:

> On the east they converge on the Red Sea from southern Egypt and Arabia and fly up alongside it until at its bifurcation they enter the peninsula of Sinai. It is here that the route of their migration would cross the path of the Children of Israel as they journeyed from Egypt to Canaan. After crossing the Sinai Desert, the quails continue their flight northwards across Israel and Syria until finally they reach Europe.[146]

The second Hebrew month is Iyar, which usually falls into April-May of the Gregorian calendar.

An article from the *Birds in Backyards* site observes that "quails rarely fly, preferring to hide unless an intruder flushes them; then they fly low to the ground, with a rapid whirring flight." [147] This may coincide with the description of Numbers 11:31: "A wind from the Lord . . . brought quails from the sea, and let them fall beside the camp . . . about two cubits above the face of the earth." A biblical cubit is about 18 to 21 inches.

Thus, this passage could be saying they were flying 36 to 42 inches above the ground (3 to 3.5 feet), alongside the sea, looking for a place to pitch. If so, it's yet another of innumerable examples of minute (in this case, botanical or ornithological) biblical accuracy, from about 3,300 years ago. Wilkinson notes that "this interpretation is accepted by Jewish commentators and by the Vulgate" and is used in the New English Bible (NEB) and the Revised English Bible (REB) translations.[148]

James L. Tullis opines,

> In analyzing the event as accurately as possible, one can place its time in either April or September, and its location in the Sinai Desert about 160 kilometers [100 miles] southeast of the Mediterranean coastline. Vast flocks of quail are known to migrate north from Africa to Europe in the spring of the year and back again each autumn.[149]

The numbers of migrating quails in the area are truly massive. An article in *The Guardian* refers to the migration southward from Egypt (in August through October) and noted that "trappers' nets . . . will catch at least 140 million birds this year."[150] An article specifically about North Sinai and quail concluded,

> Based on mean rates of capture from 2008 to 2012 in desert scrub and sand bar habitats, we estimate 2.0 million quail and 0.5 million birds of other species are killed annually in North Sinai during the forty-five days of peak migration.[151]

Wilkinson makes his best guess as to the "very great plague" resulting from eating quail, up to and including death (see Num. 11): "bacterial food poisoning," likely due to the quail being dried in the sun. The rotted condition of the meat is described by the Hebrew *zara*, commonly translated as "loathsome" or "nauseating." The resultant vomiting was so severe that it came out through their noses (v. 19). Wilkinson's best guess is that the food poisoning was "due to bacteria of the *Salmonella* group."

In conclusion, Wilkinson writes (and I fully agree),

> It was the Lord who promised through Moses that he would give them meat enough to last for a whole month (11:18–20). It was the Lord who sent the wind which drove the quail in from the sea (v. 31) and it was he who struck the people with the great plague (v. 33). This is also the view of the Psalmist in Psalm 78:26–31. . . .
>
> The question arises of whether we can still maintain that the incident was also miraculous. . . .
>
> The natural explanation of an incident need not deny its supernatural origin and significance; a supernatural event need not be unnatural in its character and mechanism. What was miraculous in the provision of the Israelites with quail meat was not how it was done, but why, when, and where it was done.

So the Israelites swallowed a lot of quail. Next comes the question of the earth swallowing up some Israelites.

> So they and all that belonged to them went down alive into Sheol; and the earth closed over them, and they perished from the midst of the assembly (Num. 16:33).

The question again (as with all of these purported miracles or extraordinary events) is whether it can be explained as a natural phenomenon. This incident clearly can. Kenneth Kitchen notes a well-known phenomenon in the area involved:

> There exists there *kewirs*, or mudflats. Over a deep mass of liquid mud and ooze is formed a hard crust of clayey mud overlying layers of hard salt and half-dry muds, about 30 centimeters [12 inches] thick. . . . Increased humidity (especially with rainstorms) causes the crust to soften and break up, turning everything into gluey mud.[152]

Another rather obvious natural possibility is an earthquake. In the article "Seismic behavior of the Dead Sea fault along Araba valley, Jordan," the authors state,

> The Dead Sea fault zone is a major left-lateral strike-slip fault. South of the Dead Sea basin, the Wadi Araba fault extends over 160 kilometers [100 miles] to the Gulf of Aqaba. The Dead Sea fault zone is known to have produced several relatively large historical earthquakes. . . .
>
> We suggest that the Dead Sea fault along the Araba valley should produce an *Mw* 7 earthquake about every 200 years on average.[153]

Or it was simply a supernatural miracle, directly brought about by God. Right after the swallowing up of Korah and his men, we have this: "And fire came forth from the Lord, and consumed the two hundred and fifty men offering the incense" (16:35). That could have been supernatural fire from God or natural lightning, in a storm that would also have naturally produced the collapse of a mudflat. The Hebrew word here, *esh*, is used, or possibly used, with the meaning of "lightning," as in 2 Kings 1:14, Job 1:16, Exodus 9:23–24 ("thunder and hail, and fire ran down to the earth . . . fire flashing continually in the midst of the hail"), Psalm 18:13–14, Psalm 148:8, and others.

Another event that is somewhat along the same lines, and

capable of possible natural interpretation, are the biblical accounts of Moses drawing water from a rock.

> "Hear now, you rebels; shall we bring forth water for you out of this rock?" (Num. 20:10; see also Exod. 17:6; Deut. 8:15; Neh. 9:15; Ps. 78:16,20, 105:21, 114:8; Isa. 48:21).

Colin Humphreys is the Goldsmiths' Professor of Materials Science at Cambridge University and Professor of Experimental Physics at the Royal Institution in London. He has published more than 500 papers on electron microscopy, semiconductors, metals, and superconductors. He is also a past president of the physics section of the British Association for the Advancement of Science. To get water from a rock, I cite material from his article "Science and the Miracles of Exodus":

> For a rock to give out water it has to be able to store water, so it has to be porous. Do porous rocks exist? The answer is yes, and porous rocks like sandstone and limestone can absorb huge quantities of water from rain. In fact, when they are underground we use them as aquifers, natural reservoirs of water, and we sink wells and boreholes into them to extract the water.
>
> If porous rocks, such as sandstone and limestone, are above ground, rainwater isn't normally stored in them: it flows out through the pores. However, in a desert region . . . porous rocks . . . can develop a hard impervious crust, rather like cement. . . . If the crust of a porous rock is broken by a sharp blow, water can indeed flow out. . . .
>
> We have seen that Moses obtaining water from a rock violates no physical laws. The biblical story fits what we know from science.[154]

We know that sandstone and limestone are porous and can contain water. The Bible refers to "flint" in this regard twice (Deut. 8:15; Ps. 114:8). It could be that this was a reference to it being mixed with limestone or chalk, since this is often how it occurs in nature. Sandstone, shale, and limestone are common in the Sinai Peninsula. Porous sandstone is "widespread in the northern Gulf area."[155]

Granite is predominant in the southern Sinai Peninsula (where Mt. Sinai is located), but there is still water to be had (from rocks at that!). Arie S. Issar, professor emeritus in the Department of Environmental Hydrology and Microbiology at Ben-Gurion University of the Negev, is the author of *Water Shall Flow from the Rock: Hydrogeology and Climate in the Lands of the Bible*. A description of this book illustrates how it supports the opinions promulgated in this section, about "water from a rock":

> Many times when the author saw the Bedouins of southern Sinai excavate their wells in the crystalline rocks, from which this part of the peninsula is built, the story of Moses striking the rock to get water came to mind. The reader will, indeed, find in this book the description for a rather simple method by which to strike the rock to get water in the wilderness of Sinai. Yet this method was not invented by the author nor by any other modem hydrogeologist, but was a method that the author learned from the Bedouins living in the crystalline mountains of southern Sinai.[156]

Thus, once we become acquainted with this scientific (geophysical) information, it's reasonable to hold that some or even all of these "water-drawing" incidents can be explained naturally. But of course, it's always possible that God led Moses and others to specific places where this phenomenon occurred.

As I've noted over and over in this book, just because a thing can be explained by natural laws and science, that does not automatically mean that it has nothing at all to do with God. God can use whatever he chooses to use for his purposes. After all, Jews and Christians who believe in the truthfulness and inspiration of the Bible believe that God created everything in the first place. *How* he did so (the process and how long it took) is another fascinating question, but we all hold that he is the Creator of all things.

10

JOSHUA AND THE CONQUEST OF CANAAN

"And there you shall build an altar to the Lord your God . . . and you shall write upon the stones all the words of this law very plainly."

—DEUTERONOMY 27:5,8

Many may not be aware that there was a second "water-parting event" in the Bible, regarding the River Jordan:

> "And when the soles of the feet of the priests who bear the ark of the Lord, the Lord of all the earth, shall rest in the waters of the Jordan, the waters of the Jordan shall be stopped from flowing, and the waters coming down from above shall stand in one heap." . . . And while all Israel were passing over on dry ground, the priests who bore the Ark of the Covenant of the Lord stood on dry ground in the midst of the Jordan, until all the nation finished passing over the Jordan (Josh. 3:13,17; see also 4:18,23).

Kenneth Kitchen stated that "some sixteen miles north of a crossing opposite Jericho, [the location] Adam is present-day

Tell ed-Damieh. It is specifically in this district that the high banks of the Jordan have been liable to periodic collapses, sufficient to block the river for a time." He notes that this happened in 1267 for sixteen hours; in 1906; and, due to an earthquake, in 1927, when it was completely obstructed for twenty-one hours.[157]

The *Israel Tours* web page "Earthquakes in History and Archaeology"—adding three more dates for the same thing happening—observes in agreement, "Historically known quakes have dammed the Jordan River repeatedly, sometimes for several days, in 1160 CE, 1267, 1534, 1834, 1906 and 1927."[158]

Jericho is the "Bible archaeology story" that "everyone" knows about (especially those who love the wonderful old spiritual, "Joshua Fit the Battle of Jericho"). Joshua and his armies blew the trumpets, and the walls fell down. Hence, it would and should be an easy matter to verify that 1) the city existed at this time and 2) that its walls fell down, through archaeological excavation, right?

Wrong. The walls from the period in question (c. 1200 B.C.) are simply not *there*. Skeptics *en masse* appear to believe that it would be *impossible* for such massive walls to vanish completely from the archaeological record, if in fact the city existed as a large fortress in the period in question.

Consequently, the example of Jericho is often brought up by biblical skeptics as a disproof of the famous biblical account, with no small amount of ridicule and intellectual condescension. The famous atheist and Bible skeptic Bart Ehrman, for example, opines,

> In the archaeological record there is no support for the kind of violent destruction of the cities of Canaan—especially the ones mentioned in Joshua. . . . Many of the

> specific cities cited as places of conquest did not even exist as cities at the time. This includes, most notably, Jericho, which was not inhabited in the late thirteenth century BCE, as archaeologists have decisively shown.[159]

Atheist Jonathan M.S. Pearce ridicules the biblical account of Jericho:

> The famous destruction of Jericho is now famously unattested as archaeology has evolved from times where archaeologists were paid up members of seminaries who were sent to verify the Bible in a time of biblical maximalism.[160]

He even cites a "Christian" source (the link no longer works, and no name is provided) to the effect that Jericho was destroyed around 1550 B.C., some 350 years before the timeline I am following in this book (following more traditional biblical archaeologists), and implies that it would have been either nonexistent or a mere unfortified small village by the time Joshua arrived.

I want to make clear here (so there is no confusion or misunderstanding) that I am *not* attempting to defend (let alone prove) the claim that the walls fell down because of Joshua and his army marching around it and blowing trumpets. I'm not sure anyone *could* prove that, and I can't conceptualize in my mind *how* they would go about doing so. I'm attempting to substantiate what *can* be objectively verified through science and am responding to the skeptical claim that the city *didn't exist*—or was in *ruins*—at the time Bible believers say it did exist and was conquered.

If it didn't *exist* in 1200 B.C., then obviously the big walls couldn't have come "tumbling down" at that time, and surely, we would then have a *big problem* defending the biblical account and the "maximalist" archaeological claim that backs it up. It would be a double-whammy. But I'm "defeating the defeaters," as Protestant philosopher Alvin Plantinga likes to say. The believer in Bible accuracy has to, at a *minimum*, prove the existence of Jericho, with significant fortifications, in c. 1200 B.C., and explain why there appears to be no current *evidence* for same.

Maximalist archaeologist Kenneth Kitchen agrees that the walls of this period (fallen or not) cannot be found, but he takes an entirely different perspective as to *why* that is.

> A great deal of the former Middle Bronze Age township was entirely removed by erosion. . . . Of the Late Bronze settlement from the mid-fourteenth century onward, almost nothing survives at all. . . . If 200 years of erosion sufficed to remove most of later Middle Bronze Age Jericho, it is almost a miracle that anything on the mound has survived at all from the 400 years of erosion between 1275 and the time of Ahab (875–853), when we hear report of Jericho's rebuilding (1 Kings 16:34) in Iron I.[161]

Following up on Kitchen's thesis, I would like to submit a possible and plausible—and scientifically corroborated—explanation of this high level of erosion in Jericho. The ancient city is only 21 miles from the Dead Sea, which is the deepest hypersaline (very salty) lake in the world and, with a salinity of 34.2 percent (in 2011), the seventh saltiest body of water in the world—almost ten times more than the oceans. It's so salty that nothing can live in it, except for small numbers of bacteria and microbial fungi.

We might reasonably suspect that this much salt in the environment would affect man-made structures as well. In fact, this is true of the famous city of Petra in present-day Jordan, which is 123 miles from the Dead Sea. A *National Geographic* article discusses a salt-induced erosion process called *haloclasty* and its effect on some buildings in Petra:

> Salt also works to weather rock in a process called haloclasty. Saltwater sometimes gets into the cracks and pores of rock. If the saltwater evaporates, salt crystals are left behind. As the crystals grow, they put pressure on the rock, slowly breaking it apart. . . .
>
> Haloclasty is not limited to coastal landscapes. Salt upwelling, the geologic process in which underground salt domes expand, can contribute to weathering of the overlying rock. Structures in the ancient city of Petra, Jordan, were made unstable and often collapsed due to salt upwelling from the ground below.[162]

Haloclasty is closely associated with arid climates, where the heat causes great evaporation and, as a result, salt crystallization. It's common along coasts as well. The Dead Sea is the lowest elevation on earth: 1,412 feet below sea level. Jericho is the lowest-elevation city in the world, at 846 feet below sea level. It has a very arid, hot desert climate, with average high temperatures in July and August of more than 100 degrees, and more than 90 in May, June, September, and October. (I visited Jericho in October 2014, and even at that time of year, it was very hot.) In January, the average high is 66 degrees.

Some archaeologists (for example, Avraham Negev and Shimon Gibson),[163] speculate that the long rainy season in Jericho (late October to April)[164] may have played a role in washing away Jericho's ruins. *Two* natural explanations thus exist, to explain the extraordinary erosion and absence of ruins dated to the time of Joshua. The water level of the Dead

Sea has also greatly fluctuated over the last several thousand years—as much as 1,300 feet, the experts tell us. This means that during the time under consideration, it likely was in some periods *much closer* to Jericho than it is now, thus exacerbating the problem of haloclasty and the city's erosion.

Certainly, the salt from the nearby Dead Sea had *something* to do with—if not being a primary cause of—the high level of erosion seen at the site.

In other words, it's not simply special pleading to explain why the site offers no evidence as to Joshua's conquest and the famous biblical text of the walls falling down. It's a perfectly plausible explanation to posit that the cause was an arid, hypersaline environment, possibly also 400 years of winter rains, and the approximately 325-year period without habitation (in other words, no repair of any crumbling buildings or other structures).

> **Deuteronomy 27:4–6, 8** "And when you have passed over the Jordan, you shall set up these stones . . . on Mount Ebal. . . . And there you shall build an altar to the Lord your God, an altar of stones; you shall lift up no iron tool upon them. You shall build an altar to the Lord your God of unhewn stones. . . . And you shall write upon the stones all the words of this law very plainly." (See also 11:26–29; Josh. 8:30–35.)

The central figure in our story about Mt. Ebal and the Bible is the late Adam Zertal (1936–2015), professor of archaeology at the University of Haifa (and its chairman from 1996–1999). He received his Ph.D. from Tel Aviv University in 1988. His dissertation was entitled "The Israelite Settlement in the Hill Country of Manasseh." Zertal is also the author of the entries on Mt. Ebal in *The New Encyclopedia of Archaeological Excavations in the Holy Land*[165] and *The Oxford Encyclopedia of Archaeology in the Near East.*[166] Additionally, he wrote five books in Hebrew about the hill country of Manasseh.

When he made his discovery of Joshua's altar in April 1980, Zertal was not inclined to support biblical texts at all. He stated later,

> I didn't even know of the story of the Joshua's altar. But we surveyed every meter of the site, and in the course of nine years of excavation, we discovered a very old structure with no parallels to anything we had seen before.[167]

Zertal published his initial findings and conclusions along these lines in his article, "Has Joshua's Altar been Found on Mount Ebal?":

> We were immediately able to date these sherds to the early part of the period archaeologists call Iron Age 1 (1220–1000 B.C.). . . .
>
> The site would prove to be the earliest and most complete Israelite cultic center ever discovered and the prototype of all later ones.[168]

What he found was a nearly square structure, almost 9 feet high, and about 25 by 30 feet in width and length. Zertal's first theory was that it was perhaps a "watchtower" or a "farmhouse." But it was not like any other farmhouse in the area that he was already familiar with. It had no entrance. He also ruled out the watchtower theory, since he saw no reason for one to be there, as no Iron Age settlement was nearby. Evidence then started surfacing as to the possibility of its being an altar:

> Bones, which were found in such large quantities in the filling . . . proved to be from young male bulls, sheep, goats and fallow deer. . . . The first chapter of Leviticus describes the animals that may be offered as sacrifices. A burnt offering must be a male without blemish (Lev. 1:3). It may be a bull (v. 5) or a sheep or a goat (v. 10). . . .
>
> Nine hundred forty-two bones were examined . . . all those that could be diagnosed were young males, approximately one year old. This correlates remarkably with the laws of sacrifice in the book of Leviticus.
>
> A great part of the bones, as we mentioned, had been burned over a fire and were cut near the joints. Being scorched in this way attests that the flesh was not intended for eating but was burned over an open fire (i.e., not in an oven).[169]

The bones corresponded to what the ancient Hebrews were allowed to eat:

> These are the animals you may eat: the ox, the sheep, the goat, the hart, the gazelle, the roebuck, the wild goat, the ibex, the antelope, and the mountain-sheep (Deut. 14:4–5).

Moreover, the structure consisted of several courts. In these were found bones of animals that had not been burned, and where the animals were eaten. This lines up with Deuteronomy 27:7 ("you shall sacrifice peace offerings, and shall eat there"). The ramp (rather than "steps") up to the top also corresponds to Exodus 20:26. Zertal describes it:

> A ramp of unhewn stones, 4 feet wide by 23 feet long, rises to the top of the platform from the southwest. The

> gentle incline, easily climbed . . . the ramp on our Mt. Ebal altar indicates a strict adherence to the law in Exodus 20:26, which requires a ramp rather than steps.

The "unhewn stones" line up with God's instructions (Deut. 27:5–6; Josh. 8:31).

Zertal, in his article, then goes into a detailed description of altars as described in the Bible and comparisons to non-Hebrew ancient Near Eastern altars. Everything fits nicely into the theory that the structure on Mt. Ebal is, in fact, an early Hebrew altar. In November 2004, Zertal made additional comments and conclusions about the Mt. Ebal excavations:

> The cultic site on Mt. Ebal satisfies the three criteria necessary to identify a biblical site: chronological (beginning of the Israelite settlement), geographical, and the nature of the site (a cultic center with a burnt-offering altar). . . . The altar on Mt. Ebal is not only the most ancient and complete altar, but also the prototype of the Israelite burnt offering altar of the First and Second Temple periods. . . .
>
> Despite the presence of wild boars in the region, not a single bone of this animal, not fit for sacrifice, was found on Mt. Ebal.[170]

Richard S. Hess, professor of Old Testament and Semitic languages at Denver Seminary (Ph.D. from Hebrew Union College), and author of more than one hundred scholarly articles, claims in his commentary on Joshua, "After reading the excavator's report and conducting a visual tour of the site, it certainly looks like an early Israelite altar such as is described in this text in Joshua."[171]

Now we shall examine the purported historical series of events known as "Joshua's conquest of Canaan." I'll be surveying a representative sample of cities or towns that the Bible states were conquered—with or without destruction—to see if 1) they *existed* c. 1200 B.C. or shortly after, and 2) any evidence of *destruction* or *change of inhabitants* (without destruction) occurred.

Hazor

> **Joshua 11:11** And they put to the sword all who were in it, utterly destroying them; there was none left that breathed, and he burned Hazor with fire.

The destruction of Hazor by fire, according to archaeology,[172] occurred in the thirteenth century B.C., probably toward the end of the century (exactly the time period of Joshua). In 1996, rather sensational charred remains of a Late Bronze Age palace were discovered in excavations led by Amnon Ben Tor. That this was the work of the Israelites was suggested (according to archaeologist James Hoffmeier) by the "deliberate decapitation and mutilation of statues of deities, in keeping with the charge of Moses to the Israelites in Deuteronomy 7:5."[173] What has been found thus far is consistent with the picture in Joshua 11.

Eero Junkkaala wrote at length specifically about this general topic and noted that four prominent Israeli archaeologists (Yadin, Aharoni, Ben Tor, and Frankel) agreed and concluded that the city was destroyed militarily by the Israelites. Frankel writes about it: "The archaeological finds ostensibly correlate with the biblical description: a Canaanite city was totally destroyed and a small Iron I village was built upon its ruins."[174]

Lachish

Joshua 10:32 And the Lord gave Lachish into the hand of Israel, and he took it on the second day.

The archaeological Level VII of Lachish has been dated to the thirteenth century B.C., and its destruction determined to be in the middle or latter part of the twelfth century B.C. According to Israeli archaeologist David Ussishkin, "the biblical description (in Josh. 10:31–32) fits the archaeological data: a large Canaanite city destroyed by fire . . . and complete desertion of the razed city explained by the annihilation of the populace." As with Hazor, a small Iron Age settlement appeared not long afterward.[175]

Bethel

Judges 1:22 The house of Joseph also went up against Bethel; and the Lord was with them.

The destruction of this Late Bronze Age town was by fire, and dated by William Albright to around 1240–1235 B.C. A relatively poor and different Israelite Iron Age I settlement then arose, according to archaeologists Amihai Mazar and Israel Finkelstein.

Junkkaala notes that "according to Finkelstein's study in 1988, Bethel is one of the earliest Israelite settlement sites, together with Mount Ebal, Giloh, Izbeth Sartah, Beth-zur, Tell el-Ful, and Tell en-Nasbeh."[176] Kitchen thinks ancient Bethel was "located at Beitin" and that it was "probably" a "new early Israelite settlement" on the ruins of the destroyed Canaanite city.[177] Negev and Gibson[178] add that "the last Late Bronze Age stratum is covered by a very thick layer of ashes and charred and fallen bricks."

Other Cities Mentioned in the Biblical Text

In his article "The Date of the Conquest," Bruce K. Waltke summarizes archaeological data about Israeli settlement at hundreds of sites in Iron Age I, citing Finkelstein:

> In Iron I there was a dramatic swing back in the population of the hill country. About 240 sites of the period are known in the area between the Jezreel and Beer-Sheva valleys; 96 in Manasseh, 122 in Ephraim . . . and 22 in Benjamin and Judah.[179]

Then Waltke notes Canaanite cities that underwent "catastrophic destructions":

> Hazor (Tell el-Qedah), Megiddo (Tell el-Mutesellim), Succoth (Tell Deir *Alla*), Bethel (Beitin), Beth Shemesh (Tell er-Remeileh), Ashdod (Esdud), Lachish (Tell ed-Duweir), Eglon (Tell el-*esi*), and Debir or Kiriath-Sepher (Tell Beit Mirsim or Khirbet Rabud).

On the other hand, he differentiates cities mentioned in the Bible that show no sign of destruction, in line with the biblical accounts:

> Gibeon (el-Jib) (Joshua 9), Taanach (Tell *Taaannak*) (Judg 1:27), Shechem (Tell Balatah) (Josh 24), Jerusalem (el-Quds) (Josh 15:63; 2 Sam 5:6–9), Beth-shean (Tell el-*husn*) (Judg 1:27–28), and Gezer (Tell Jezer) (Josh 10:33).[180]

Kitchen assesses the overall evidence and harmony with the scriptural accounts and concludes that "eighteen or nineteen" sites out of twenty "were in being in Late Bronze (II)," according to what we have determined by archaeology. He states that Makkedah was an exception to the rule because "most of that site is not accessible, hence is not decisive."[181]

Kitchen summarizes Joshua's "conquest" of Canaan, as described in the Bible, in relation to archaeological research: "The text of Joshua does *not* imply huge and massive fiery destructions of every site visited (only Jericho, Ai, and Hazor were burned)."[182] Archaeologist James K. Hoffmeier concurs:

> A close look at the terms dealing with warfare in Joshua 10 reveals that they do not support the interpretation that the land of Canaan and its principal cities were demolished and devastated by the Israelites.[183]

Joshua does not describe a widespread destruction of the land. Rather, as Joshua admits (13:1), there was still much land not in Israelite hands, and the book proceeds to outline those areas (vv. 2–8).[184] So the idea of a group of tribes coming to Canaan, using some military force, partially taking a number of cities and areas over a period of some years, destroying (burning) just three cities, and coexisting alongside the Canaanites and other ethnic groups for a period of time before the beginnings of monarchy does not require blind faith.[185]

No one is claiming that we will likely find a bumper sticker anywhere in Israel (formerly Canaan) saying (Julius Caesar-like), "Joshua came and saw and conquered in 1199 B.C.!" Archaeology can verify only whether the facts regarding any given site are *consistent* with the biblical account and do not directly *contradict* or refute it. Kitchen continues, explaining some of the constant difficulties of archaeological research and the true nature of the "conquest" of Canaan:

> Usually less than about 5 or 10 percent of any given mound is ever dug down to Late Bronze (or any other) levels; hence between 85 and 95 percent of our potential source of evidence is never seen. . . .
>
> We should speak of an Israelite *entry* into Canaan, and settlement: *neither* only a conquest (although raids and attacks were made), *nor* simply an infiltration (although some tribes moved in alongside Canaanites), *nor* just re-formation of local Canaanites into a new society "Israel."[186]

A lot more verifying data from archaeology concerning many of the cities mentioned in the book of Joshua can assuredly be produced. I researched twenty-eight more of them in one of my apologetics articles, if brave and hearty souls want to pursue the topic further.[187] But for my present purposes, it would belabor the point and be too tedious in its painstaking detail. The above is sufficient to provide a general "traditional" outline of archaeological support for the biblical narrative of Joshua's conquest.

It may come as a shock to many (including hundreds of minimalist archaeologists), but the data in this regard "fit" what we know from history and archaeology. The great maximalist archaeologist and Egyptologist Kenneth Kitchen, after concluding his research concerning these matters, mildly complained about this very thing and tweaked his minimalist and skeptical academic colleagues:

> This review shows up the far greater deficiencies in some critiques of the Joshua narratives and list that are now already out of date and distinctly misleading.[188]

11

KING DAVID VERSUS KING ARTHUR

Then all the tribes of Israel came to David at Hebron, and said, "Behold, we are your bone and flesh."

—2 SAMUEL 5:1

The substantial historicity of the united monarchy of Judah (reigns of King Saul: c. 1037–c. 1010 B.C., King David: c. 1010–c. 970 B.C., and King Solomon: c. 970–c. 931 B.C.) was widely accepted in the middle years of the twentieth century, even within secular archaeological circles.

But by the 1990s, what is called archaeological or biblical *minimalism* became quite the fashionable view to take among a new generation of archaeologists who worked in Israel. It was the high-water mark of skepticism, influenced and infused by a marked "anti-biblical" or "anti-traditional," or what could be called a "vehemently secular," spirit. Older "truths" were no longer accepted as established or given. Many archaeologists in the 1990s, and continuing until the present time, held or hold a view similar to the following:

> Nadav Na'aman, an authority on Jewish history . . . at Tel Aviv University, describes David's story as "extraordinary

fiction." But he believes that it contains kernels of truth, preserved as the tale was passed down by oral tradition.[189]

In other words, among the minimalists, David is regarded similarly to how most historians view King Arthur: a real person (not nonexistent), but vastly mythologized, to such an extent that the "kernel" of historical truth and fact has been mostly lost amid the colorful and memorable legends built up around him. The late Philip R. Davies, Bible scholar at the University of Sheffield, confidently proclaimed the same: "I'm not the only scholar who suspects that the figure of King David is about as historical as King Arthur."[190]

Ze'ev Herzog, archaeologist at Tel Aviv University, took an even more extreme view in a 1999 front-page story in the Israeli newspaper *Haaretz*, titled "The Bible: No Evidence on the Ground":

> Following seventy years of intensive excavations in the Land of Israel, archaeologists have found out: The patriarchs' acts are legendary, the Israelites did not sojourn in Egypt or make an exodus, they did not conquer the land. Neither is there any mention of the empire of David and Solomon, nor of the source of belief in the God of Israel. These facts have been known for years, but Israelis are a stubborn people, and no one wants to hear it.[191]

I submit that stubbornness and excessive dogmatism are traits not unknown among minimalist archaeologists. Tom Meyer, a biblical scholar at Shasta Bible College in California, described this sort of skepticism among scholars, who thought King David "never existed and was a figment of the imagination of a post-exilic Jewish community who, after returning to Jerusalem from Babylonian captivity in the fifth century B.C., invented King David as a national figure which the fledgling nation could rally around as they rebuilt their country."[192]

Thomas L. Thompson, professor of Old Testament at the University of Copenhagen, and author of *Early History of the Israelite People* (1992), stated,

> It is out of the question that Saul, David, and Solomon, as described as kings in the Bible, could have existed. I think the biblical accounts are wonderful stories, invented at the time when Jerusalem was part of the Persian Empire in the fifth century B.C.[193]

God has a wonderful sense of humor, and it is often exhibited (or so it seems to me) in the particular timing of new archaeological findings that support the truthfulness and historical trustworthiness of the Bible.

In March 1993, all biblical scholars and archaeologists (minimalist and maximalist alike) agreed that there was no "concrete evidence" outside the Bible (such as in written monuments or documents) of the existence of King David. Then, lo and behold, in July 1993, just four months after the above article that cites Thompson, definitive evidence of this nature (the Tel Dan Stele) was found in Israel. Eric H. Cline, chairman of the Department of Classical and Semitic Languages and Literatures at the George Washington University, told the story in his book, *Biblical Archaeology: A Very Short Introduction.* A portion of it was adapted for an internet article, "Did David and Solomon Exist?":

> As it is currently reconstructed, the inscription describes the defeat of both Joram, king of Israel, and Ahaziyahu,

> king of Judah, by a king of Aram-Damascus in the ninth century BCE.[194]

"House of David" is also biblical terminology (1 Sam. 20:16; 2 Sam. 3:1–6; 1 Kings 12:19–26; 2 Chron. 10:19; and many other instances in the RSV). The language of the inscription is a dialect of Aramaic. Most scholars think King Hazael of Damascus (ninth century B.C.) is the author. Prominent Israeli archaeologist Israel Finkelstein, who regards himself as neither a minimalist nor a maximalist (somewhere in the middle of the spectrum), described the decisive importance of this find:

> Much of the minimalist effort has been invested in the claim that David and Solomon . . . are not historical figures. They argued that, like Abraham, Moses, Joshua, David, and Solomon are not mentioned in any extra-biblical texts, and should therefore be seen as legendary personalities. This argument suffered a major blow when the Tel Dan basalt stele was discovered in the mid-1990s. . . .
>
> Moreover, it most probably specified the names of the two later kings—Joram of Israel and Ahaziah of Judah—both of whom are mentioned in the biblical text.[195]

Arguably, a second mention of the "House of David" occurs in the Mesha Stele[196] (c. 840 B.C.), connected with King Mesha of Moab, written using a variant of the Phoenician alphabet, closely related to paleo-Hebrew script. It was discovered in August 1868 in Dibhan, Jordan, but re-interpreted in light of the Tel Dan Stele, so that many think it refers to the "House of David" and contains a possible second mention of David. Opposing views exist, as always. Some think it refers to Balak, a Moabite in the Bible, who lived 200 years before David.

French epigrapher, historian, and philologist André Lemaire had actually suggested a reading of "House of David" in 1992, before the Tel Dan Stele was discovered.[197] An article written by Amanda Borschel-Dan notes how Michael Langlois, of the Center for Judaic Studies at the University of Michigan, used his own fancy high-tech methods to discover something further:

> After layering the images together, in a startling discovery, Langlois found a previously overlooked dot, which indicates a break between words throughout the entire tablet, as was customary among scribes at the time. . . .
>
> "In my paper I'm not trying to discuss whether King David exists, just trying to read the stone, and my conclusion for line 31 is that the most likely reading is Beit David, which takes into account the traces of letters and the combination of them," said Langlois.[198]

Many exciting, Bible-affirming discoveries have been occurring in the City of David portion of Jerusalem—the ancient city that dates back to King David and before, directly south of the Temple Mount.

The late Israeli archaeologist Eilat Mazar discovered in February 2005 what is called the "Large Stone Structure," and what she believed to be the palace of King David. Two notable finds were bullae—a *bulla* being

> an oval or round object made of clay . . . bearing a seal impression reflecting the identity and public standing of an individual witnessing a document. Sealed documents of this sort, usually made of papyrus, were placed in private or public/municipal archives.[199]

The first of these bullae was of a government official named Jehucal, son of Shelemiah, son of Shevi. This person seems to be mentioned in Jeremiah 37:3 and 38:1, and thus presumably lived in the late seventh or early sixth century B.C., when Jeremiah lived. A second bulla at the site was from another government official, Gedaliah, son of Pashhur, who also seems to be named in Jeremiah 38:1–4.

Several artifacts found in the vicinity corroborate eleventh- to tenth-century dates. Mazar also discovered, in 2015, the royal bulla of the biblical king Hezekiah (r. 715–687/6 B.C.). It reads, "Belonging to Hezekiah [son of] Ahaz king of Judah" and has been dated to between 727 and 698 B.C. It was the first time that such a seal from an Israelite or Judean king had ever been found.

Hezekiah is the king who dug the famous tunnel bearing his name (2 Kings 20:20; 2 Chron. 32:2–4,30; Isa. 22:11). I was thrilled to walk through it in 2014. The *Encyclopedia Britannica* writes about him: "The dates of his reign are often given as about 715 to about 686 B.C., but inconsistencies in biblical and Assyrian cuneiform records have yielded a wide range of possible dates." Thus, it states that he flourished between c. 750 and c. 651 B.C. In any event, these dates sufficiently line up with the archaeologically determined date of the bulla bearing his name.

Science News in July of 2021 reported a discovery of a section of a First Temple-period city wall of Jerusalem.[200] The First Temple was built soon after David's death, during Solomon's reign (c. 970–c. 931 B.C.). The new find is in the eastern section of the City of David.

The tunnels and shafts under Jerusalem are also archaeologically verifiable (and quite interesting as well). Hezekiah's Tunnel, or the Siloam Tunnel, was designed to bring water from the Gihon Spring (the primary source of water in the area) to Jerusalem during times of siege warfare. It has long been widely accepted as dating to the time of King Hezekiah. The famous Warren's Shaft, a forty-three-foot-high vertical natural "chimney" under ancient Jerusalem discovered in 1867, has also been equated with the biblical "shaft" that was the means by which David's soldiers captured the previously Jebusite city that developed into Jerusalem:

> **2 Samuel 5:7–8** Nevertheless David took the stronghold of Zion, that is, the City of David. And David said on that day, "Whoever would smite the Jebusites, let him get up the water shaft." (Compare 1 Chron. 11:5–8.)

Another exciting support of the time frame of David's kingdom is Khirbet Qeiyafa, 20 miles west of Jerusalem on the top of a hill in the Elah Valley, overlooking the spot where the Bible reports that young David killed Goliath. I was privileged to visit it in 2014, and with the permission of our guide, we even "dug" on the (unoccupied) site a bit, and I found several specimens of pottery to bring home as souvenirs. Nearly 6,500 square feet of an Iron Age IIA city has been uncovered. Based on pottery styles and two burned olive pits tested for carbon-14, excavators Yosef Garfinkel and Saar Ganor have dated the site to 1025–975 B.C.

The presence of two gates, and the location, caused Garfinkel and Ganor to identify the city with the biblical Shaaraim ("two gates" in Hebrew: Josh. 15:35–36; 1 Sam. 17:52; 1 Chron. 4:31–32). Others have speculated that it is one of the following biblical cities: Azekah (Josh. 10:10–11, 15:20,35), Netaim (1 Chron. 4:23), or Adithaim (Josh. 15:36).

Garfinkel, Ganor, and Michael G. Hasel summed up the results of their excavation research in their book, *In the Footsteps of King David: Revelations from an Ancient Biblical City*:

> The tens of thousands of animal bones found at Khirbet Qeiyafa . . . include bones of goats, sheep, and cows, but no pig bones [i.e., the inhabitants followed Mosaic dietary requirements—see, e.g., Lev. 11:7].
>
> The rich Canaanite or Philistine iconography . . . is unknown. . . . It appears that the inhabitants of Khirbet Qeiyafa obeyed the commandment: "Thou shalt not make unto thee any graven image" (Exod. 20:4). . . .
>
> We obtained seventeen different radiometric dates from olive pits . . . which clearly indicate that the city had been destroyed no later than 980 to 970 BCE. . . . Khirbet Qeiyafa can be dated to the time of David or Saul, but not to Solomon's reign, which is later than the results obtained.[201]

A potsherd, or *ostracon*, of momentous significance was found at the site:

> The epigrapher, Haggai Misgav, determined that the language is Hebrew, making this the most ancient known Hebrew inscription.[202]

A second inscription was also discovered during the 2012 excavations:

> The inscription includes a personal name: Eshbaal, son of Beda. . . . the name Eshbaal is known from the Bible, but has never before appeared in an ancient inscription. All the occurrences of this name come from the tenth century BCE and are mostly connected with the reign of King David. . . .
>
> In the Bible, Eshbaal was the second king of Israel, the son of King Saul and a rival of David (1 Chron. 8:33). . . .

> In the following centuries, however, the personal name Eshbaal, or any other personal name including the element Baal, disappears from the biblical text.[203]

Some think three other men bore the name Eshbaal, with the Baal element replaced so that the final form became *Jashobeam*. All three of these men (if the hypothesis is correct) fought alongside King David: a warrior (1 Chron. 11:11), the Korahite who was with David at Ziklag (12:6), and the leader of David's first division (27:2).

Biblical Eglon is mentioned eight times in the book of Joshua, during the period about two centuries before David. It is believed that Tel Eton is a remnant of this city. It's located about 12 miles south of Khirbet Qeiyafa, which itself is 20 miles southwest of Jerusalem; and it's about 10 miles west of Hebron, which in turn is 18 miles south of Jerusalem.

In ancient times, cities in the same political jurisdiction, or "nation," if you will, were usually spaced no more than 18 miles from one another (within one long day's walk). These four locations—Jerusalem, Hebron, Khirbet Qeiyafa, and Eglon—fit that pattern, and all existed during King David's reign, suggesting indeed some sort of united "kingdom" of Judah (albeit a small one) under King David and his son and successor, Solomon.

Major Israeli newspapers announced this exciting find in 2018, including *Haaretz*[204] and *The Times of Israel.*[205]

Another way to support biblical accuracy in general, and particularly with regard to King David, is to demonstrate from archaeology that cities associated with King David in the Bible existed at the purported period of his life (c. 1040 B.C.–c. 970 B.C.). If they *didn't exist* during his time, that would constitute a problem of biblical chronology or accuracy. If they *did*, it's not *proof* of David, but it's *consistent* with the biblical report.

An inspired document, as Christians and Jews believe the Hebrew Bible is, *would* be historically trustworthy and exhibit many evidences that it's not mere mythology or fiction or legend. The sort of argumentation I am presenting is not so much intending to prove that King David existed as to *disprove the alleged disproofs* of his existence—"defeating the defeaters," so to speak. The two endeavors are logically and epistemologically distinct.

Ziklag

Based on excavations from 2015–2019, researchers believe that a site near the present-day city of Kiryat Gat in southern Israel (Khirbet al-Rai) is the biblical Ziklag, where David found refuge from the paranoid King Saul, who was pursuing him (1 Chron. 12:1). A *Fox News* article observed:

> "Above the remains of the Philistine settlement was a rural settlement from the time of King David, from the early tenth century B.C.," the researchers added. "This settlement came to an end in an intense fire that destroyed the buildings" [see 1 Sam. 30:1].[206]

Bethsaida

Rami Arav, associate professor at the University of Nebraska, discovered a city gate here from the time of David. The city had been founded in the eleventh century B.C. and was destroyed in 920 B.C. (about fifty years after David's death).[207] *The Jerusalem Post* reported that the gate likely dates from the time of the First Temple, built by Solomon (r. c. 970–c. 931 B.C.), when the city was known as Zer (Josh. 19:35).[208] Archaeologists Negev and Gibson concur:

"A substantial settlement existed at the site in Iron Age II [1000 to 920 B.C.]."[209]

Bethlehem

This was David's hometown (1 Sam. 17:12,15,58, 20:6), where he was anointed by the prophet Samuel (16:1–13). Negev and Gibson state:

> The archaeological record at present shows the earliest settlement existed amid the fertile fields of Bait [or Beit] Sahur on the lower ground half a mile to the east, where remains of all periods from the Chalcolithic to the Iron Age have been found. Perhaps ancient Bethlehem was located there.

The earliest known mention of Bethlehem is in the Amarna correspondence of 1350–1330 B.C. Jacob's wife Rachel (eighteenth century B.C.) was buried there (Gen. 35:19, 48:7), and in the book of Ruth, set during the time of the judges (c. 1200–c. 1037 B.C.), it's mentioned seven times, five of them in the first chapter.

Gath

Archaeological consensus seems to place this city at Tel es-Safi, between Ashkalon and Beth Shemesh. In the Bible, it is said to be the hometown of Goliath (1 Sam. 17:23), and the place where the Philistines ran and were slain after Goliath's death (v. 52; see also 2 Sam. 1:20). Negev and Gibson inform us that "excavations have uncovered explicit stratigraphic evidence of the LB, Iron I and Iron II [1000–586 B.C.]."

Ashkelon

Ashkelon is mentioned in the Bible at the time of Saul's death and David's ascension to the throne (2 Sam. 1:20), and three times in the earlier books of Joshua and Judges. Negev and Gibson state that "Philistine remains . . . were uncovered dating from 1100 B.C." and that it wasn't destroyed until "604 B.C."; therefore, it was present during David's life dates.

Ekron

Ekron is also mentioned as a place where the Philistines fled in terror after Goliath's defeat at the hands of David (1 Sam. 17:52), so it would have to, of course, *be* there at the time (c. 1024 B.C.) for the Bible to be accurate. It is believed to be Tel Miqne. Negev and Gibson verify that "Stratum V," discovered during the thirteen seasons of excavations between 1981 and 1996, is dated "the first half of the eleventh century B.C." (1100–1050). Stratum IV was destroyed "in the first quarter of the tenth century B.C." (1000–975). This means that it was occupied when David killed Goliath but no longer when David was forty to sixty-five years old and reigning as king. Accordingly, the Bible doesn't mention it as an existing city during this latter period. It is mentioned again by the prophet Jeremiah (c. 650–c. 570 B.C.) as fit for judgment (Jer. 25:15–17,20).

Sure enough, Negev and Gibson note that Ekron revived at "the beginning of the seventh century B.C." but was again destroyed "at the end of the seventh century"—in other words, after Jeremiah's birthdate, so his prophecy of doom is seen to be accurate. The same prophecy was applied to Ashkelon, and we saw above that it was annihilated at the same time (604 B.C.). The "remnant of Ashdod" (Jer. 25:20) "prospered until the Hasmonean Revolt [167–160 B.C.]. During the rebellion Judas Maccabeus 'took it, and laid it waste.'"[210] These events qualify as divine judgments according to biblical criteria, and we can also conclude (as Christians who believe in God and the supernatural) that Jeremiah gave accurate prophecies concerning divine wrath.

Gibeah

Saul is mentioned as being there while David was evading him (1 Sam. 22:6). Archaeologists identify it as Tell el-Ful, which is well attested as having existed during Saul's and David's time. Negev and Gibson noted that "the remains of a tower-like structure" were "identified by the excavators as the Citadel of Saul. . . . The pottery from the earliest phase of this tower is typical of the eleventh-tenth centuries B.C." Saul reigned here for twenty-two years, according to 1 Samuel (chs. 8–31).

Gibeon

Gibeon is mentioned in conjunction with David seven times in 2 Samuel 2, 3, 20, and 21. Negev and Gibson state that "except for some traces of settlement in the Late Bronze Age all the remains on the site are from the Iron Age and later periods." In other words, again, archaeology verifies the Bible's chronology, including the time of David. There is indeed a (fully excavated) large "pool" there (2 Sam. 2:13), which is "37 feet in diameter and 82 feet deep."

Hebron

David reigned in Hebron during his first seven years as king of Judah (c. 1010–1003 B.C). Leibel Reznick, in his article "Did Hebron Disappear?", notes the skepticism of many "noted historians and archaeologists . . . [who] boldly claimed that Hebron was . . . uninhabited during Early Iron age (1250–1000 BCE)."[211] He contended that this cynicism is unwarranted and based on "six serious blunders." These are too detailed to examine in this short survey, but the link to the article may be followed for those who wish to pursue the discussion in depth.

12

DIGGING UP PROOFS OF THE PROPHETS

"Oh Jerusalem, Jerusalem, killing the prophets and stoning those who are sent to you! . . . Behold, your house is forsaken."

—LUKE 13:34,35

Up until now we have been examining the trustworthiness of the biblical text by seeing if (and how often) it lines up with what we know from archaeology, history, and other sorts of science. With the prophets, it's a little different, because they (as their name suggests!) make prophecies, which can be objectively verified. But they also mention things in passing that are able to be corroborated or disconfirmed as well.

Our first "test case" will be the prophet Amos:

> For behold, the Lord commands, and the great house shall be smitten into fragments, and the little house into bits (Amos 6:11; see also 1:1, 8:8, 9:1,5; Zech. 14:5).

Amos the prophet, according to the *Encyclopedia Britannica*, "flourished during the reigns of King Uzziah

(c. 783–742 B.C.) of Judah (the southern kingdom) and King Jeroboam II (c. 786–746 B.C.) of Israel." His recording of this verified earthquake is evidence of when he lived, and also of the historical accuracy of what he wrote.

A 2000 article in *International Geology Review* verifies the basic known facts of this event:

> Widely separated archaeological excavations in Israel and Jordan contain late Iron Age (Iron IIB) architecture bearing evidence of a great earthquake. Masonry walls best display the earthquake, especially walls with broken ashlars, walls with displaced rows of stones, walls still standing but leaning or bowed, and walls collapsed with large sections still lying course-on-course. Debris at six sites (Hazor, Deir Alla, Gezer, Lachish, Tell Judeideh, and En Haseva) is tightly confined strati-graphically to the middle of the eighth century B.C., with dating errors of ~30 years. Biblical and post-biblical sources indicate a single, regionally extensive earthquake in the year 750 B.C. The epicenter was north of present-day Israel, probably in Lebanon. . . . The earthquake was at least magnitude 7.8, but likely was 8.2, the magnitude being estimated by scaling of isoseismal radii relative to smaller historic earthquakes in Israel and Lebanon.[212]

Ruth Schuster offers much information in her article on this topic:

> An earthquake that ripped apart Solomon's Temple was mentioned in the Bible and described in colorful detail by Josephus—and now geologists show what really happened. . . .
>
> Evidence of catastrophe in eighth-century BCE northern Israel is legion. A destruction layer at Hazor was dated

> by Israel Finkelstein and Yigal Yadin to 760 BCE, the right time frame for Amos. At Lachish, David Ussishkin found a destruction level from the same time. . . .
>
> Moving onto Megiddo (which the Christians call Armageddon), the archaeologists describe "tilted walls and pillars, bent and warped walls, fractured building stones, dipping floors, liquefied sand, mudbrick collapse and burnt remains" (Shmuel Marco and Israel Finkelstein of Tel Aviv University, with Amotz Agnon of Hebrew University and Ussishkin).[213]

She mentions also Tel Abu Hawam, which "had been settled from the Bronze Age" but was destroyed by the quake and not rebuilt. Tel Dan also "fits the timeline of the biblical quake." In Tel Shafi (the Philistine city of Gath), "a 4-meter-thick (13-foot) wall . . . fell onto its side in the eighth century BCE." There is also corroborating evidence from the Dead Sea, published in *Tectonophyics*, "from layered sediment at Ein Feshkha and Nahal Tze'elim (next to Masada)."[214]

Note that all of the above evidence is from outside Jerusalem. That changed in the summer of 2021, when archaeologists at the City of David National Park in Jerusalem discovered—for the first time—proof in that hallowed location. Rossella Tercatin, conveys what happened:

> "When we excavated the structure and uncovered an eighth-century BCE layer of destruction, we were very surprised, because we know that Jerusalem continued to exist in succession until the Babylonian destruction, which occurred about 200 years later," IAA excavation directors Dr. Joe Uziel and Ortal Chalaf said.
>
> "We asked ourselves what could have caused that dramatic layer of destruction we uncovered. Examining the

> excavation findings, we tried to check if there is a reference to it in the biblical text. Interestingly, the earthquake that appears in the Bible, in the books of Amos and Zechariah, occurred at the time when the building we excavated in the City of David collapsed."[215]

A more detailed report appeared in *The Times of Israel* on the same day,[216] and *Smithsonian Magazine* took note two days later.[217]

Our second "test case" is the prophet Isaiah, who lived from c. 740 to c. 681 B.C.[218] The current buzz about archaeological evidence and Isaiah revolves around a bulla (that is, a seal—see chapter eleven) with his name on it, found in 2018 in Jerusalem.

The late Israeli archaeologist Eilat Mazar announced in February 2018 that her team had discovered the bulla. Her team had already found a bulla from King Hezekiah (with whom Isaiah was closely associated) in 2015,[219] literally within six and a half feet of the Isaiah bulla, between the Temple Mount and the City of David (an area known as the *Ophel*). She detailed the Isaiah discovery in an article and stated,

> According to the Bible, the names of King Hezekiah and the prophet Isaiah are mentioned in one breath fourteen of the twenty-nine times the name of Isaiah is recalled (2 Kings 19–20; Isa. 37–39). No other figure was closer to King Hezekiah than the prophet Isaiah. . . .
>
> Without an *aleph* at the end, the word *nvy* is most likely just a personal name. Although it does not appear in the Bible, it does appear on seals and a seal impression on a jar handle, all from unprovenanced, private collections. . . .
>
> Reut Livyatan Ben-Arie, who studied the bullae from the Ophel with me, suggests that there is enough space for

two more letters at the end of the second register: a "*w*" (*vav*), the last letter in the name *Yeshayahu*, and an "*h*," the definite article "the" for the word *navy'* ("prophet"), rendering it *hanavy'* ("the prophet").[220]

Now, does this *prove* that Isaiah the prophet (the biblical figure) existed? Technically, or in the strictest sense, no. But I would draw an analogy of Isaiah's "status" to someone like Homer, the Greek epic poet, who is also thought to have lived in the eighth century B.C., though many scholars believe he never existed. Hence this comment in a *Washington Post* article from 2015:

> Homer's existence has been in doubt for years. In fact, there's an academic field of inquiry that examines everything involving Homer called the "Homeric Question." Homer has puzzled just about every scholar who has studied him for the simple reason that there isn't much to study. There's no reliable historical information about him.[221]

We have no *indisputable* or *definitive* proof of Homer's existence, as all agree. Yet that hasn't stopped his *works* (or those of someone *like* what we believe to be "him"), the *Iliad* and the *Odyssey*, from having a huge (and very real) impact on Western civilization and literature in particular.

Something is going on there. The influential *ideas* were thought of and promulgated by *someone*, whether Homer or someone else. But—as also in the case of Isaiah—we can attempt to *verify specific references to the world and history* contained in Homer. The famous example is Troy, the ancient city on the west coast of Turkey, the locus of Homer's account of the Trojan War.

Until the late nineteenth century, this war was thought by scholars to be entirely legendary. But starting in 1871, Heinrich Schliemann excavated the site of classical-era Troy, under which were found the ruins of numerous earlier settlements. This led several historians and archaeologists to believe that there is at least a kernel of historical truth in Homer's famous accounts. Opinions run the gamut of "essentially legendary" to "essentially historical," with probably the majority position being the in-between view of "partly historical." In any event, it's possible that these propositions can be *verified* or *proven false*. That's the point. This applies to Isaiah and other figures referred to in the Bible, just as it does to the alleged (or actual?) Trojan War, referred to in the epics of Homer.

The Isaiah bulla is the most exciting find in this regard, but there is more where the book of Isaiah is concerned. Rabbi Leibel Reznick, a senior lecturer in Talmudic studies, describes in an article[222] many archaeological finds that verify persons mentioned in the book of Isaiah, and hence, we could argue, also Isaiah's existence and his accuracy as a chronicler. For example, Reznick writes, "King Ahaz of Judah (r. 732–716 B.C.) is mentioned seven times in Isaiah. He also appears in the cuneiform Annals of King of Assyria Tiglath-pileser III (r. 745–727 B.C.)."[223]

There are a number of other events and personages Isaiah mentions whose taking place and historical existence are scientifically verifiable—and, indeed, verified. We'll examine a few.

Esar-haddon (king of Assyria, r. 681–669 B.C.)—see Isaiah 37:37–38 (see also Ezra 4:2)—is referred to in many cuneiform chronicles.[224] "Sennacherib king of Assyria" (same passage) also appears in Isaiah 36:1 and 37:21. He writes in his own *Chronicles* about his invasions of Israel and Jerusalem.

A seal (almost exactly citing Isa. 7:1) was discovered that included the following: "Belonging to Ahaz (son of) Jotham, King of Judah."[225] Pekah (also Isa. 7:1) was the second-to-last king of Israel, before it was conquered by the Assyrians. He is mentioned twice in the *Annals* of Tiglath-pileser III.[226] "Rezin the king of Syria" (same verse again; see also three additional appearances in 7:4,8 and 8:6) is also referred to in the *Annals* of Tiglath-pileser III.[227]

Merodach-baladan ("son of Baladan, king of Babylon") was friendly to King Hezekiah of Judah (Isa. 39:1–2). He appears in the cuneiform texts of Assyrian kings Tiglath-pileser III, Sargon II (r. 722–705 B.C.), and Sennacherib (r. 705–681 B.C.).[228]

King Sargon II of Assyria (r. 722–705 B.C.)—see Isaiah 20:1—is cited in countless cuneiform chronicles.

Shebna, a servant of King Hezekiah of Judah, appears five times in Isaiah (22:15, 36:3,11,22, 37:2). He is described as "over the household" (Isa. 22:15)—that is, in charge of the king's household affairs. The "Shebna inscription" was found in 1870 in the area of the City of David (precisely where he would have been expected to be, in service to the king). It was the first ancient Hebrew inscription found in modern times.

King Tirhakah of Ethiopia (Isa. 37:9; see also 2 Kings 19:19) is Taharqa, a pharaoh of the Twenty-Fifth Dynasty of Egypt and king of the Kingdom of Kush (present-day Sudan), from 690 to 664 B.C. He lived in the same general period as King Hezekiah.[229]

That adds up to eleven archaeological verifications of the accuracy of the text of the book of Isaiah. In my opinion, this makes it more likely than not that there was a person, Isaiah, who claimed to be a prophet, speaking for God, in the service of King Hezekiah of Judah, who was himself indisputably an actual person according to the criteria of archaeology and historiography. The fact that the two bullae bearing their names were literally found six feet apart is seemingly compelling evidence of Isaiah's historical existence.

Next we shall examine the archaeological evidence for the prophet Jeremiah, who lived c. 650 to c. 570 B.C. I will outline nineteen separate and independent archaeological verifications of the text of the book of Jeremiah. Certainly, the cumulative impact and strength of this evidence in relation to the extraordinary accuracy of this biblical book cannot be dismissed.

An article for the Archaeological Institute of America states,

> Austrian Assyriologist Michael Jursa recently discovered the financial record of a donation made to a Babylonian chief official, Nebo-Sarsekim [Babylonian: "Nabu-sharussu-ukin"—Jer. 39:3: "Sarsechim the Rab-saris"]. The find may lend new credibility to the book of Jeremiah, which cites Nebo-Sarsekim as a participant in the siege of Jerusalem in 587 B.C.
>
> The tablet is dated to 595 B.C., which was during the reign of the Babylonian king, Nebuchadnezzar II.[230]

An *Express* article provides more evidence for a real historical figure and prophet named Jeremiah:

> Tom Meyer, a professor in Bible studies at Shasta Bible College and Graduate School in California . . . told Express.co.uk: . . . "In 1982, Israeli archaeologists were excavating the layer of ruins from the time of Jerusalem's destruction by Babylon in 586 B.C.
>
> "In a place that has now been labeled 'The Bullae House,' archaeologists discovered over 50 bullae or seals dating to the time of the famous Jeremiah the prophet."[231]

One of the seals mentioned "Gemariah the son of Shaphan." He was a "secretary" who was cited in precisely the same way in Jeremiah 36:10 (see also 36:11–12, 25). Two more of these seals were inscribed with "Baruch son of Neriah." Baruch was Jeremiah's scribe, described in the Bible also as "son of Neriah" (Jer. 36:4; see also 36:5, 8, 10, 13–19, 26–27,-32).

Another article concurs:

> In 1975 a collection of 250 clay seals (scarabs) were found about 44 miles southwest of Jerusalem. These seals were used to authenticate letters from their senders. One of them was from "Berekhyahu, son of Neriyahu the scribe." This is almost certainly the Baruch of Jeremiah. . . . If we can establish beyond reasonable doubt that the Baruch of Jeremiah is a real person in the position we know he had in the book of Jeremiah, then we can conclude that, almost certainly, the biblical prophet Jeremiah was a real person as well.[232]

Leibel Reznick provided several physical items that verified persons mentioned in the book of Jeremiah. He noted, "When outside confirmation of the minor characters surfaces, it lends great strength to those who firmly believe in the veracity and accuracy of the biblical narrative."[233]

The phrase "Ahikam, son of Shaphan" occurs six times in the book of Jeremiah in the RSV, and also in 2 Kings 25:22. Archaeologists have found bullae bearing the name "Ahikam son of Shaphan."[234]

Reznick notes that Jeremiah 40:14 ("Baalis the king of the Ammonites") is "attested to by two seals found in Jordan, the Milqom Seal and the Baalisha Seal, which reads Baalisha (Baalis) king of the sons of Ammon."[235] Reznick states that the "Melqart Stele mentions [the] king of Aram, Bir-hadad."[236] This corresponds to Jeremiah 49:27 ("the strongholds of Ben-hadad").

A biblical false prophet, "Gedaliah the son of Pashhur" (Jer. 38:1,4,6), was attested in a bulla found in Jerusalem in the City of David, just south of the Temple Mount in August 2008 by Israeli archaeologist Eilat Mazar.[237]

Jeremiah 36:12,20–21 mentions "Elishama the secretary" (of King Jehoiakim); compare Jeremiah 41:1. A bulla from that time period reads, "Elishama, servant of the king."[238]

"Hezekiah king of Judah" appears in Jeremiah 15:4 and 26:18–19. He has been verified by many seals and bullae.[239]

Hilkiah was a high priest mentioned in Jeremiah 29:3 (compare 2 Kings 22 and 23; Ezra 7; Neh. 11 and 12; 2 Chron. 34 and 35). A signet ring with his name has been found and dated to Jeremiah's era.[240]

"Pharaoh Hophra king of Egypt" (Jer. 44:30) is Pharaoh Apries, of the Twenty-Sixth Dynasty, who reigned from 589 to 570 B.C.—all within Jeremiah's lifetime. The different names are a matter of transliteration (*Apries* being Greek and *Hophra*, Hebrew). He is also known as Wahibre Haaibre.

Jehoiachin, king of Judah (Jer. 52:31) is cited in the Ration Tables of Babylon.[241]

Jehucal, as Reznick noted, was an "official in the court of Zedekiah. A bulla bearing the name 'Jehucal the son of Shelemiah' was discovered in the archaeological City of David in Jerusalem [in 2005] together with other bullae dating to the period of Zedekiah."[242] Sure enough, this proves Jeremiah accurate, since Jeremiah 37:3 refers to "Jehucal the son of Shelemiah."

Jerahmeel was the son of king Jehoiakim. A bulla has been found, reading, "Jerahmeel, the king's son"—precisely as Jeremiah 36:26 states.[243]

Manasseh, "son of Hezekiah, king of Judah" (Jer. 15:4), is thought to have reigned from 687 to 643 B.C. and is archaeologically verified in the annals of Assyrian kings Esarhaddon (r. 681–669 B.C.) and Assurbanipal (r. 669–631 B.C.).[244]

"Seraiah the son of Neriah" (Jer. 51:59) has been verified by a bulla with the name "Seraiah ben Neriah."[245]

Zedekiah was in the court of King Jehoiakim of Judah (r. 609–598 B.C.). A bulla found in the City of David in Jerusalem bore the name "Zedekiah the son of Hananiah," echoing and verifying Jeremiah 36:12.[246]

Our fourth and last example of biblical prophets in relation to archaeology and other sciences—and arguably the most interesting for our present purposes—is Daniel, who, according to biblical chronology and maximalist archaeologists, lived in the sixth to the fifth century B.C.

Many if not most modern scholars, however, think Daniel is merely a mythical or legendary figure or that, at best, the book bearing his name dates to the second century B.C. One Jewish scholar certainly speaks for many when he writes:

> Specialists are united in dating the book to the second century BCE, sometime around the Maccabean revolt. . . . I don't see anything like extraordinary evidence that Daniel was composed in the sixth century. Quite the contrary.[247]

We're sadly familiar with this story by now. A lot of scholars didn't think King David existed, either, until (as we saw in the previous chapter), in 1993, an artifact was found with "House of David" written on it. We live and learn—and once in a while, even some members of schools of erroneous thought in archaeology admit that they got it wrong.

Remember, just seventy years ago, most astronomers believed in a "steady state" universe—that is, an eternal one that had no beginning. Even Einstein agreed with that, before he changed his mind. Then Big Bang cosmology came along, and virtually all astronomers (an overwhelming turnaround) now believe that the universe had a beginning. I won't belabor where *that* notion had been residing for the last three thousand or more years.

Many more such examples could be given. Thus, the mere fact that there may be a particular *scholarly consensus* at any given time is significant and noteworthy from a sociological perspective, but not *compelling*. In fact, technically, it is the *ad populum* fallacy—"a lot of (smart) folks *believe* in *x*; therefore, *x* must be true." But points of view are only as good as the evidence provided for them.

Persian Kings Cyrus and Darius

The British Museum web page for the "Cyrus Cylinder" features a

> clay cylinder; a Babylonian account of the conquest of Babylon by Cyrus in 539 B.C., of his restoration to various temples of statues removed by Nabonidus, the previous king of Babylon, and of his own work at Babylon. The cylindrical form is typical of royal inscriptions of the Late Babylonian period, and the text shows that the cylinder was written [in cuneiform] to be buried in the foundations of the city wall of Babylon. It was deposited there after the capture of the city by Cyrus in 539 B.C., and presumably written on his orders.[248]

The text is regarded by more traditional biblical scholars as evidence of Cyrus's policy of the restoration of the Jewish people following their Babylonian captivity—an act that the book of Ezra (1:1–4) attributes to King Cyrus. By implication, this (at least indirectly) supports the historical accuracy of the book of Daniel, which portrays Daniel as a servant of King Darius I ("the Great"), who ruled over the Achaemenid Empire from 522 to 486 B.C. and (seemingly) also of the prior king, Cyrus the Great (r. 559–530 B.C.):

> It pleased Darius to set over the kingdom a hundred and twenty satraps, to be throughout the whole kingdom; and over them three presidents, of whom Daniel was one, to whom these satraps should give account, so that the king might suffer no loss. . . . So this Daniel prospered during the reign of Darius and the reign of Cyrus the Persian (Dan. 6:1–2, 28).

> And as for me, in the first year of Darius the Mede, I stood up to confirm and strengthen him (Dan. 11:1).

Daniel presents King Darius as being tolerant of Judaism, just as Cyrus had been (6:25–26).

With regard to these kings and their actions, secular history broadly agrees with the above picture. The book of Ezra, in chapter 6, likewise recounts how King Cyrus ordered—in his first year (approximately 559 B.C.)—the rebuilding of the Jewish temple in Jerusalem, with the restoration of stolen temple items that the Babylonians had carried away, and that Darius followed this policy. Ezra 6:15 proclaims that the Temple was "finished . . . in the sixth year of the reign of Darius the king." This would be approximately 516 B.C.

Flavius Josephus (c. A.D. 37–c. 100), the eminent Roman Jewish historian, verifies the biblical accounts of Cyrus and

Darius regarding the Jews and specifically the rebuilding of their Temple.[249]

King (?) / Regent Belshazzar

Belshazzar was a figure formerly found only in the Bible, and so scholars could and did question his historicity, since he couldn't be documented anywhere else. He is mentioned eight times in Daniel—chapters 5, 7, and 8—and nowhere else in Holy Scripture.

But lo and behold, in 1854, four cuneiform cylinders[250] with inscriptions from King Nabonidus of Babylonia (r. 556–539 B.C.) were found in Ur, in the foundation of a ziggurat or compound. And they contained a mention of Belshazzar, who was Nabonidus's eldest son:

> As for me, Nabonidus, king of Babylon, save me from sinning against your great godhead and grant me as a present a life long of days, and as for Belshazzar, the eldest son—my offspring—instill reverence for your great godhead in his heart and may he not commit any cultic mistake, may he be sated with a life of plenitude.

Nabonidus is not mentioned in the book of Daniel or anywhere in the Bible, as far as I can tell. Why would that be, seeing that he was the last king of Babylon before it was conquered by Cyrus the Great and the Persians? Instead, we have a chapter devoted to Belshazzar, who is called "king of Babylon" (Dan. 7:1) and "the Chaldean king" (5:30), and elsewhere "king" (5:1, 5–10, 13, 8:1).

Is this not a serious historical error? No, it's not, once the full story is understood. It turns out that Nabonidus wasn't present in Babylon for nine or ten years (552–543 or 542 B.C.). In those years, he resided, according to historians of Babylon, in Tema (or Tayma), in Arabia. During this period, Belshazzar acted as regent in Babylonia, and Nabonidus continued to be recognized as the king.[251] Thus, Belshazzar, ruling in Nabonidus's absence or stead, could sensibly be called "king," since he was the regent—the one in charge during the true king's absence. And this is what the prophet Daniel called him.

The regency itself is documented in another artifact called the Nabonidus Chronicle, acquired by the British Museum in 1879. It contains cuneiform descriptions mostly concerning Nabonidus's reign. Thought to be written during the late sixth or early fifth century B.C.,[252] it refers to Nabonidus's self-imposed exile, and how Babylon was administered during that time by his son, Bel-shar-usur.

The book of Daniel, therefore, is shown to be historically accurate in this particular account. The Bible is always "blunt" and pragmatic and phenomenological (i.e., "going by appearances") in its approach. Belshazzar was acting as regent in place of the king (which has happened many times in history), and so he was called "king" based on his *appearance* as king. We speak in the same way today. The sun looks to us as though it rises and sets in relation to the horizon, and so we refer to it that way, when in fact it is only the *appearance* of same, since the sun's seeming "motion" is determined by the rotation of the earth.

If the Bible called Belshazzar king, yet he was in fact not even a *regent*, and could not be independently verified at all, then that would be a serious error, or at least potentially so. But this is *not* the case. And we know this from direct archaeological evidence.

Chief Eunuchs

Then the king commanded Ashpenaz, his *chief eunuch*, to bring some of the people of Israel, both of the royal family and of the nobility (Dan. 1:3).

While undertaking an excavation of the Babylonian city of Sippar (Tell Abu Habbah) in 1880–1882, Assyriologist Hormuzd Rassam discovered almost 130,000 inscribed cuneiform tablets, presently housed at the British Museum. One of these is called the Nebo-Sarsekim Tablet, presently in the British Museum, dated to 595 B.C. It includes the following section:

> [Regarding] 1.5 minas (~850 grams / 27 troy oz) of gold, the property of Nabu-sharrussu-ukin, *the chief eunuch*, which he sent via Arad-Banitu the eunuch to [the temple] Esangila: Arad-Banitu has delivered [it] to Esangila. In the presence of Bel-usat, son of Alpaya, the royal bodyguard, [and of] Nadin, son of Marduk-zer-ibni. Month XI, day 18, year 10 [of] Nebuchadnezzar, king of Babylon.[253]

According to Michael Jursa (associate professor at the University of Vienna), the rarity of the Babylonian name, the high rank of the *rab ša-rēši*, and the closeness in time make it almost indisputable that the person mentioned on the tablet is identical to the biblical figure described as a "chief eunuch" (Dan. 1:3) or "Sarsechim the Rab-saris" (Jer. 39:3). Moreover, the tablet is dated within eight years of the events recorded in Jeremiah. A Christian Bible study site offers further related insight, which will clarify this confusing subject matter:

> The Akkadian name Nabu-sharrussu-ukin, phonetically Nebo-Sarsekim, was equivalent to the Hebrew name Sar-sekim, and to this name, the Bible attached the title "the Rab-saris," which meant "chief eunuch."
>
> Eunuchs were common in Assyrian and Neo-Babylonian courts, and there were several with the title of "chief eunuch" functioning as officials for the king (2 Kings 18:17; Jer. 39:13).[254]

Daniel had the English term, and the earlier text from Jeremiah had the Babylonian equivalent title. These are all translation issues. They are conveying the same message. Daniel also refers to a "chief eunuch" as a position in Babylonian government (1:3), near the time that Jeremiah did the same.

Once again, the Bible remarkably reflects actual history, in the fairly minute details of the office of "chief eunuch" and at least one such historically documented person.

King Nebuchadnezzar Eating Grass

Daniel 4:33 informs us that the Babylonian king, Nebuchadnezzar, "was driven from among men, and ate grass like an ox . . . and his nails were like birds' claws."

Prima facie, what Daniel describes in this section looks ridiculous, and we might perhaps be excused for thinking it is myth or legend. No doubt, this has not infrequently been used as fodder for cynical biblical skeptics, quick to mock the Bible as ahistorical (and Christians for believing that it *does* record actual history). In fact, however, what happened to this famous king is a documented medical and psychiatric condition.

The condition is called *boanthropy*. The website *Online Psychology Degree Guide* has an article that includes a section on this disorder.

> Those who suffer from the very rare—but very scary—mental disorder boanthropy believe they are cows, often going as far as to behave as such. Sometimes those with boanthropy are even found in fields with cows, walking on all fours and chewing grass as if they were a true member of the herd. . . . Interestingly, it is believed that boanthropy is even referred to in the Bible, as King Nebuchadnezzar is described as being "driven from men and did eat grass as oxen."[255]

Shadrach, Meshach, and Abednego

"If you do not worship, you shall immediately be cast into a burning fiery furnace; and who is the god that will deliver you out of my hands?" (Dan. 3:15).

My purpose here is to overcome the objection that such things "never happen" or happen so rarely as to cast doubt, *prima facie*, on the Daniel story.

James A. Montgomery, in his volume *A Critical and Exegetical Commentary on the Book of Daniel*, states that the fiery furnace "must have been similar to our common lime-kiln, with a perpendicular shaft from the top and an opening at the bottom for extracting the fused lime," and notes "the existence of similar ovens in Persia for the execution of criminals."[256] Tawny L. Holm, in his article "The fiery furnace in the book of Daniel and the ancient Near East," provides further examples in Mesopotamia of execution by burning:

> With regard to historical inscriptions, one finds the burning of prisoners in Neo-Assyrian texts, especially from the ninth-century [883–859 B.C.] reign of Assurnasirpal II.... As another example, one notes the Assur ostracon, an Assyrian letter written in Aramaic, in which an Assyrian military officer considers the fate of defectors; he asserts that the practice of past Assyrian kings was to burn them."[257]

I think that enough evidence has now been shown (of such a thing actually happening) to overcome hostile and "automatic" claims that the text of Daniel is mere fiction or legend, *simply* because of its description of one attempted execution by burning.

Daniel in the Lions' Den

The famous story of Daniel in the lions' den can be found in chapter 6:

> Then the king commanded, and Daniel was brought and cast into the den of lions. The king said to Daniel, "May your God, whom you serve continually, deliver you!" And a stone was brought and laid upon the mouth of the den, and the king sealed it with his own signet and with the signet of his lords, that nothing might be changed concerning Daniel. Then the king went to his palace, and spent the night fasting; no diversions were brought to him, and sleep fled from him.
>
> Then, at break of day, the king arose and went in haste to the den of lions. When he came near to the den where Daniel was, he cried out in a tone of anguish and said to Daniel, "O Daniel, servant of the living God, has your God, whom you serve continually, been able to deliver you from the lions?" Then Daniel said to the king, "O king, live for ever! My God sent his angel and shut the lions' mouths, and they have not hurt me, because I was found blameless before him; and also before you, O king, I have done no wrong." Then the king was exceedingly glad, and commanded that Daniel be taken up out of the den. So Daniel was taken up out of the den, and no kind of hurt was found upon him, because he had trusted in his God (vv. 14–23).

The British Museum has an article entitled "Lion-hunting: the sport of kings." It states,

> Some of the most spectacular depictions of the hunt were found in the palace of king Ashurnasirpal II (883–859 B.C.) at the city of Nimrud (in the north of present-day Iraq).

> They show the king hunting lions and wild bulls from his chariot. . . . More than 200 years later, King Ashurbanipal [r. 669–631 B.C.] revived the royal lion hunt and decorated his North Palace at the city of Nineveh (also in the north of present-day Iraq) with brilliantly carved reliefs that show his prowess as a brave hunter. . . . Although Ashurbanipal represented himself hunting animals in the wild, the hunting scenes that decorated Ashurbanipal's palace were staged events within the game parks of the city. These were public spectacles, comparable to Roman arena games.[258]

The *Joy of Museums* website concurs:

> The Lion Hunt of Ashurbanipal, a sequence of Assyrian palace reliefs from the North Palace at Nineveh dating from about 645 B.C., shows King Ashurbanipal hunting lions.
>
> The Assyrian "royal lion hunt" was the staged and ritualized killing by the king of lions already captured and released into an arena.[259]

The idea, then, in light of the above information, was that Assyrian kings necessarily had to keep lions in some sort of confinement (in the above instance, a "cage") for the purpose of having spectacles of lion-hunting in their arenas (much as the Romans later did, to kill Christians for the purpose of morbid spectacle). In the Bible, 2 Samuel 23:20 and 1 Chronicles 11:22 refer to a man who "went down and slew a lion in a pit."

The Persians followed this practice of glorifying royal lion-hunting:

> There are some echoes . . . of the staged lion-hunting imagery in the Persian palaces, which displays the lion as

a dangerous creature. At Persepolis, its presence is recurrent: in several buildings there are images in the Palace of Darius showing a figure fighting beasts, including lions.[260]

The argument and hypothesis, then, is that perhaps Daniel was cast into one of these places of confinement (a "den") of lions, possibly also for the purpose of staged-spectacle hunting. And if that was indeed the case, we see that the Bible was again accurate for the umpteenth time.

Aramaic Chapters

Daniel 2:4 through to chapter 7 is written in Aramaic. This fact has been used as an argument for the book having supposedly been written in the second century B.C. rather than in the sixth or fifth century B.C., because Aramaic was at the later date the *lingua franca* in the area (that is, the accepted "standard" language for "all," much as English is today in many parts of the world).

But the underlying assumption is fallacious. Aramaic was clearly in use as far back as the tenth century B.C. in Mesopotamia, and over time, the western regions of Assyria spoke both Akkadian and Aramean at least as early as the mid-ninth century B.C. Assyrian king Tiglath-Pileser III (r. 745–727 B.C.) made Aramaic the empire's second official language, and it eventually supplanted Akkadian. From about 700 B.C., it began spreading in all directions, but with different dialects—not only in Assyria, but also in Babylonia, the Levant, and Egypt. We know, for example, that Adon, a Canaanite king, wrote to a pharaoh in Aramaic in around 600 B.C.[261]

Zdravko Stefanovic, in a doctoral dissertation on this topic, [262] analyzed ninth- to seventh-century B.C. Old Aramaic inscriptions that exhibited a significant similarity to Daniel's Aramaic.

Persian Words

The book of Daniel also contains about fifteen Persian words. Biblical linguist S.R. Driver famously (or infamously) contended,

> The Persian words presuppose a period after the Persian Empire had been well established; the Greek words demand, the Hebrew supports, and the Aramaic permits, a date after the conquest of Palestine by Alexander the Great (332 B.C.).[263]

Typical of the skeptical arguments of Bible critics, this one has been regurgitated for over 130 years now, even though, arguably, it has long been refuted—before it was even asserted, by professor of Hebrew E.B. Pusey in 1868.[264]

Here is how the rebuttal goes. None of Daniel's Persian words is found in Persian literature after 300 B.C. Two of them have been found in sixth- and fifth-century B.C. texts. Kenneth Kitchen notes that "the Persian words in Daniel are specifically, *Old Persian* words."[265] According to an expert on the matter, by the fourth century B.C., the inscriptions of Artaxerxes II (r. c. 405–358 B.C.) and Artaxerxes III (r. c. 358–338 B.C.) differ enough from the language of Darius's inscriptions to be called a "pre-Middle Persian," or "post-Old Persian."[266]

The argument is simple, decisive, and devastating. Daniel couldn't have used Old Persian words that were obsolete by the fourth century, two centuries later—the time that he (or, more accurately, some unknown person called "Daniel") supposedly wrote his book, according to the skeptics. Once again, then, we see that the book of Daniel (like many other biblical books, as I have shown throughout this book), is remarkably upheld in its accuracy by many external archaeological and historical sources.

13

ASTRONOMERS TRACK THE STAR OF BETHLEHEM

"Where is he who has been born king of the Jews? For we have seen his star in the East, and have come to worship him."

—MATTHEW 2:2

The "wise men" or *Magi* were originally a Median (northwest Persian) tribe:

> In classical literature, they are presented to us almost exclusively in connection with Medo-Persian history. Herodotus represents them as one of the six tribes into which the Median people were divided.[267]

They performed priestly functions, perhaps due to Zoroaster (Zarathustra) *possibly* having belonged to the tribe (or the belief that he did), and studied astronomy and astrology, in part learned from Babylon. Daniel (1:20, 2:27, 5:15) uses the word to denote "wise men" or "astrologers who interpret dreams and messages."

Several Church Fathers agree with this general picture:

> Clement of Alexandria, Diodorus of Tarsus, Chrysostom, Cyril of Alexandria . . . and others are probably right in bringing them from Persia. Sargon's settlement of Israelites in Media (circa 730–728 B.C. [2 Kings 17:6]) accounts for the large Hebrew element of thought. . . . Median astronomers would thus know Balaam's prophecy of the star out of Jacob (Num. 24:17). . . .
>
> East of Palestine, only ancient Media, Persia, Assyria, and Babylonia had a Magian priesthood at the time of the birth of Christ. From some such part of the Parthian Empire the Magi came.[268]

The Bible doesn't mention how many Magi there were. The number three is deduced from the three gifts they gave (gold, frankincense, and myrrh—Matt. 2:11). Some of the Church Fathers refer to three wise men. No Church Father regarded them as kings. They were *not* magicians, but rather, "fundamentally," Zoroastrians—members of a religion that forbade sorcery—and astrologers in the ancient Mesopotamian definition, where the appearance of the heavens was seen as a reflection of what happened on earth but not an actual cause.

They may have arrived either a little over a year after Jesus' birth or up to two years after. Our clue for this chronology comes from Herod wanting to kill all the male children in Bethlehem and its surroundings under two years old (Matt. 2:16). He had determined the likely age of the Messiah based on his discussions with the wise men about when the star first appeared (2:7; see also v. 16).

My own educated guess, based on my studies and research, is that the visit of the wise men occurred when Jesus was a year old and that they told Herod the star had appeared a year and three months previously (thinking Jesus may have been born *then*), based on the conjunction of Jupiter (thought by ancient astrologers to be the "king" of planets) and Regulus (the star of kingship, and brightest in the constellation Leo) in September, 3 B.C. Herod then decided to kill all children under two just to make extra-sure that he killed Jesus.

The *Catholic Encyclopedia* elaborates on the nature of the journey of the wise men:

> From Persia, whence the Magi are supposed to have come, to Jerusalem was a journey of between 1,000 and 1,200 miles. Such a distance may have taken any time between three and twelve months by camel.[269]

Camels "can easily carry an extra 200 pounds and can walk about 20 miles a day through the harsh desert climate."[270] Using this figure and the high estimate of the distance above, it comes out to exactly sixty days for the journey (barring various difficulties that might arise). Presumably, there were resting periods and side journeys to towns to replenish supplies, etc., which might add another month, bringing the duration to three. Persia would have been about twice as far as Babylon, but it depends on preparation time, how many stops and breaks, etc. A six-month "window" for the journey is required, to incorporate their seeing the star both in Persia (or Babylon) and in Israel when they arrived.

Skeptics of the story (mostly the "anti-theist" type of atheist—those who delight in mocking Christianity and trying to make it and Christians look ridiculous) seem to find it unthinkable that such a journey could be made with the simple aid of a star in the West.

But it's not rocket science (then or now) to know and understand that Jerusalem was west of Persia—so a star to the west having to do with a king (Jupiter and Regulus were associated with a king) and a lion (of Judah), the constellation Leo, provided that there was an existing familiarity with Judaism, would logically lead to Jerusalem, both geographically and in the context of the religions of that time.

I examined my own globe of the world and saw that Jerusalem is almost exactly due west from northwest Persia, where the Magi likely came from. In current maps, Baghdad and Amman, Jordan are roughly on the line due west from this area. Baghdad was built in the eighth century. Ancient Babylon lies about 53 miles south of Baghdad, but it was conquered by the Persians in 539 B.C. and was never the same again, eventually becoming a ruin and wasteland.

Amman (ancient Ammon, in the region of the Ammonites in current-day Jordan) was not religiously significant enough at this time, either, and after the fourth century B.C., it was conquered by the Greeks, Egyptians, and Romans. It was no extraordinary astronomical deduction, then, to conclude that some important happenings due *west* were to occur in Jerusalem.

The question then becomes: *how* did they journey from Persia to Jerusalem? Was it just a fly-by-night random affair, or were there known routes? The latter was in fact the case. An ancient "superhighway" of sorts, called the Royal Road, was constructed by the Persian king Darius I (the Great) of the first (Achaemenid) Persian Empire in the fifth century B.C. We know the course of the road from the historian Herodotus, other historical sources, and archaeology. The *Encyclopedia Britannica* states that it ran "from Susa, the ancient capital of Persia, across Anatolia to Sardis and Smyrna on the Aegean Sea." This was a distance of about 1,500 miles.

The Royal Road was well north of Israel—even north of Damascus, Syria. Therefore, it couldn't have been the *entire* route of the Magi. Most of the rest likely would have been the equally famous road called the King's Highway, an "ancient thoroughfare that connected Syria and the Gulf of Aqaba by way of what is now Jordan." During the Roman period, it was called *Via Regia* and *Via Traiana Nova*. The King's Highway is mentioned in the Old Testament, in conjunction with the journeys of Moses and the Hebrew nation (Num. 20:17,19, 21:22), and is said to have run through or near Kadesh at the southern border of Canaan (now Israel), which is historically accurate.[271] The Silk Road, a sort of successor to the Royal Road, at least in part, was also greatly flourishing as a means of east-west trade at the time the Magi would (or could) have traveled on it.

The Magi simply would have had to follow the Royal Road or Silk Road to Damascus and proceed to Jerusalem via the King's Highway. Among these three, and possibly some relatively short connecting routes (just as it was with, for example, the Oregon Trail and various "shortcuts" in the American West), the entire journey can be visualized and mapped with a fair degree of likelihood or probability, just as most travelers by car in America are likely to take interstate freeways on long trips.

In any event, they weren't following a star *literally every moment*. The Bible doesn't state that. It's merely the stuff of Christmas carols, which are not exactly inspired revelation. My point is that the "celestial navigation" played a relatively minor role in the journey of the wise men.

Not everything in the Bible is "mysterious" or miraculous. Most of the journey was "predetermined" according to well-known travel and trade routes already long established. To travel to Jerusalem from Persia, they had to go around the Arabian Desert and Syrian Desert via the Fertile Crescent. They didn't need a star to guide them all that way. They simply followed the water and the fertile land outside the desert, with the understanding that they were making their way to Jerusalem.

The more difficult and interesting question about their journey is, what route did they take *back*? The Bible states that "being warned in a dream not to return to Herod, they departed to their own country by another way" (Matt. 2:12). Probably most likely, they would have followed the coastal route on the Mediterranean Sea until they were out of reach of Herod, or else they went across the Arabian Desert. There are various ways to find water, even in the desert.[272] And since their land was likely due east, the rising sun is all they required for broad navigation—especially taking a more direct route across the desert. The camels did the rest.

One seeming difficulty of the well-known story of the journey is the meaning of the wise men seeing the star "in the East," but then traveling *west* to Bethlehem. John Mosley, program supervisor at the Griffith Observatory in Los Angeles, provides a perfectly reasonable explanation:

> This has been interpreted to mean either that the star was in the eastern part of the sky or that the wise men were in the eastern part of the world when they saw it, but the actual situation is not so ambiguous. The Greek phrase, "en te anatole" simply means "as it rose" or "at its rising" which of course is always in the eastern sky, and does not refer to the location of the observer. Some authors interpret the phrase to mean that the Magi observed the star's predawn heliacal rising with the sun. . . . The New English Bible . . . [reads,] "We observed the rising of his star" and "the star which they had seen at its rising."[273]

Other Bible versions are similar to the NEB.

Starting in August, 3 B.C., Jupiter rose in the east as a morning star and then came into conjunction with Venus. This started a series of six conjunctions in that year and the next, five with other planets and one with Regulus. At the end of 2 B.C., Jupiter (always one of the brightest objects in the sky) appeared to be moving westward, toward Jerusalem from the east.

Another central consideration in the dating of these events has to do with the date of the death of Herod the Great. The conventional wisdom is that he died in 4 B.C. Jesus' birth is believed by all to be one to two years before Herod died. If we have a different year for Jesus' birth, then we have to look at different astronomical data for when the star of Bethlehem appeared, what it was, etc.

Historians have primarily relied on the Jewish historian Josephus (A.D. 37–c. 100) for determination of this date, as influentially interpreted by Protestant theologian and historian Emil Schürer in his 1891 book, *A History of the Jewish People in the Time of Jesus Christ*. But physicist John A. Cramer notes that the lunar eclipse preceding Herod's death, as noted by Josephus, may have been at a later date than the usually accepted one:

> This date [4 B.C.] is based on Josephus's remark in *Antiquities* 17.6.4 that there was a lunar eclipse shortly before Herod died. This is traditionally ascribed to the eclipse of March 13, 4 B.C. Unfortunately, this eclipse was visible only very late that night in Judea and was additionally a minor and only partial eclipse. There were no lunar eclipses visible in Judea thereafter until two occurred in the year 1 B.C. Of these two, the one on December 29, just two days before the change of eras, gets my vote since it was the one most likely to be seen and remembered.

> That then dates the death of Herod the Great into the first year of the current era, four years after the usual date.[274]

This argument was also advanced in the nineteenth century by scholars Édouard Caspari, Florian Riess, and others, so it's not new. Josephus also notes that Herod died before the Jewish Passover holy day.[275]

These are our two historical clues. John Cramer, continuing his analysis based on Josephus, concludes,

> Only four lunar eclipses occurred in the likely time frame: September 15, 5 B.C., March 12–13, 4 B.C., January 10, 1 B.C. and December 29, 1 B.C. . . .
>
> The December 29 eclipse, the moon rose at 53 percent eclipse, and its most visible aspect was over by 6 P.M. It is the most likely of the four to have been noted and commented on.[276]

Noted professor of New Testament history and archaeology Jack Finegan (1908–2000) took a different approach and examined the manuscript evidence in Josephus:

> The currently known text of Josephus's *Ant.* 18.106 states that [Herod] Philip died in the twentieth year of Tiberius (A.D. 33/34). . . . This points to Philip's ascension at the death of Herod in 4 B.C. . . .
>
> In 1995 David W. Beyer reported to the Society for Biblical Literature his personal examination in the British Museum of forty-six editions of Josephus's *Antiquities* published before 1700 among which twenty-seven texts, all but three published before 1544, read "twenty-second year of Tiberius," while not one single edition published prior to 1544 read "twentieth year of Tiberius." . . .

> [This] points to 1 B.C. . . . as the year of death of Herod. . . . Accordingly, if the birth of Jesus was two years or less before the death of Herod in 1 B.C., the date of birth was in 3 or 2 B.C., presumably precisely in the period 3/2 B.C., so consistently attested by the most credible early Church Fathers.[277]

Jack Finegan noted some early writers' reckoning of 3 or 2 B.C. for the birth of Jesus, including Irenaeus, Clement of Alexandria, Tertullian, Julius Africanus, Hippolytus of Rome, Hippolytus of Thebes, Origen, Eusebius of Caesarea, and Epiphanius of Salamis.

Another argument that can be made is the date of coins issued by Herod the Great's successors. The evidence shows that none can be dated before A.D. 1. These coins were controlled by Rome, and only after Herod the Great's death could such coins be issued. It would be odd for a five-year gap to occur.

As we shall see, a tentative acceptance of Herod's death in 1 B.C. or A.D. 1 (if Finegan and others of the same opinion are in fact right) will be significant in terms of lining up the known astronomical data regarding an extraordinary "bright star" in the sky that can ostensibly or speculatively be equated with the star of Bethlehem.

Now let's examine Matthew 2:9: "the star which they had seen in the East went before them." This refers (in context) to the wise men being in Jerusalem and talking to Herod (2:1, 7–9). He "sent them to Bethlehem," which is south of Jerusalem, about six miles. (I traveled this route in 2014.) Therefore, this, I submit, is what the Bible (which habitually uses phenomenological language[278]) means by saying the star "went before" them. In other words, it would always have been "ahead of" or "in front of" or "before" them as they traveled, much as we say we are "following the sun west" or how American slaves (in folklore, at least, if not in fact) attempting to escape to the north followed the "drinking gourd" (the Big Dipper) north.

Thus, we could say the Big Dipper or North Star "went before" the slaves, just as we say they "followed" it. The North Star would also lead anyone to the North Pole if he kept following it—that is, by our vantage point, it would "go before" him. It's all phenomenological language, which we use all the time, just as the biblical writers also did.

We know from the astronomical charts that Jupiter, in later November and early December in 2 B.C., was to the south from Jerusalem; therefore, it "went before" the wise men as they traveled south to Bethlehem—the journey that the text refers to. Jupiter wouldn't have moved much on the way from Jerusalem to Bethlehem.

A camel travels about 3 miles per hour on average, so it would have taken two hours to get to Bethlehem. That's roughly the entire time the Bible refers to them (in non-literal language, I believe) following a star. In the language of appearance (non-literal language), it "went before them" not in perceived motion, but because it was always ahead of them on the way.

Dag Kihlman provided a more specific view:

> Jupiter—if this was the star of Bethlehem—was not seen in the early evenings in December in 2 B.C. It rose very late, at roughly 9 P.M. . . .
>
> A more realistic view (if Jupiter was the star of Bethlehem) is that the Magi traveled early in the morning, when Jupiter was still visible. . . .
>
> If the Magi started at a suitable hour, they would have had Jupiter in front of them as they left Jerusalem. If they

> traveled by donkey, camel, or horse . . . they would have had Jupiter in front of them all the way to Bethlehem.[279]

And so "the star . . . came to rest over the place where the child was" (Matt. 2:9).

We know from astronomical data that Jupiter entered into *retrograde motion*. Astronomer Christopher Crockett explains this phenomenon:

> Typically, the planets shift slightly eastward from night to night, drifting slowly against the backdrop of stars. From time to time, however, they change direction. For a few months, they'll head west before turning back around and resuming their easterly course. Their westward motion is called *retrograde motion* by astronomers. . . . [It's] an illusion caused by the motion of earth and these planets around the sun.[280]

As an analogy, when we pass a car on the freeway, it temporarily seems to be moving backward. In December, 2 B.C., Jupiter (because of its retrograde motion) appeared to come to a stop above Bethlehem and—according to some researchers—remained there, seemingly motionless (the "rest" in the biblical text), for six days. Ernest L. Martin contends that at dawn on December 25 in that area, Jupiter would have been at an elevation of 68 degrees, above the southern horizon, shining down on Bethlehem. It would have been the brightest "star" in the sky on that day and at that location.[281]

Let's examine more closely what the author may have been describing in saying that the star "came to rest over the place where the child was." First of all, the text doesn't indicate that it shone *specifically* on a "house." This is a common misconception. Matthew 2:11, just two verses later, simply says they *went* "into a house"—not that the star was shining on it, *identifying* it. We must be precise about what any given text under consideration actually *asserts* and does *not* assert.

Two of the best Protestant Bible commentators and exegetes of our time, R.T. France and D.A. Carson, agree:

> It is not said to indicate the precise house, but the general location *where the child was*.[282]

> The Greek text does not imply that the star pointed out the house where Jesus was or that it led the travelers through twisty streets; it may simply have hovered over Bethlehem as the Magi approached it.[283]

The Greek "adverb of place" in Matthew 2:9 is *hou*. In the RSV, *hou* is translated by "the place where" (in the KJV, simply "where"). It applies to a wide range of meanings beyond something as specific as a house. In other passages in the RSV, it refers to a mountain (Matt 28:16), Nazareth (Luke 4:16), a village (Luke 24:28), the land of Midian (Acts 7:29), and the vast wilderness that Moses and the Hebrews traveled through (Heb. 3:9). Thus, it can easily, plausibly refer to "Bethlehem" in Matthew 2:9.

This is an important point because it goes to the issue of supernatural or natural. A "star" (whatever it is) shining a beam down on *one house* would be (I agree) supernatural—not any kind of "star" we know of in the natural world. But a star shining on an *area*, in the *direction* of an area (which a bright Jupiter was to Bethlehem in my scenario, at 68 degrees in the sky), is a perfectly natural event.

Matthew 2:9 is similar to how we would speak in English: "*Where* I was, I could see the conjunction very well." "Where" obviously refers to a *place*. And a person's place is many things simultaneously. Thus, when I saw the "star of Bethlehem"-like conjunction in December 2020, I was in a field, near my house (in my neighborhood), in my town (Tecumseh), in my county (Lenawee), in my state (Michigan), and in my country (the United States).

This is my point about "place" in Matthew 2:9. It can mean larger areas beyond just "house." If the text doesn't *say* specifically, "The star shone on the house," then we can't say for sure that this is what the text *meant*.

I have found eighteen other English Bible translations of Matthew 2:9 that also have "the place where" (Weymouth, Moffatt, Confraternity, Knox, NEB, REB, NRSV, Lamsa, Amplified, Phillips, TEV, NIV, Jerusalem, Williams, Beck, NAB, Kleist & Lilly, and Goodspeed). In all these cases, they are translating *hou*, literally meaning "where" but at the same time implying *place* (which is the "where" referred to). The Living Bible (a very modern paraphrase) has "standing over Bethlehem," which bolsters my argument (because it doesn't say "house").

But what about Luke 2:8–9?

> And in that region there were shepherds out in the field, keeping watch over their flock by night. And an angel of the Lord appeared to them, and the glory of the Lord shone around them, and they were filled with fear.

Note that it is the light from an angel (rather than a star) that "shone around them," and they were not yet visiting Jesus. Thus, Luke 2:15 states, "Let us *go over to Bethlehem* and see this thing that has happened." They were not in the same place. When I visited Bethlehem in 2014, I saw exactly how far it was, at least according to local tradition. The birth site is a considerable distance away, and at a higher elevation.

We mustn't be led astray by extraneous factors when exegeting Holy Scripture. I believe that the explanation I am contending for is feasible and in harmony with both science and the biblical texts. To say, then, that the star "came to rest over the place" is to observe that they didn't see it moving much over Bethlehem *once they arrived there*. I'm not an astronomer, but I can cite scientists and other experts who know much more about these aspects. If the wise men hit the right day (in Bethlehem), Jupiter would have *appeared* to be stationary.

In the Christian view, God in his providence could have arranged that the wise men, exercising their own free will, arrived at just the right time, when the bright Jupiter appeared to be a sign above Jerusalem for this king, who they believed was indicated by what they saw in Persia or Babylon (both due east).

Commentator Peter Pett stated that Jupiter "was actually stationary on December 25, interestingly enough, during Hanukkah, the season for giving presents."[284] That was in 2 B.C. Note that I am not claiming that this is when Jesus was *born*, but rather when he was at least a year old.

Ivor Bulmer-Thomas opines,

> As a planet approaches a stationary point and then moves away from it its motion is very slow, hardly detectable by the naked eye for about a week. The Magi would have noticed the slowing down of the planet as they approached Bethlehem, and they would have recognized that a stationary point was near.[285]

Now, what is even more interesting is Bulmer-Thomas's documentation that *the ancients knew about retrograde motion* of the planets and stationary points:

> There is a wealth of material showing directly that for several centuries before the birth of Christ and round about the time of his birth Babylonian astronomers were deeply interested in retrogradations and stationary points. It is contained in hundreds of cuneiform texts excavated in Babylon and Uruk. . . . The three volumes of Neugebauer's *Astronomical Cuneiform Texts* (1955) give a vast collection of Babylonian inscriptions dealing with retrogradations and stations.

This is highly significant because it means not only that Matthew 2:9 uses phenomenological language, but also that the Magi understood retrograde motion of planets, which may lie behind the terminology (received from oral tradition) of "came to rest over" Bethlehem. In my opinion, these facts support my natural interpretation all the more, because it's not just (as a critic might say) "projecting" our modern scientific understanding onto the Bible, but (fascinatingly) an understanding *that already existed* and was known by the wise men.

But (we might wonder at this point) if the star didn't shine right on the "house" (Matt. 2:11) where Jesus was, then how did the wise men *find* the house? We often make things too complicated by over-analyzing them. They would simply have to ask the locals about this child who had generated so much excitement one or two years previously and inquire as to where he lived. Word about notable events travels fast in small towns, and people know one another.

It would be like when I visited Woodstock, New York, in 1992 and asked someone at a gas station if he knew where "Big Pink" was: the famous house (to rock music fans of a certain age) where Bob Dylan and The Band (some of whom lived there) recorded *The Basement Tapes* in 1967. It so happened that this man *lived* there, so he took me right to it. That's how small towns are.

The population of Bethlehem at the time of Jesus' infancy was estimated to be only 300 by eminent archaeologist William F. Albright. Other Bible scholars think it was no more than a thousand.

Let's take a look now at what we know from astronomy in the period of 3–2 B.C. Christians who have written about this topic have previously mostly concentrated on celestial events in the years 7–5 B.C., based on the assumption of Herod's death in 4 B.C. But if he in fact died in 1 B.C. or A.D. 1 (I'm not claiming that it's *certain*, but based on legitimate scholarly *speculation*), then we should look instead to the events of 3–1 B.C.

We know that in the time between September of 3 B.C. and May of 2 B.C., Jupiter—the "king," as it was known—made (from the vantage point of Babylon) three very bright conjunctions with Regulus, a star that also had royal connotations for both the Romans and the Persians. The Magi may very well have taken note of these stellar events. On June 17 of 2 B.C., Jupiter also made another rendezvous with Venus, producing one of the most brilliant stars that anyone would have ever seen. This would have been seen in the west, over Judea, by observers in Babylon and Persia.

In December, 2 B.C. (possibly on December 25), the wise men arrived and visited Jesus in Bethlehem, when he was (by my previous "biblical calculations") about a year old. Jupiter was right above Bethlehem in December (viewed from Jerusalem), in its paused retrograde motion (and seeming not to move at all for six days). Thus, we possibly have the wise men visiting Jesus on the date later recognized as Christmas, or at least in the month of December, but without Jesus being a newborn baby, which lines up with Patristic thought.

In that year, the feast of Hanukkah began on December 23. It's a gift-giving feast. The Magi would have observed the entire Jewish nation in a happy holiday spirit. The wise men, if they saw Jesus on the twenty-fifth, would in turn have presented gifts to him on the third day of the festival. Provided my chronology is accurate, history would remarkably line up with the biblical account, as we have seen over and over in this book.

Jesus was a toddler when the wise men visited him. We're so used to thinking otherwise that this may be difficult to accept at first. But we must bow to what the Bible actually teaches (as opposed to what Hallmark greeting cards present). The word for *child* in Matthew 2:8–9 is *paidion*, defined as "a young child . . . properly, a child under training . . . a younger child (perhaps seven years old or younger)."

"Babe," on the other hand (Luke 2:12,16, RSV and KJV) is the English translation for *brephos*, which means "an unborn or a newborn child" and is used in Luke 1:41,44 of children in the womb. In Luke 2, it's the day of Jesus' birth. So the use of "babe" and "child" in English (RSV) obviously includes the meaning here of "newborn."

I believe that Jesus was a year old when the wise men visited. Commentators generally believe he was two years old or younger, but not a newborn. The Magi visit a "house," not a baby in a "manger," and no angels or shepherds or animals are in sight.

A summary of all the dates I have brought to bear might be helpful, in conclusion.

1) September, 4 B.C.: conception of John the Baptist. Zechariah was a priest from the class of Abijah (Luke 1:5). These classes served for a week in the Temple, two times a year (see 1 Chron. 24:10; see also vv. 1–19). German Catholic theolo-

gian Josef Heinrich Friedlieb (1810–1900) documented that Zechariah's class would have been serving in the Temple in the second week of the Jewish month Tishri (late September). While Zechariah was thus serving, the archangel Gabriel revealed to him that his wife Elizabeth was to bear a son. That means that John the Baptist was conceived in September (in the year 4 B.C. in the timeline I am proposing). This would mean that the day of John's birth came at the end of June, 3 B.C. The Catholic Church celebrates the Nativity of St. John the Baptist on June 24.

2) c. March 25, 3 B.C.: conception of Jesus Christ, the Annunciation. Luke informs us of how Gabriel told the Blessed Virgin Mary that Elizabeth was six months pregnant (Luke 1:36), which means that the Annunciation occurred at or around March 25 (again, the date that the Catholic Church celebrates *that* great occasion). Nine months from this date is December 25, which the Catholic Church and virtually all Christians celebrate as the date of Christ's birth, and it is reasonable to believe (based on the Bible and historical data) that this was indeed the actual date of his birth.[286]

3) c. June 24, 3 B.C.: birth of John the Baptist.

4) September, 3 B.C.: conjunction of Jupiter and Regulus (astronomical data).

5) c. December 25, 3 B.C.: birth of Jesus. This is a deduction from #1 and #2, with early Church agreement.[287]

6) June 17, 2 B.C.: Jupiter was in a close and spectacularly bright and striking conjunction with Venus, after a series of spectacular conjunctions, causing the wise men—for reasons given above—to decide to journey from Persia

to Jerusalem. This is all based on astronomical data and deduction from biblical data on the wise men seeing "the star" both in Persia and again specifically in Jerusalem and Bethlehem, when they arrived months later, to visit and worship a non-newborn Jesus.

7) August 26–27, 2 B.C.: Jupiter and Mars were in close conjunction, and Venus and Mercury were also close by, thus further leading the wise men on to the west and Jerusalem. I base this on astronomical data and extrapolation from biblical texts regarding their journey and arrival.

8) December 23, 2 B.C.: Hannukah began in Israel.

9) December, 2 B.C. (possibly December 25): The wise men arrived and visited Jesus in Bethlehem, after talking to Herod in Jerusalem, when Jesus was about a year old. Jupiter was right above Bethlehem then, viewed from Jerusalem, at 68 degrees above the horizon, and the brightest object in the sky at that time and place (Matt. 2:9). This was during its paused apparent retrograde motion. It began "moving" again after December 25. This view derives from astronomical and biblical data, and an extrapolation of known historical facts, with biblical and early Church corroboration of a non-newborn Jesus visited by the wise men, guided by the star.

10) 1 B.C. or A.D. 1: Herod the Great died. The date is derived from historical and archaeological data; from Josephus, who mentions a lunar eclipse (corroborated from astronomy); and from the time of Jewish feasts. It's also based on early Josephus manuscript evidence and Roman coinage.

Lastly, the Catholic Church, to my knowledge, is not *dogmatic* about Jesus being born on the twenty-fifth of

December or, for that matter, being visited by the wise men literally on the sixth of January, which is now regarded as the Feast of the Epiphany. These are the days that these momentous events are *celebrated* in the Church (or, I should say, large portions of the Church, since some observe different liturgical calendars), but Catholics—again, as far as I know—aren't *required* to believe that these events literally occurred on these dates.

I have offered speculations and hypotheses about the timing of these events, both the years and months. I noted a certain "tantalizing" correspondence of astronomical data with the now-established date of the celebration of Christmas and even the traditional Catholic dates concerning John the Baptist. It *may* be that the visit of the wise men occurred on or about the sixth of January. After all, I have found evidence (in my own apologetics research) of various sorts for the authenticity of the twenty-fifth of December date.

We might speculate on a possible scenario, for example, where the wise men were led to Bethlehem in the month of December, by an extraordinary "star," in the manner I have described, but, for whatever reason, didn't actually see (toddler) Jesus until January 6, twelve days later. Perhaps Jesus and his parents were out of town in the interim. Various theories can be proposed, if we want to seek or provide objective, secular evidence for a correspondence. In the Catholic Church, different opinions on such matters are allowed, just as there is (surprisingly to many!) a wide latitude permitted in much biblical exegesis.

14

ST. LUKE KNOWS HIS STUFF

It seemed good to me . . . to write an orderly account for you, most excellent Theophilus, that you may know the truth concerning the things of which you have been informed.

—LUKE 1:3–4

A widespread bias against the historical accuracy of the four Gospels is rampant among various types of scholars and biblical skeptics, and particularly atheists. Sometimes, the Gospel of Luke in particular is attacked because it's believed that Luke was not its author, or that the manuscripts were late, or because he supposedly contradicts the other Gospels (alleged internal discrepancies) or the book of Acts, traditionally believed to be authored by the same Luke.

I highly suspect that a big factor in such cynical skepticism is what the great Anglican apologist C.S. Lewis described as "chronological snobbery." It's casually assumed that documents almost 2,000 years old cannot possibly be accurate. When it's pointed out that the same skeptics accept various reports of secular historians (including ones that presuppose the existence of miraculous occurrences), they retort that the

Gospel writers had a "religious agenda," and therefore wanted to pass that along, while neglecting historical accuracy—as if the two things are inevitably mutually exclusive.

I submit that such criticisms are quite often more a matter of knee-jerk anti-Christian or anti-religious bias than conclusions based on an actual open-minded examination of the texts in question. Many of these critics have never cracked a book written by those who believe in biblical accuracy or inspiration.

My goal in this chapter is simple: I will attempt to show that we have massive reason to believe that the Gospel of Luke is relentlessly, remarkably accurate in its historical and geographic details, and able to be extraordinarily substantiated from secular archaeology and other sciences. In a word, the skepticism is unfounded, and the evidence contrary to it has a powerful cumulative impact that cannot be easily dismissed.

> **Luke 2:51** And he [Jesus] went down with them [Mary and Joseph] and came to Nazareth.

Skeptics, for many years, have asserted that Jesus' hometown of Nazareth did not exist at all in his time. Their judgments were premature and erroneous, as usual. *The Times of Israel* (which cannot be accused of Christian bias), addressed this topic and the latest archaeology:

> Nazareth . . . as British-Israeli archaeologist Yardenna Alexandre notes . . . existed well before and well after [Jesus'] lifetime. . . .
>
> Among her digs, in 2009, Alexandre discovered the first example of a residential building from the time of Jesus. It was found near today's Church of the Annunciation.

> . . . In her report, Alexandre describes the structure as "a simple house comprising small rooms and an inner courtyard . . . inhabited in the late Hellenistic and the Early Roman periods [late second century B.C. to early or mid-second century A.D.]." . . .
>
> Among the artifacts is a coin of Emperor Claudius that was uncovered on the floor of a corridor that led into a three-story pit complex. According to the report, "the coin was minted in Akko-Ptolemais in 50–51 C.E."[288]

> **Luke 3:1** In the fifteenth year of the reign of Tiberius Caesar [A.D. 29], Pontius Pilate being governor of Judea, and Herod being tetrarch of Galilee, and his brother Philip tetrarch of the region of Ituraea and Trachonitis, and Lysanias tetrarch of Abilene.

The Gospel of Luke can be historically verified in scores of particulars, as I will demonstrate throughout this chapter, beyond argument. Luke 3:1 is an excellent example of Luke's relentless accuracy in the finest points of nomenclature; geographical places; and historically verifiable events, reigns of rulers, etc.

A temple inscription found at Abila (dated from between A.D. 14 and 29) named Lysanias as the tetrarch of the locality.[289] The first-century Roman Jewish historian Josephus also made note of "Abila of Lysanias."[290] Josephus also verifies that Philip ruled over Trachonitis: "Herod . . . also gave Gaulonitis [the Golan Heights], and Trachonitis, and Paneas [Caesarea Philippi] to Philip, who was his son."[291]

The existence and office of Pontius Pilate have been verified in mentions by ancient historians Josephus, Philo, and Tacitus—and, notably (as the first physical proof), in the "Pilate Stone,"[292] found in 1961 at Caesarea Maritima, on the Mediterranean coast of Israel. That location was made the Roman administrative capital of Judaea in A.D. 6; hence, it was where Pilate would have often resided. The palace and amphitheater and much else remain. Luke records that Paul spent two years as a prisoner there (Acts 23:33,35, 24:27, 25:4,6). The Pilate Stone includes his *whole* name: "Pontius Pilate." Luke—characteristically—is most minutely accurate, since "Pontius Pilate" occurs only three times in the New Testament. It appears twice in Luke (Luke 3:1 and Acts 4:27) and once in Paul's epistles (1 Tim. 6:13). "Pilate" is used in the New Testament fifty-three times.

Luke's accuracy extends beyond Roman puppet rulers to Jewish religious leaders.

Annas and Caiphas (see Luke 3:2) are mentioned by Josephus in the *Antiquities of the Jews*:

> He also deprived him in a little time, and ordained Eleazar, the son of Ananus, who had been high priest before, to be high priest [A.D. 25]. Which office when he had held for a year, Gratus deprived him of it, and gave the high priesthood to Simon, the son of Camithus [A.D. 26]. And when he had possessed that dignity no longer than a year, Joseph Caiaphas was made his successor.[293]

In 1990, construction workers ran across an ornate limestone ossuary while paving a road in the Peace Forest near the North Talpiot neighborhood of Jerusalem:

> One especially beautiful ossuary is twice inscribed "Joseph, son of Caiaphas" and holds, together with other remains, the bones of a sixty-year-old male. This ossuary may well be the final resting place of the Caiaphas known from the New Testament as the high priest who

> conducted the initial interrogation of Jesus before handing him over to Pontius Pilate.[294]

In 2011, archaeologists from Bar-Ilan and Tel Aviv Universities announced the discovery of an ossuary inscribed with the text "Miriam, daughter of Yeshua, son of Caiaphas, Priest of Maaziah from Beth Imri." It demonstrated that Caiaphas descended from the priestly course of Maaziah, instituted by King David.[295]

Archaeologists have even found evidence regarding boats used in the Sea of Galilee in Jesus' time for fishing (see, for example Luke 8:22).

A largely intact boat was discovered on the northwest shore of the Sea of Galilee, not far from Peter's hometown Capernaum, in 1986.[296] The "ancient Galilee boat" was made of cedar and rowable (see John 6:19) and had a mast for a sail (see Luke 8:23). The dimensions were 27 feet by 7.5 feet—large enough for Jesus and his twelve disciples to fit in. Radiocarbon dating came out to 40 B.C. (give or take 80 years), and dating based on pottery was 50 B.C. to A.D. 50. Thus, the time and the place fit. Surely, the disciples had a vessel much like this one.

This is minor evidence in terms of proving Bible accuracy, yet the details still harmonize nicely with biblical texts regarding the fishing profession of several of the disciples.

Another excellent test case for Luke's accuracy is an examination of the evidence for the first-century existence of the towns of Chorazin and Bethsaida (Luke 10:13) and Capernaum, Peter's hometown (v. 15).

Capernaum was abandoned after the eleventh century, and as a result many thought it never existed. But it was discovered in 1838, properly identified in 1866, and excavated between 1905 and 1926. Resumed excavations in 1968 discovered an ancient house, believed to be Peter's. It also has a glorious white limestone synagogue from a later date, built on top of a synagogue with black basalt walls, dating from the first century, where Jesus would have worshiped and spoken.[297] Leen Ritmeyer observed,

> Digging deeper down in 1981, walls made of basalt stones and a basalt floor turned up 4 feet below the surface. These walls were located underneath the walls of the white synagogue. . . . When first-century material was found on and below the basalt floor, it became evident that these basalt walls belonged to a synagogue of the first century, i.e., the synagogue in which Jesus taught.[298]

Excavations occurred in Chorazin (known as Tell Khirbat Karraza) in 1962–1964 and 1980–1987. Excavations in 1980 found remains going back to the first century.[299]

As for Bethsaida: in 2019, what has been described as the "Church of Apostles" was unearthed by the El-Araj excavations team in the fourth season at the site of Bethsaida-Julias/Beithabbak (El-Araj), on the north shore of the Sea of Galilee, near where the Jordan River enters the lake. Excavations were undertaken by Mordechai Aviam of Kinneret College and R. Steven Notley of Nyack College. The Byzantine-period church is believed by some to have been built over the house of the apostle brothers Peter and Andrew. The findings suggested that the city's economy was primarily based on fishing on the Sea of Galilee. A coin from the time of Philip the Tetrarch (a son of Herod the Great; r. 4 B.C.–A.D. 34) was discovered at the site.[300] According to Notley:

> We have a Roman village, in the village we have pottery, coins, also stone vessels which are typical of first-century

Jewish life, so now we strengthen our suggestion and identification that El-Araj is a much better candidate for Bethsaida than e-Tell.[301]

How about the crucifixion of Jesus? That would seem to be an event that could be verified according to archaeological science. In the Gospel of John (20:25), Jesus' disciple Thomas refers to "the print of the nails" in the "hands" of the risen Jesus, and Luke records Jesus saying, "See my hands and my feet" (Luke 24:39), referring to the scars left by his crucifixion, as proof of his identity.

Perhaps surprisingly, until 1968, no *physical* evidence of crucifixion (despite much *literary* and *historical* evidence) had been produced. Accordingly, some (thinking like "doubting Thomas") doubted the veracity of the biblical descriptions of crucifixion, and some of these held that crucifixion victims were attached to crosses with ropes and not nails.

But in that year, Greek-Israeli archaeologist Vassilios Tzaferis found the long-lost proof in Jerusalem: a man named Jehohanan, who had been crucified in the first century. The remains included a heel bone with a nail driven through it from the side, suggesting that in this case of crucifixion, the heels had been nailed to opposite sides of the upright. Moreover, a discovery in Cambridgeshire (U.K.) in November 2017 of the heel bone of a man with an iron nail through it is believed by archaeologists to confirm the use of this execution method in ancient Rome.[302]

Another argument made by skeptics is that Jewish crucifixion victims were supposedly never buried in tombs due to ritual defilement and the criminality usually involved. The Jehohanan find upends that notion, too, since his remains were found in the usual type of rock-hewn tomb in first-century Jerusalem, and also in an ossuary (or box serving as a coffin).

Let's move on to a fascinating and unique proof of Lucan accuracy, having to do with (of all things) acoustics and the capacity of large crowds to hear speakers. Skeptical scholar Robert M. Grant argues that it would have been "impossible" for Peter to address more than three thousand (Acts 2:6, 14, 41) or five thousand people (Acts 4:4) without a microphone.[303] Moreover, he claims that since the population of Jerusalem then was about 30,000 (estimates vary from 20,000 to 100,000),[304] it was demographically quite unlikely that 3,000 of them or 5,000 *men* at one time could become Christians. I shall attempt to rationally and objectively consider both of these claims.

Successfully addressing three to five thousand people or even many more is not impossible at all. History attests to this. But what does science tell us? It's reported that Protestant evangelist George Whitefield (1714–1770) preached to crowds of 20,000 or more as a young man (up until about 1739). Those who heard him said he had a voice "like a lion." Benjamin Franklin did some sort of experiment in that same year to test Whitefield's range.

Braxton Boren, who was in 2014 a doctoral candidate at the Music and Audio Research Laboratory at New York University, did an "updated Franklin" study.[305] His specialty is the physics of sound and acoustic simulation techniques. In a separate interview,[306] readers were informed of what he discovered.

Utilizing a variety of reported variables, the loudness of Whitefield's voice was estimated to be an amazing 90 decibels (usually, what is considered "loud" is 74 or more, and normal conversation is 60). Actors and opera singers were enlisted to test voice loudness, and the highest they could attain was, sure enough, around 90 decibels.

The study concluded that Whitefield could be heard by as many as 50,000 people. Certainly 20,000 to 30,000 could easily hear him. Moreover, buildings in the surroundings add some six decibels to the loudness of a voice. That was the case with Jerusalem and Peter. Thus, Peter could have easily talked to more than 5,000 people, according to the documented findings of acoustical science. All he needed was a loud voice. Paul (whom the New Testament records giving many speeches and sermons) was said to have a "loud voice" (Acts 14:10, 16:28). Peter isn't described in this way, but it's a reasonable assumption to make.

Another factor in public speaking to large crowds (minus microphones) is the *topography* of an environment. The tour guide when my wife Judy and I visited Israel in 2014 explained how Jesus probably gave the Sermon on the Mount from the *bottom* of the mountain. The hills at the spot form a natural amphitheater, which allows easy hearing. My tour group later tested the theory in a similar "amphitheater": the location where Jesus fed the 4,000 (across the Sea of Galilee). It was absolutely correct: we could hear one another—talking fairly softly, to test it—perfectly, from bottom to top and vice versa.

Jesus is described five times as having a "loud voice," even on the cross (Matt. 27:46,50; Mark 15:34; Luke 23:46; John 11:43). Besides the Sermon on the Mount, he is described in other instances as preaching from a boat in the Sea of Galilee (Matt. 13:1–9; Mark 4:1–9), which generally has large slopes by its shore. He spoke to "great crowds" (Matt. 13:2), "a very large crowd" (Mark 4:1), and "a great crowd" (Luke 8:4). If he had a loud voice and the acoustics were right, he could have *easily* spoken to many thousands. Lay archaeologist B. Cobbey Crisler and professional sound engineer Mark Miles tested this in the same spots on the Sea of Galilee as I did and got the same results, albeit more precisely.[307]

When Peter spoke on the day of Pentecost (Acts 2), and 3,000 people got baptized and joined the Church, the location (the Upper Room, near the present tomb of David) was the present-day Mt. Zion, a western hill of Jerusalem. He could have, then (quite possibly), been preaching to crowds *down* the hill from Mt. Zion, where the day of Pentecost and the receiving of the Holy Spirit took place (after which he spoke). That would make it easier to be heard—and all the more so if indeed he had a loud voice.

The second speech to a large group by Peter was in the Temple complex (Acts 3:1–2, 11–12). As noted above, buildings or walls increase the loudness of the voice, and the crowd would have been more compact.

With regard to Grant's claim that 5,000 converts would be far too large a percentage of Jerusalem's population, he neglects to see that Jerusalem was, at the time of the day of Pentecost, filled with many thousands of pilgrims, since Shavuot, or the Feast of Weeks, was being observed (it falls between May 15 and June 14 in our calendar). It was one of three "pilgrimage festivals," along with Passover (Pesach) and the Feast of Booths (Sukkot), when all Israelites were expected to make the trip to the Temple in Jerusalem.

Not only Jews in Israel, but from *all over the ancient world* came to worship together during this period,[308] and the crowds could have swelled to possibly several hundred thousand. Grant relied on a 1943 article by the well-known German Lutheran scholar Joachim Jeremias (1900–1979) for his calculation of Jerusalem's population. Jeremias himself estimated that Jerusalem's population could reach 125,000 during pilgrimage festivals.[309]

Acts 2 notes this influx of Jews from all over in stating, "Now there were dwelling in Jerusalem Jews, devout men from every nation under heaven" (v. 5; see also vv. 9,11). Therefore, the population was temporarily far larger than usual, and Grant's clever but shortsighted "demographic" objection to the text vanishes.

The sermon in Acts 4 may have very well been during Shavuot as well, since Acts 3 appears to give no indication of significant time passing.

Another way to verify the text of Luke for accuracy is to check whether his mention of a significant famine (Acts 11:28) lines up with what we are able to determine about past events of this sort.

As Craig S. Hawkins notes, Suetonius, the first- and second-century Roman historian, referred to the bad conditions "in the days of Claudius" (Acts 11:28) brought about by "a scarcity of provisions, occasioned by bad crops for several years." Roman historian Tacitus (A.D. 55–120) wrote about two famines in Rome in the first century. Jewish historian Josephus (A.D. 37–95), also documents severe famines in Asia Minor and Judea in the first century.[310]

Luke's precision extends to particular titles of rulers. For example, King Agrippa I is accurately titled "king" (Acts 12:1) rather than "tetrarch"—like other seemingly similar rulers (see Matt. 14:1; Luke 3:1,19, 9:7; Acts 13:1)—and history records that he was the last ruler with the title of "king" who reigned over Judea.

How about a more "dramatic" and seemingly "fantastic" (and Old Testament-like) alleged event, such as Herod (Agrippa) being "eaten by worms" (Acts 12:21–23)? Christians can't possibly defend *that*, can they?

Actually, we can plausibly do so. Jewish-Roman historian Josephus provides a corroborating parallel account:

> Now when [Herod] Agrippa had reigned three years over all Judea . . . he exhibited shews, in honor of Cesar. . . . And presently his flatterers cried out . . . that "he was a God." And they added, "Be thou merciful to us. For although we have hitherto reverenced thee only as a man,

> yet shall we henceforth own thee as superior to mortal nature." Upon this the king did neither rebuke them, nor reject their impious flattery. . . . A severe pain also arose in his belly; and began in a most violent manner. . . . His pain was become violent. Accordingly he was carried into the palace. . . . And when he had been quite worn out by the pain in his belly, for five days, he departed this life.[311]

Some might counter Josephus's account by saying that it has nothing directly to do with "worms" and so is irrelevant. But it can't be *ruled out*, since there is a condition called *ascariasis*, in which roundworms can become parasites in human intestines. A Mayo Clinic article states,

> Most infected people have mild cases with no symptoms. But heavy infestation can lead to serious symptoms and complications. . . .
>
> The larvae mature into adult worms in the small intestine, and the adult worms typically live in the intestines until they die.[312]

A scientific article on this condition confirms that it can indeed be fatal: "In some rare cases, ascariasis may cause serious consequences" and "even sudden death."[313]

Other medical conditions also entail worms or similar creatures infesting the human body. *Myiasis* involves "the infection of a fly larva (maggot) in human tissue."[314] Histopathologist A.T. Sandison wrote an article about Herod the Great's death and also speculated that myiasis could have been the cause:

> Herod Agrippa I, grandson of Herod the Great, died in somewhat similar circumstances to his grandfather in

> A.D. 44. He developed abdominal pain while at the theater and died within five days. . . . Josephus does not mention myiasis in this case but in Acts (12:23) we read that "he was eaten of worms."[315]

We see, then, that "eaten by worms" is not some fantastical and mythical account that can be immediately dismissed with derision. The Bible, in its usual phenomenological, pre-scientific language, describes a death in blunt and revolting terms, which correspond with at least two known conditions in which worms or other parasites literally eat the interior of the human body. The biblical description, strikingly corroborated by Josephus, is (far from being impossible) entirely *plausible*, understood as myiasis or ascariasis. In other words, known reputable history and solid science offer confirmation of what might—not knowing of these evidences—be seen as an improbable or impossible death.

As mentioned above, familiarity with the proper titles of various political figures is a mark of Luke's accuracy. We'll see more of those here. Acts 13 mentions Paul and his companions sailing to the island of Cyprus and meeting Sergius Paulus, a "proconsul" (vv. 4,7). Cyprus became a "senatorial province" in 22 B.C. and hence was governed by a proconsul. As for Sergius Paulus himself, a Bible reference work noted in 1897,

> A remarkable memorial of this proconsul was recently (1887) discovered at Rome. On a boundary stone of Claudius his name is found, among others, as having been appointed (A.D. 47) one of the curators of the banks and the channel of the River Tiber. After serving his three years as proconsul at Cyprus, he returned to Rome, where he held the office referred to.[316]

Another inscription mentioning "proconsul Paulus" was discovered at Soloi, Cyprus, in 1878.[317] Two more evidences also exist: "a fragmentary inscription discovered near Pisidian Antioch, currently housed in the Yalvac Museum, on which the name L. Sergius Paulus is visible" and "an inscription near Pisidian Antioch which was copied by Sir William Ramsay and J.G.C. Anderson in 1912 that refers to L. Sergius Paullus, the younger, son of Lucius."[318]

Another example having to do with particular titles in specific places at the time of the writing of Luke is found in Acts 14:8,11–13, an account of Paul's and Barnabas's visit to Lystra, in central ancient Anatolia, in the southwest of present-day Turkey. Here the people lauded them as "gods" and called them "Zeus" and "Hermes." A "priest of Zeus" in the region was also mentioned. Two inscriptions from the area, found in 1909, referred to "priests of Zeus" as well as worship or veneration of both Zeus and Hermes.[319]

Philippi, mentioned in Acts 16:12 (see also 20:6), was "the leading city of the district of Macedonia," according to Luke. But scholars fretted over his use of the Greek word *meris* ("district" in RSV), which was thought to be highly improbable and inaccurate. But lo and behold, in time, they were "foiled again," as Bible scholar Merrill F. Unger notes,

> Excavations in the papyri-rich sands of the Fayum in Egypt have demonstrated that the resident colonists there, many of whom had emigrated from Macedonia where Philippi was located, idiomatically employed this very word *meris* to denote the divisions of a district. Now all scholars own that the word was used correctly by Luke.[320]

Remarkable specific and meticulous details abound in Luke's writings. He refers to "Lydia, from the city of

Thyatira, a seller of purple goods" (Acts 16:14). It turns out that, as a result of inscriptions, we now know that Thyatira had many trade guilds, and one that was "particularly strong" was the "production of purple dye."[321] Indeed, fifteen of twenty-eight inscriptions found in Thyatira regarding dye were related to this trade of *purple* dye.[322]

Similarly, Luke used the Greek word *politarchos* for "city authorities" in reference to Thessalonika in Macedonia (Greece—see Acts 17:1,6,8). For a long time, this was dismissed as a mistake. But sure enough, seventeen examples of this terminology, covering about 150 years over the first and second centuries, were found on inscriptions.[323]

One Roman road entered the city of Thessalonika at the Vardar Gate, a Roman arch. It included the inscription (dated to the second century): "In the time of Politarchs" and alludes to six of them. A marble building block including this inscription was removed from the gate in 1877. It can be viewed in the British Museum. That's "hard evidence" (literally!):

> In 1960, Carl Schuler published a list of 32 inscriptions bearing the term *politarchas*. Approximately 19 out of the 32 came from Thessalonica, and at least three of them dated back to the first century.[324]

By now the pattern is clear: Luke was not only a *reliable* historian, but a *remarkably and extraordinarily accurate* one. Therefore (and this is the underlying point), he can be trusted when he reports things about Jesus and Peter and Paul, too. We can't go by one standard for secular matters and another for religious ones. Anyone who thinks Luke was merely a fanatical religious zealot who arbitrarily made up myths for the sake of the promulgation of Christianity is himself—ironically—engaging in myth-making.

But we have a long way to go yet in our survey. There is much more.

Luke's attention to meticulous detail was so comprehensive that it extended even to particular terms of disdain used by Stoic philosophers in Athens, who insulted Paul when he preached to them in that famous city.

The Greek noun *spermologos*—literally "seed-picker" ("babbler" in Acts 17:18, RSV)—was usually used to describe a type of finch.[325] Luke, in his use of this Greek word (only here in the New Testament), exhibits an extraordinary awareness of Athenian Stoic culture and slang, since this was a word used by Zeno of Citium, the founder of Stoicism, to insult one of his followers (see *Diog. Laert. Zeno*, c. 19).

While Paul was in Athens, he referred in his preaching to "an altar" with the inscription, "To an unknown god" (Acts 17:23). Greek geographer Pausanias (c. A.D. 110–c. 180) and Greek biographer of philosophers Diogenes Laertes (fl. third century), both mentioned such altars to anonymous gods in Athens.[326]

Luke notes that "Claudius had commanded all the Jews to leave Rome" (Acts 18:2). This event was attested to by Roman historian Suetonius in *The Lives of the Twelve Caesars* and Roman historian and Senator Cassius Dio in his *Roman History*.

Luke again proves that he was recording actual history and real people in the right places and time periods when he refers to "Gallio," who was "proconsul of Achaia" (Acts 18:12). Gallio (c. 5 B.C.–A.D. 65) was a Roman Senator and elder brother of the famous Stoic philosopher Seneca, who alludes to him, saying, "I remembered my master Gallio's words, when he began to develop a fever in Achaia."[327] He is also described as "my friend and proconsul" by Roman emperor Claudius in the Delphi Inscription, dated around A.D. 52, confirming that he became *proconsul* of Achaia in

July, A.D. 51. Thus, this is considered one of the most certain dates of Paul's missionary travels or of any event of his life, since he appeared before Gallio (Acts 18:12–16).

Even the word translated "tribunal" in Acts 18:16 is accurate:

> The word, tribunal, is the Greek word *bema*, meaning judgment seat. This was a speaker's platform where official proclamations were publicly read, and where citizens appeared before civic officials. The *bema* of Corinth was discovered in 1935, and was identified because of a Latin inscription, which read, "He revetted the *rostra* [the Latin equivalent of a *bema*] and paid personally the expense of making all its marble."[328] The *bema* of Corinth is a large, stone speakers' platform. It is here that the apostle Paul was acquitted by Gallio.[329]

Luke, when describing Paul's missionary journeys, was acquainted with the prevailing practices in any given region. He mentions those in Ephesus "who practiced magic arts" (Acts 19:19). Ephesus was, in fact, so renowned for widespread sorcery and occultic practices that the description *Ephesia grammata* or "Ephesian writings" became synonymous with "magical texts." Some papyri of these writings have been found.[330]

Luke mentions "asiarchs" who were friends of Paul in Ephesus (Acts 19:31), and "106 specific *asiarchs* have now been identified in Ephesus, within fifty years of the time of Paul."[331]

"Town clerk" (*grammateus*), a term used by Luke with regard also to Ephesus (Acts 19:35), has been another object of attack, used to discredit the Bible and Luke's trustworthiness. But it was corroborated over 120 years ago:

> The title is preserved on various ancient coins. . . . It would appear that what may have been the original

> service of this class of men [was] to record the laws and decrees of the state and to read them in public. . . . They were authorized to preside over the popular assemblies and submit votes to them.[332]

Luke describes one such town clerk as addressing the crowds and acting in a supervisory and administrative manner, eventually dismissing the assembly (Acts 19:35–41), which is in complete harmony with what we know about this office in this place and time.

Luke in Acts 21:27–28 notes that "Jews from Asia" accused Paul of having "brought Greeks into the Temple," which "defiled" it. This is true to history, too. Non-Jews could go no farther than the Court of the Gentiles in Herod's temple. There were warning signs that sought to prevent such occurrences. One such plaque was discovered in 1871 by French archaeologist Charles Clermont-Ganneau. It reads, "No foreigner is to enter within the railing and enclosure around the Temple. And whoever is caught will be responsible to himself for his subsequent death."[333] A second fragmented warning sign was found near the Old City of Jerusalem, close to the Lion's Gate, in 1935.

Luke's knowledge extends to fine points of Roman law as well. (More specifically, we could say he was simply recording the apostle Paul, who possessed such knowledge.) Luke records Paul saying to a Roman centurion, "Is it lawful for you to scourge a man who is a Roman citizen, and uncondemned?" (Acts 22:25). Here, Paul was appealing to what is known as the Porcian laws, particularly Lex Porcia II (*Lex de Porcia de tergo civium*), possibly proposed by Cato the Elder, consul in 195 B.C. and 184 B.C. It extended the right to *provocatio* (appeal to the plebeian tribune) against flogging.[334]

Similarly, in Acts 22:28, Luke correctly verifies two ways to become a Roman citizen: by *birth* (Paul saying, "I was born a citizen"), as is well known, or—much more rarely and expensively, as he also notes—by *purchasing* it (the Roman tribune saying, "I bought this citizenship for a large sum").[335]

Luke refers to the "high priest Ananias" (Acts 23:2, 24:1). Ananias and his rank are corroborated by Josephus: "But now Herod King of Chalcis removed Joseph, the son of Camydus, from the high priesthood and made Ananias, the son of Nebedus, his successor."[336]

Luke notes that "Felix came with his wife Drusilla, who was a Jewess" (Acts 24:24). Josephus verifies the office of Felix and his Jewish wife Drusilla:

> While Felix was procurator of Judea, he saw this Drusilla; and fell in love with her. . . . She . . . was prevailed upon to transgress the laws of her forefathers, and to marry Felix.[337]

Luke gets the successor of Felix correct, too—"Felix was succeeded by Porcius Festus" (Acts 24:27). Josephus again corroborates this: "Porcius Festus"—"the procurator"—"was sent as successor to Felix by Nero."[338]

According to Luke's account in Acts 25:11, Paul says during one of his trials, "I do not seek to escape death; but if there is nothing in their charges against me, no one can give me up to them. I appeal to Caesar." This is true to Roman history and law:

> The right to appeal was re-affirmed by the promulgation in Augustus's reign of the *Lex Iulia de vi publica et privata*. This law basically forbade an official holding the *imperium* to bind, torture, or kill a Roman citizen who had appealed to Rome.[339]

Luke refers to "Agrippa the king" (Acts 25:13). King Agrippa II was accurately titled "king" as opposed to "tetrarch." In A.D. 53, Agrippa was forced to give up the tetrarchy of Chalcis, but in exchange, Claudius made him ruler with the title of "king" over the territories previously governed by Philip.[340] Josephus calls him "king" at least eighteen times in his writings.[341] His name has also been found on Jewish coins of the time.[342] Luke got it right again.

In another instance of Luke's uncanny knowledge of political titles, he reports that Procurator Festus referred to the infamous Roman emperor Nero as "my lord" (Acts 25:24–26). This was formerly thought to be a serious error. But it's been shown that Roman emperors before and during Paul's time were indeed called "lords." One town in the Greek region of Boeatia, for example, called Nero "lord of the whole world."[343]

The great Bible scholar F.F. Bruce commented upon the extraordinary accuracy of Luke's use of the many different titles for officials:

> One of the most remarkable tokens of his accuracy is his sure familiarity with the proper titles of all the notable persons who are mentioned in his pages. . . . The accuracy of Luke's use of the various titles in the Roman Empire has been compared to the ease and confident way in which an Oxford man in ordinary conversation will refer to the Heads of Oxford colleges by their proper titles—the *Provost* of Oriel, the *Master* of Balliol, the *Rector* of Exeter, the *President* of Magdalen, and so on. . . . But Luke had a further difficulty in that the titles sometimes did not remain the same for any great length of time; a province might pass from senatorial government to administration by a district representative of the emperor,

> and would then be governed no longer by a proconsul but by an imperial legate.[344]

Lastly, Luke mentions that prisoner Paul "was allowed to stay by himself" (Acts 28:16) and lived "two whole years at his own expense" (v. 30). This accurately reflects the widespread Roman practice of keeping less dangerous criminals under house arrest.[345]

Considerations such as the many recounted above—and, no doubt, many more—led the prominent German Lutheran historian and theologian Adolf von Harnack to conclude,

> Judged from almost every possible standpoint of historical criticism, it [the book of Acts] is a solid, respectable, and in many respects an extraordinary work.[346]

15

ST. JOHN WRAPS IT UP

And after this he said to him, "Follow me."

—JOHN 21:19

Ironically, though the Gospel of John has subject matter that can be subjected to archaeological examination, many seem to think the book is almost entirely non-historical and confines itself to theology and a sort of vague accompanying or underlying Greek-influenced philosophy. Some have even opined that topographical aspects of the Gospel are only symbolic. It's a classic example of presuppositions leading folks astray.

It's true that John's Gospel has many elements that are more or less unique to itself, but it's assuredly *not* lacking a solid grounding in historical reality. There are many compelling elements involved in probing the "archaeology of the Gospel of John."

Bethsaida

This important city in biblical history, mentioned as Peter's and Andrew's hometown (John 1:44; see also 12:21) was located on the north shore of the Sea of Galilee. It has been well excavated since 1987, when Rami Arav, professor of religion and philosophy at the University of Nebraska at Omaha, rediscovered the site and identified it (et-Tell) as Bethsaida.[347]

Jacob's Well

> **John 4:12** "Are you greater than our father Jacob, who gave us the well, and drank from it himself, and his sons, and his cattle?"

The location of Jacob's Well is in Sychar (John 4:5–6), between Mt. Ebal and Mt. Gerizim, near Shechem and Nablus (or Neapolis). No excavations have taken place as of yet, but it's well attested to in the second-century B.C. Jewish *Book of Jubilees*[348] and in the Mishna[349] ("the plain of Ein Soker"). Jacob's Well is indeed located in the vicinity, about half a mile southeast of Nablus, at the foot of Mt. Gerizim. Jews, Samaritans, Muslims, and Christians all agree on its location and connection to Jacob, and there is scarce reason to doubt this strong tradition. Nor should John be doubted in writing that Jacob's Well existed in Sychar.

John 4:6 (twice) and 4:14 use the Greek word *pégé*, which means "spring" or "fountain" (compare 2 Pet. 2:17; James 3:11). On the other hand, in 4:11–12, a different Greek word is used: *phrear*, which means "well" or "cistern" (see Luke 14:5). This perfectly describes Jacob's Well, which is "a combination of dug-out well and running spring"[350] and is "cut through alluvial soil and soft rock [limestone], receiving water by infiltration through the sides."[351]

Its water "is supplied in two ways—through underground sources that make it a true well and by percolated surface water, which makes it a cistern. This may have prompted Jesus' remark about living water in v. 14."[352] Thus, we observe an uncanny accuracy of description through the use of two Greek words that fit the actual site like a hand in a glove. "Bible and science"—contrary to unfortunately popular conceptions—is always a harmonious combination. This is a classic example.

The Pool of Bethesda

> **John 5:2** Now there is in Jerusalem by the Sheep Gate a pool, in Hebrew called Beth-zatha, which has five porticoes.

Until the nineteenth century, clear archaeological evidence for the existence of this pool was lacking. But in archaeological digs in that century, Conrad Schick discovered a large tank about 100 feet northwest of St. Anne's Church, which he believed to be the Pool of Bethesda. Evidence for a pool under this name ("Beth Eshdathayin") is found in the Copper Scroll from Qumran,[353] dated to between A.D. 25 and 68. Israeli historian Benjamin Mazar (1906–1995) believed that Jewish high priest Simon the Just built the pools in the third century B.C.[354] Urban C. von Wahlde elaborates:

In John 5:2 the Pool of Bethesda is described as having five porticoes or colonnades. For centuries, scholars thought that the notion of a five-sided pool was purely symbolic, intended to represent the five books of the Torah that were somehow superseded by the miracle of Jesus. Beginning in the 1880s, however, archaeologists discovered the remains of a pool north of the Pool of Israel, and continuing excavation ultimately exposed a rectangular pool with a wall in the middle that divided it in two. With porticoes on the four sides of the pool and on the central wall, this was indeed a "five-sided" pool.[355]

The Pool of Siloam

John 9:7 "Go, wash in the pool of Siloam.". . . So he went and washed and came back seeing.

The Pool of Siloam was built during the reign of King Hezekiah, to leave besieging armies without access to the spring's waters. The pool was fed by the newly constructed Siloam tunnel ("Hezekiah's Tunnel"). During its early period, it was sometimes known as the Lower Pool (Neh. 3:15; Isa. 22:9). It was rediscovered during work on a sewer in the autumn of 2004. Archaeologists Eli Shukron and Ronny Reich uncovered some stone steps, and it quickly became evident that they were likely part of the Second Temple-period (516 B.C.–A.D. 70) pool. Shukron commented in an article announcing the exciting find,

> The moment that we revealed and discovered this four months ago, we were 100 percent sure it was the Siloam Pool. . . . We know today that the Siloam Pool is connected to the Temple Mount. There is a road that connects the two elements. The entire system is clearer today.[356]

Once excavation commenced, four coins were soon found: all coins of Alexander Jannaeus (103–76 B.C.), a Hasmonean Jewish king. This is a strong indication that the newly rebuilt pool dates from the late Hasmonean or early Herodian period. A dozen coins later found date to the time of the First Jewish Revolt (A.D. 66–70).[357]

Portico of Solomon

John 10:23 refers to Jesus "walking in the Temple, in the portico of Solomon." Flavius Josephus, the famous first-century Roman Jewish historian who lived in Jerusalem, referred to the wall and porch (or "cloister") that King Solomon had built east of the Temple House:

> Now this temple, as I have already said, was built upon a strong hill. At first the plain at the top was hardly sufficient for the holy house and the altar, for the ground about it was very uneven, and like a precipice; but when King Solomon, who was the person that built the temple, had built a wall to it on its east side, there was then added one cloister founded on a bank cast up for it.[358]

Josephus verifies that the porch, east of the outer court (Woman's Court), along the east wall of Solomon's and Herod's Temple complex, was indeed built by King Solomon.[359]

Caiaphas

Caiaphas was indeed Annas's son-in-law, as John 18:13 notes, and as we know from Josephus,[360] and he was the high priest (as John 18:13 also notes) from the years A.D. 18 to 36, having been appointed by Valerius Gratus (Prefect of Judaea from A.D. 15 to 26). Annas had been high priest from A.D. 6 to 15.

Mosaic Law, in referring to "the death of the high priest" (Num. 35:25, 28) implies that high priests were still called by that title even after leaving office (much as we address former presidents of the United States as "Mr. President." This easily explains Luke 3:2 ("in the high priesthood of Annas and Caiaphas"). Matthew calls Caiaphas "high priest" twice (26:3, 57).

POSTSCRIPT

Most of the things I have dealt with in this chapter and throughout the entire book will never be heard about in a Sunday sermon or a Sunday school class or a Wednesday-night Bible study. They *should* be, because they demonstrate that the Bible and science and reason are not at odds at all, and that is a sorely needed emphasis. But they're not, so people must deliberately seek them out and learn about them in books like this and related apologetics and archaeological articles.

New archaeological discoveries in relation to the Bible continue to be made all the time. It's an exciting period for biblical archaeology. Ten years from now (mark my words!), an entire book could likely be filled with just the new Bible-related discoveries in Israel from now until then. The Bible's historical trustworthiness has been verified in the pages of this book. The new finds that will keep arriving will verify it all the more.

How can I say that before the fact? Because archaeology has remarkably substantiated the biblical text, again and again, over the past 150 years, and especially the last thirty years. Therefore, we have little or no reason to believe that future discoveries won't continue to do the same thing. The pattern has long since been set.

Perhaps Bible believers like me can be forgiven if we indulge in a little bit of gratuitous "I told you so!" or "That doesn't surprise me in the slightest!" rhetoric now and then, after hearing of the latest corroboration of the Bible from secular archaeology.

Having reached the end of this volume, I'd like to add a personal touch and a wish. My own Christian faith, though it was fairly strong already, has been strengthened all the more in researching and writing this book. It's my hope that readers who already identify as Christians (or practicing Jews, for that matter, who can also resonate with most of this book, since it concentrates on the Hebrew Bible) will have the same experience.

Perhaps also skeptics and unbelievers will, after reading this volume, consider more seriously the proposal and the possibility that this Bible we're familiar with, to varying degrees, is something quite special. I submit that they must admit, in honesty (having read this book and its hundreds of demonstrations), that the Bible is historically accurate—a necessary aspect of divine inspiration, though I have not attempted to prove the latter in this book and don't expect an atheist to easily accept that much deeper and more complex belief.

This project began in discussions with atheists, and so it's appropriate to end it with an appeal to reason, open-mindedness, and a challenge to all skeptics. Let them be intellectually courageous enough to open themselves to archaeological and other scientific evidence, and solid historical research, when it comes to the Bible—and to not to make the Bible a special exception to the normal rules of demonstration, as if it can't possibly be verified by such evidences, just as any other document can.

Thanks for reading, and for joining me on this journey!

APPENDIX A

YES, THERE WERE CAMELS

The question of the dating of camels and when they were domesticated in Israel is hotly debated, and biblical skeptics (at least the more "aggressive" ones) love to bring it up in the attempt to challenge or even embarrass those who believe that the Bible is historically trustworthy and, indeed, divinely inspired.

I contend that it's much ado about nothing, as I think I sufficiently demonstrated in chapter six. But if some readers (including those not convinced by my explanation) want to further study the issue, here are some great resources:

Megan Sauter, "Did Camels Exist in Biblical Times? (5 reasons why domesticated camels likely existed)," Biblical Archaeology Society/*Bible History Daily* (November 12, 2018): https://www.biblicalarchaeology.org/daily/ancient-cultures/ancient-near-eastern-world/did-camels-exist-in-biblical-times.

Mikel del Rosario, "Were There No Camels During the Time of Biblical Patriarchs?", *Apologetics Guy* (December 1, 2017): http://apologeticsguy.com/2017/12/camels-in-the-bible-were-there-no-camels-during-the-time-of-biblical-patriarchs.

Alice C. Linsley, "Yes, Abraham Had Camels," *Just Genesis* (2-9-17): http://jandyongenesis.blogspot.com/2008/12/abrahams-camels.html.

Christopher Eames, "Camels: Proof That the Bible Is False?," *Watch Jerusalem* (3-29-19): https://watchjerusalem.co.il/590-camels-proof-that-the-bible-is-false.

"Patriarchal Wealth and Early Domestication of the Camel," *Associates for Biblical Research / Bible and Spade* (Summer 2000): https://biblearchaeology.org/research/patriarchal-era/3444-patriarchal-wealth-and-early-domestication-of-the-camel.

"Research: Did the Patriarchs Have Camels? Adulterating the Bible," *Ministry: International Journal for Pastors* (May 1953): https://www.ministrymagazine.org/archive/1953/05/research.

KJ Went, "Abraham, Camels and Egypt, or, Where did Abram get his Camel from?: Genesis 12:16," *Difficult Sayings* (2021): https://www.studylight.org/language-studies/difficult-sayings.html?article=518.

Glenn Miller, "Was the Bible wrong about Abraham having camels that early?," *Christian Thinktank* (4-18-98): https://www.christianthinktank.com/qnocamel.html.

T.M. Kennedy, "The Date of Camel Domestication in the Ancient Near East," *Associates for Biblical Research* (2-17-14): https://biblearchaeology.org/research/contemporary-issues/3832-the-date-of-camel-domestication-in-the-ancient-near-east.

APPENDIX B

THE WRATH OF JOSHUA

The issue of how Canaan was transformed in a relatively short period into Israel and Judah is one of the most contentious in biblical and Near Eastern or Israeli archaeology (with stark divides along the usual minimalist-maximalist lines). In chapter ten, I did my best to demonstrate that a surprising amount of archaeological and historical evidence exists in favor of the "traditional" (biblical) conception of a military conquest of Canaan, led by Joshua. But the larger picture can often get lost in the details, so I thought it best to relegate some of these "finer points" to an appendix, so as to not exhaust the reader's patience or attention. But here they are, for sticklers for detail.

Another issue that will no doubt arise in the minds of many readers is the question of widespread killing entailed in this conquest. It appears at first glance intuitively unjust and even "evil" for God to command the killing of men, women, and children, and even all livestock in some cases. It is difficult to comprehend, and so it is a legitimate question to address (even in a book such as this). I've done so many times, as a Christian apologist these past forty years.

In a nutshell, Christians—along with believing Jews—hold God, our Creator, has prerogatives as the "cosmic judge." He gave us many gifts and privileges and blessings, and in turn, he urges us—for our own good and well-being—to follow rules of morality and conduct that he has spelled out and also placed in our individual consciences.

Often in history (as both the Bible and historical records in general amply attest), human beings reject these moral standards and become progressively more rebellious against God and the good. A point can be reached at which certain segments of the human population are beyond all hope of redemption, and so God judges them, up to and including sentencing them to death. He usually uses human agents to do so—in this instance, Joshua's army. In the case of Sodom and Gomorrah (if my reasoning is correct), he appears to have utilized a meteor airburst. It must be stressed that the Bible records that Israel—God's "chosen people"—was also repeatedly judged by God.

God exercised no double-standards or "exemptions"! Jerusalem was destroyed, along with Solomon's Temple, by the Babylonians, with all remaining Jews taken into captivity, in the sixth century B.C. This was what the prophet Jeremiah warned (for an estimated sixty years) would happen if the inhabitants there didn't repent of their idolatry and other evils. It happened again in the first century A.D., when the Romans destroyed Herod's beautiful rebuilt Temple (as Jesus had predicted) and devastated Jerusalem, killing tens of thousands, and turning it into an utterly non-Jewish Roman town.

I understand that it's hard to accept or conceptualize such massive judgments. I've struggled with it myself at times. But I think we can grasp it to a large extent by understanding that God, as Christians and Jews believe him to be, exercises *justice* as well as *mercy*. We can comprehend this by analogy and our own experience and feelings about those who break the law and commit heinous crimes against others. After all, we have human judges who sentence people to life imprisonment or sometimes to death because they violated human laws or moral codes. It works the same on the cosmic scale with God—except that he is far *above* us (what is called *transcendence* in theistic theology), not like a mere human judge. The one who granted us life in the first place can also take it away.

For further reading, in much more depth, here are several of my own related articles, from my blog, *Biblical Evidence for Catholicism* (which offers a lot of material far broader in scope than what its title implies):

"God's Judgment of Humans (Sometimes, Entire Nations)," February 16, 2007: https://www.patheos.com/blogs/davearmstrong/2016/03/gods-judgment-humans-sometimes-entire-nations.html.

"'How Can God Order the Massacre of Innocents?' (Amalekites, etc.)?", November 10, 2007: https://www.patheos.com/blogs/davearmstrong/2017/01/can-god-order-massacre-innocents-amalekites-etc.html.

"Did Moses (and God) Sin in Judging the Midianites (Numbers 31)?", May 21, 2008): https://www.patheos.com/blogs/davearmstrong/2016/09/did-moses-god-sin-by-judging-the-midianites.html.

"Israel as God's Agent of Judgment," September 28, 2014: https://www.patheos.com/blogs/davearmstrong/2014/09/israel-as-gods-agent-of-judgment.html.

"God's Judgment of Sin: Analogies for an Atheist Inquirer," September 6, 2018): https://www.patheos.com/blogs/davearmstrong/2018/09/gods-judgment-analogies-for-an-atheist-inquirer.html.

"'Why Did God Kill 70,000 Israelites for David's Sin?'", April 13, 2020: https://www.patheos.com/blogs/davearmstrong/2020/04/why-did-god-kill-70000-israelites-for-davids-sin.html.

Having dealt with the contention about God's alleged cruelty, we can now move on to a survey of Joshua's conquest of Canaan, for those who are interested.

Kenneth Kitchen undertook a survey of many of the biblical archaeological sites mentioned in Joshua, to see if they verify or are consistent with (as opposed to "proving") the biblical accounts. I will incorporate archaeologists' summaries from others as well and include the relevant Bible passages.

Joshua's "conquest" is generally dated during the thirteenth and twelfth centuries B.C.—roughly 1250–1150—in other words, on the borderline between the Late Bronze Age and the Early Iron Age.

Azekah

> **Joshua 10:10** And the Lord threw them into a panic before Israel, who slew them with a great slaughter at Gibeon, and chased them by the way of the ascent of Beth-horon, and smote them as far as Azekah and Makkedah. (cf. 10:11; 15:35).

Azekah was occupied right through the Early, Middle, and Late Bronze periods, as well as through the Iron Age.[361]

Libnah

> **Joshua 10:29–30** Then Joshua . . . fought against Libnah; and the Lord gave it also and its king into the hand of Israel; and he smote it with the edge of the sword, and every person in it; he left none remaining in it.

"Libnah . . . can be plausibly identified with Tell Bornat (Tel Burna), which was inhabited in the Late Bronze Age, in agreement with the probable date of Joshua's raids."[362]

The city was "settled in the Early Bronze Age and Iron Age I–II."[363]

Eglon

> **Joshua 10:34–35** And Joshua passed on with all Israel from Lachish to Eglon; and they laid siege to it, and assaulted it; and they took it on that day, and smote it with the edge of the sword; and every person in it he utterly destroyed that day.

"Eglon . . . is in all likelihood to be sited at present-day Tell Aitun (Tell Eton), occupied in the Late Bronze II period."[364]

Debir

> **Joshua 10:38–39** Then Joshua, with all Israel, turned back to Debir and assaulted it, and he took it with its king and all its towns; and they smote them with the edge of the sword, and utterly destroyed every person in it; he left none remaining.

"Debir . . . is more securely located at Khirbet Rabud . . . this site was inhabited in the fourteenth/thirteenth centuries, in the Late Bronze II period, and was reoccupied directly in Early Iron I (twelfth century)."[365]

Ashtaroth

> **Joshua 9:10** Og king of Bashan, who dwelt in Ashtaroth.

Ashteroth (Tell Ashtara) appears twice (as *Aštartu*) in the cuneiform letters from Tell El-Amarna in 1350 B.C.

(letters EA 256 and EA 197). It's also mentioned in the Egyptian sources: the Execration Texts and the campaign list of Ramesses III (r. 1186 to 1155 B.C.).

Chephirah and Kiriath-jearim

Joshua 9:17 And the people of Israel set out and reached their cities [the Hivites': see 9:7] on the third day. Now their cities were Gibeon, Chephirah, Be-eroth, and Kiriath-jearim.

Dutch archaeologist Karel J.H. Vriezen extensively surveyed Chephira ("Khirbet Kefireh") in 1970, 1973, and 1974. He discovered pottery shards from the Early Bronze, Iron I, and Iron II periods. The walls of the site had nine towers and three gates. Excavation at Kiriath-jearim began only in 2017.[366] Thus, the digging likely has not yet reached the Bronze Age level to determine if the city existed then.

Jarmuth

Joshua 10:3 "Piram king of Jarmuth."

"In Late Bronze II [1400–1200 B.C.] the upper citadel was resettled."[367]

"It was a Canaanite city-state and appears as 'city of Yaramu' on the mid-fourteenth century B.C. tablet from Tell el-Hesi (Inscriptions). . . . The resettlement of the site took place in Late Bronze II."[368]

Makkedah

Joshua 10:28 And Joshua took Makkedah on that day, and smote it and its king with the edge of the sword; he utterly destroyed every person in it, he left none remaining.

"May be located at Khirbet el-Qom, very plausibly. . . . Only very limited survey and excavations could be done there, as the modern Arab village overlies much of the site. Thus Late Bronze remains have not yet been found."[369]

"Some archaeologists (for example, Z. Kallai) think it is located at Tel Arani. If so, that was 'settled in Late Bronze IIB (thirteenth century B.C.). Parts of a massive structure were uncovered.'"[370]

Gezer

Joshua 10:33 Then Horam king of Gezer came up to help Lachish.

"Gezer is firmly located at Tell Jazari by inscriptions, and it certainly existed in Late Bronze Age IIB, when Merneptah of Egypt captured it in circa 1209/1208 ("Israel Stela"). Stratum XV of excavations in the mound would likely represent the Gezer of this period."[371]

Negev and Gibson devote a long entry to Gezer and confirm many Late Bronze findings.[372]

Gaza

Joshua 10:41 And Joshua defeated them from Kadesh-barnea to Gaza . . . (cf. 14:6–7; 15:3).

"Archaeological soundings . . . in 1922 . . . uncovered a series of walls, the earliest of which was associated with Late Bronze Age pottery . . . Egyptian texts dating to the reign of Thutmosis II [r. 1493–1479 B.C.] refer to Gazat 'a prize city of the governor,' indicating at least a fifteenth century B.C. date for the occupation of the site. Gaza is also mentioned in the El-Amarna [c. 1350 B.C.] and Taanach tablets [also c. 1350 B.C.] as an Egyptian administrative center."[373]

Shimron and Achshaph

Joshua 11:1 When Jabin king of Hazor heard of this, he sent to . . . the king of Shimron, and to the king of Achshaph.

"In the Amarna letters [c. 1350 B.C.] and the Execration Texts [end of nineteenth or early eighteenth century B.C.], the city is referred to as *Shimon*. The latter source mentions Endaruta as the 'mayor' of Akšapa (Achshaph) in a perfectly preserved letter from Pharaoh (EA 367). Its topic was to guard and defend Akšapa and to prepare for 'troop arrivals.' Achshaph is also referenced in the Amarna letters (EA 366).

"[Shimron] also figures in the list of Palestinian towns of Thutmosis III [r. 1479–1425 B.C.]."[374]

"One of the earliest Canaanite cities, it [Achshaph] is mentioned for the first time in the later group of Execration Texts. It is also listed among the cities conquered by Thutmosis III in the middle of the fifteenth century B.C. . . . It also appears in the Egyptian papyrus Anastasi I of the thirteenth century B.C."[375]

Chinneroth

Joshua 11:2 And to the kings who were in the northern hill country, and in the Arabah south of Chinneroth.

"Kinneret is mentioned in the fourteenth century B.C. Aqhat Epic of Ugarit, an ancient city of Syria. The remains have been excavated at Tel Kinrot. It's also mentioned as *Kennartou* in the Annals of Thutmose III (r. 1479–1425 B.C.).

"Only after another gap was the city reestablished, during Iron Age I. . . . The whole city seems to follow the Canaanite tradition of the Late Bronze Age."[376]

Merom

Joshua 11:5 And all these kings joined their forces, and came and encamped together at the waters of Merom, to fight with Israel.

"It is apparently mentioned in the list of conquests of Thutmosis III [r. 1479–1425 B.C.], and a fortified town in Galilee by the name of *mrm* is drawn, together with other Galilean cities, on the reliefs of Pharaoh Rameses II [r. 1279–1213 B.C.]."[377]

Great Sidon and Misrephoth-maim

Joshua 11:8 And the Lord gave them into the hand of Israel, who smote them and chased them as far as Great Sidon and Misrephoth-maim.

"In the El-Amarna letters [1350 B.C.] Zimrida, King of Sidon, is mentioned."[378]

"Identified with Khirbet el-Meshrifeh, south of Ras en-Naqura, which was inhabited in all periods."[379]

Gath and Ashdod

Joshua 11:22 There was none of the Anakim left in the land of the people of Israel; only in Gaza, in Gath, and in Ashdod, did some remain.

Gath (Tel Zafit) is mentioned in the El-Amarna letters [c. 1350 B.C.] as *Gimti/Gintu*. Late Bronze Canaanite remains at the site are impressive. Ashdod is thought to date from the seventeenth century B.C. It was excavated by archaeologists nine times between 1962 and 1972. It's first mentioned in written documents from Late Bronze Age Ugarit (thirteenth to twelfth century B.C.).

Aroer

Joshua 12:2 Sihon king of the Amorites who dwelt at Heshbon, and ruled from Aroer.

"It is identified with Khirbet Arair on the River Mogib (Arnon), where remains of Bronze Age and Iron age settlements . . . have been found. . . . It was resettled at the end of the Late Bronze Age."[380]

Edrei

Joshua 12:4 And Og king of Bashan, one of the remnant of the Rephaim, who dwelt at Ashtaroth and at Edre-i.

Daraa was an ancient city dating back to the Canaanites. It was mentioned in Egyptian hieroglyphic tablets of Pharaoh Thutmose III between 1490 and 1436 B.C. (known in those days as *Atharaa*). In the Old Testament, it's called Edrei (the capital of Bashan).

Aphek

Joshua 12:18 The king of Aphek.

"From the thirteenth century, a central fortified residence has been dug. . . . Other traces exist as well, such as tombs."[381]

"In the ruins of the palace were discovered Egyptian, Hittite and Akkadian documents. . . . Most of these documents date from the fourteenth to thirteenth centuries B.C."[382]

Taanach

Joshua 12:21 The king of Taanach.

"Tell Ta'annek. Occupied from the seventeenth to mid-fifteenth century, then not visibly until the late thirteenth into the twelfth century. The former date suits Joshua, and the latter Deborah in Judges."[383]

"To Late Bronze Age II belongs another large palace, whose walls were 7 feet thick."[384]

Megiddo

Joshua 12:21 The king of Megiddo.

"Tell el-Mutesillim. Megiddo was an important place through the sixteenth to early twelfth centuries (strata X to VIIA, series of palaces, etc.)."[385]

At the Battle of Megiddo (1457 B.C.), the city was subjugated by Thutmose III (r. 1479–1425 B.C.), and an elaborate government palace was built in the Late Bronze Age. Amarna Letter E245 (c. 1350 B.C.) mentions local ruler Biridiya of Megiddo.

Kedesh and Jokneam

Joshua 12:22 The king of Kedesh, one; the king of Jokneam.

"Possibly the present-day Tell Abu Qudeis in Jezreel; its stratum VIII goes back to the thirteenth century at least; more is not known. Another Qedesh, at tell Qudeish, is reported northwest of Lake Huleh, also of this period."[386]

"A name which may possibly refer to Kedesh appears in the lists of Thutmosis III [r. 1479–1425 B.C.] and in the El-Amarna letters [c. 1350 B.C.]."[387]

"Joqneam . . . Tell Qemun. With a very long history. Its stratum XIX in the thirteenth century ended in destruction."[388]

"Yoqneam is mentioned in the Karnak inscription recording the campaign of Thutmosis III into Canaan (c. 1486 B.C.)."[389]

Dor

Joshua 12:23 The king of Dor in Naphath-dor.

"Traces of Late Bronze Age I-II materials have turned up, but systematic excavation has not yet reached beyond circa 1100 levels."[390]

"The earliest known appearance of Dor is from an Egyptian inscription from Nubia, dated to the time of Rameses II (thirteenth century B.C.)."[391]

Tirzah

Joshua 12:24 The king of Tirzah.

"The first Iron Age remains (period VIIa) were built upon a Late Bronze wall."[392]

"The burials, both of children and of adults, were the same [in the Late Bronze Age] as those of the preceding period. . . . This settlement must have been abandoned either at the end of the fourteenth century or early in the thirteenth century B.C."[393]

Archaeology is often (so its practitioners tell us) a speculative and inexact science. But I submit that there is more than enough verification in the above information to establish that the Bible—the book of Joshua, in this instance—is, yet again, substantially accurate in its claims.

ABOUT THE AUTHOR

Dave Armstrong is the author of fifty-one books: ten published by major Catholic publishers, with several bestsellers. He has defended Christianity as an apologist since 1981 and Catholicism in particular since 1990 (full-time since 2001). His blog, *Biblical Evidence for Catholicism*, went online in 1997 and contains more than 4,000 articles. Dave has been a regular columnist for *National Catholic Register* since 2016, and has additionally been published in *Catholic Answers Magazine*, *The Catholic World Report*, *Catholic Herald*, and several other well-known Catholic periodicals.

ENDNOTES

1 Nelson Glueck, *Rivers in the Desert* (New York: Farrar Strauss and Cudahy, 1959), 31: https://archive.org/stream/riverinthedesert012851mbp/riverinthedesert012851mbp_djvu.txt.

2 Kenneth A. Kitchen, *On the Reliability of the Old Testament* (Grand Rapids and Cambridge: Wm. B. Eerdmans Publishing, 2003), 469.

3 Thomas L. Thompson, *The Historicity of the Patriarchal Narratives* (Harrisburg, PA: Trinity Press International, 2002), 2.

4 The dates in this timeline are drawn from Kenneth A. Kitchen, *On the Reliability of the Old Testament*.

5 Carol A. Hill, "The Garden of Eden: A Modern Landscape," *Perspectives on Science and Christian Faith* 52 (March 2000), 31–46: https://www.asa3.org/ASA/PSCF/2000/PSCF3-00Hill.html.

6 "Havilah," *International Standard Bible Encyclopedia* (Grand Rapids, MI: Wm. B. Eerdmans Publishing, 1915): https://www.studylight.org/encyclopedias/eng/isb/h/havilah.html.

7 James Sauer, "The River Runs Dry: Creation Story Preserves Historical Memory," *Biblical Archaeology Review* 22:4 (1996), 52–57, 64: https://www.baslibrary.org/biblical-archaeology-review/22/4/3.

8 Gordon Govier, "Do Photos Evidence Lost Edenic River?", *Christianity Today* Vol. 40, No. 11 (October 7, 1996): https://www.christianitytoday.com/ct/1996/october7/6tb92a.html.

9 See "Mahd Adh Dhahab Mine (Mahad Dahahab Mine; Cradle of Gold Mine), Wejh, Tabuk Region, Saudi Arabia," mindat.org.: https://www.mindat.org/loc-15176.html.

10 *New American Bible* (Nashville: Catholic Bible Press: a division of Thomas Nelson Publishers, with revised New Testament, 1987). Quotation is from the footnote for Genesis 2:10–14 (p. 3).

11 Gihon [1]," *International Standard Bible Encyclopedia*: https://www.studylight.org/encyclopedias/eng/isb/g/gihon-1.html.

12 Kevin Burrell, *Cushites in the Hebrew Bible* (Leiden, Netherlands: Brill, 2020), 134: https://books.google.com/books?id=CfHJDwAAQBAJ&newbks=1&newbks_redir=0&dq=Cushites_in_the_Hebrew_Bible&source=gbs_navlinks_s.

13 "Cush," *The McClintock and Strong Biblical Cyclopedia* (New York: Harper and Brothers, 1880): https://www.biblicalcyclopedia.com/C/cush.html.

14 The map is found in Dora Jane Hamblin, "Has the Garden of Eden been located at last?," *Smithsonian Magazine*, vol. 18, no. 2 (May 1987): http://www.ldolphin.org/eden. The map itself: http://www.ldolphin.org/eden/fig2.gif.

15 Kurt Lambeck, "Shoreline reconstructions for the Persian Gulf since the last glacial maximum," *Earth and Planetary Science Letters* 142 (1996), 43–57: http://people.rses.anu.edu.au/lambeck_k/pdf/171.pdf.

16 "Is the Cradle of Civilization hidden under water?," *Archaeology Mysteries* (December 2020): https://archaeologymysteries.com/2019/02/11/sea-level-rise-and-its-impact-on-human-civilization/.

17 "Deluge," *Catholic Encyclopedia* (1908): https://www.newadvent.org/cathen/04702a.htm.

18 Bernard Ramm, *The Christian View of Science and Scripture* (Grand Rapids, MI: Wm. B. Eerdmans Publishing, 1954; hardcover edition reprinted in 1966), 240–241: https://archive.org/stream/christianviewofscienceandscripture/christianviewofscienceandscripture_djvu.txt.

19 Carol A. Hill, "A Time and a Place for Noah," *Perspectives on Science and Christian Faith*, vol. 53, no. 1 (March 2001), 24–40: https://www.asa3.org/ASA/PSCF/2001/PSCF3-01Hill.html.

20 Anthony Slaven, *The Development of the West of Scotland 1750–1960* (London: Routledge, 1975; reprinted in 2006), 131; text can be accessed through a Google Book search on the book's page: https://books.google.com/books?id=yUH-AQAAQBAJ&newbks=1&newbks_redir=0&dq=wooden+boats,+size+limit,+300+feet&source=gbs_navlinks_s.

21 For information about this phenomenon, see Bijoy Chandrasekhar, "What is hogging and sagging of ships?," *MarineSite.Info*: https://www.marinesite.info/2021/04/what-is-hogging-and-sagging-of-ships.html.

22 Alan E. Hill, "Quantitative Hydrology of Noah's Flood," *Perspectives on Science and Christian Faith* Vol. 58, No. 2 (June 2006): https://www.asa3.org/ASA/

PSCF/2006/PSCF6-06Hill2.pdf.

23 *Ibid.*

24 James G. Titus et al., "Greenhouse Effect, Sea Level Rise, and Coastal Drainage Systems," *Journal of Water Resources Planning and Management*, vol. 113, vo. 2. (March 1987): http://papers.risingsea.net/downloads/sea-level-rise-coastal-drainage.pdf.

25 E.C.L. During-Caspers, "New archaeological evidence for maritime trade in the Persian Gulf during the Late Protoliterate period," *East West* 21, 21–44, 1971. During-Caspers was a lecturer in the Department of Archaeology, Leiden University. https://www.jstor.org/stable/29755644.

26 Kurt Lambeck, "Shoreline reconstructions for the Persian Gulf since the last glacial maximum," *Earth and Planetary Science Letters* 142 (1996), 43–57: http://people.rses.anu.edu.au/lambeck_k/pdf/171.pdf.

27 For detailed information on this storm, see "A Report on the Super Cyclonic Storm 'GONU' during 1–7 June, 2007," India Meteorological Department (February 2011): https://rsmcnewdelhi.imd.gov.in/images/pdf/gonu.pdf.

28 Alan E. Hill, "Quantitative Hydrology."

29 See also Hamlet Petrosyan, "The Sacred Mountain," in Levon Abrahamian and Nancy Sweezy, ed., *Armenian Folk Arts, Culture, and Identity* (Indiana University Press, 2001), 36: https://archive.org/details/isbn_9780253337047/page/36/mode/2up.

30 Alan E. Hill, "Quantitative Hydrology of Noah's Flood."

31 Carol A. Hill, *A Worldview Approach to Science and Scripture: Making Genesis Real* (Grand Rapids, MI: Kregel Publications, 2019). The chapter in question is accessible on the Google Books page: https://books.google.com/books?id=qmy1DwAAQBAJ&printsec=frontcover&dq=Carol+A.+Hill,+A+Worldview+Approach+to+Science+and+Scripture:+Making+Genesis+Real&hl=en&newbks=1&newbks_redir=0&sa=X&ved=2ahUKEwic9dmf89j7AhX_jIkEHeXcBHAQ6AF6BAgCEAI#v=onepage&q=Carol%20A.%20Hill%2C%20A%20Worldview%20Approach%20to%20Science%20and%20Scripture%3A%20Making%20Genesis%20Real&f=false.

32 Baghdad, Iraq, located near ancient Babylon, has a latitude of 33.312805, according to *LatLong.Net*: https://www.latlong.net/place/baghdad-iraq-12885.html. Vicksburg, Mississippi, located on the Mississippi River about halfway

between New Orleans and Memphis, has a latitude of 32.363724, according to the same source: https://www.latlong.net/place/vicksburg-ms-usa-4482.html.

33 "World: Greatest Twenty-four-Hour (1 Day) Rainfall," Arizona State University: World Meteorological Organization's World Weather & Climate Extremes Archive: https://wmo.asu.edu/content/world-greatest-twenty-four-hour-1-day-rainfall.

34 "No. 988 - Cherrapunji, India, Holds New Record for 48-Hour Rainfall," World Meteorological Organization April 4, 2014: https://public.wmo.int/en/media/press-release/no-988-cherrapunji-india-holds-new-record-48-hour-rainfall.

35 Zoë Schlanger, "Why do all our climate data start in 1880?," *Quartz* (August 17, 2017; updated July 20, 2022): https://qz.com/1055629/why-does-all-our-climate-data-start-in-1880.

36 See Jürgen Herget et al., "Altai megafloods—The temporal context," *Earth-Science Reviews* Vol. 200 (January 2020): https://www.sciencedirect.com/science/article/abs/pii/S0012825219301540.

37 See ValentinaYanko-Hombach et al., "Controversy over the great flood hypotheses in the Black Sea in light of geological, paleontological, and archaeological evidence," *Quaternary International* Vols. 167–168 (June 2007), 91–113: https://www.sciencedirect.com/science/article/abs/pii/S1040618206001984.

38 See "Missoula Floods," *Columbia River Images*: http://columbiariverimages.com/Regions/Places/missoula_floods.html.

39 See Daniel Garcia-Castellanos et al., "The Zanclean megaflood of the Mediterranean—Searching for independent evidence," *Earth-Science Reviews* Vol. 201 (February 2020): https://www.sciencedirect.com/science/article/pii/S0012825219302521.

40 See J. O'Connor, "The Bonneville Flood—A Veritable Débâcle," *Developments in Earth Surface Processes* Vol. 20 (2016), 105–126: https://www.sciencedirect.com/science/article/abs/pii/B9780444635907000068.

41 "Monster hurricanes reached U.S. during prehistoric periods of ocean warming," *Woods Hole Oceanographic Institution* (February 11, 2015): https://www.whoi.edu/press-room/news-release/prehistoric-hurricanes.

42 Gary Rendsburg, "Ur Kasdim: Where Is Abraham's Birthplace?," *Torah.com*, 2019: https://www.thetorah.com/article/ur-kasdim-where-is-abrahams-birthplace.

43 Cyrus H. Gordon, "Where Is Abraham's Ur?," *Biblical Archaeology Review* 3.2 (1977): 20–21, 52: https://webcache.googleusercontent.com/search?q=cache:XOWrpKQfIXcJ:https://www.baslibrary.org/biblical-archaeology-review/3/2/5.

44 M. Bözdeniza et al, "Vernacular domed houses of Harran, Turkey," *Habitat International*, vol. 22, no. 4 (December 1998), 477–485. Citation from page 478: https://www.sciencedirect.com/science/article/abs/pii/S0197397598000277.

45 Tamara M. Green, *The City of the Moon God: Religious Traditions of Harran* (Leiden, Netherlands: Brill, 1992), 19: https://books.google.com/books?id=qLK9CwAAQBAJ&q=2000#v=snippet&q=2000&f=false.

46 Kenneth A. Kitchen, *On the Reliability of the Old Testament* (Grand Rapids and Cambridge: Wm. B. Eerdmans Publishing, 2003), 359.

47 See Ephraim Stern (ed.), *The New Encyclopedia of Archaeological Excavations in the Holy Land*, Vol. 4 (Carta, Jerusalem: The Israel Exploration Society, 1993); "Shechem," 1,345–1,353. Citations from p. 1,347 and p. 1,352: https://www.mq.edu.au/__data/assets/pdf_file/0010/527734/NEAEHL-Shechem.pdf.

48 David G. Hansen, "Shechem: Its Archaeological and Contextual Significance," *Bible and Spade* (Spring 2005): https://biblearchaeology.org/research/new-testament-era/2365-shechem-its-archaeological-and-contextual-significance?highlight=WyJzaGVjaGVtIiwic2hlY2hlbSdzIiwic2hlY2hlbSciXQ==

49 Avraham Negev and Shimon Gibson, *Archaeological Encyclopedia of the Holy Land* (New York: Continuum, 2001), 224: https://books.google.com/books?id=27nq65cZUIgC.

50 "The History of the 4,000-Year-Old Steps in Hebron" (October 26, 2018): http://en.hebron.org.il/history/956.

51 John J. Bimson, "Archaeological Data and the Dating of the Patriarchs," chapter in A.R. Millard & D.J. Wiseman (ed.), *Essays on the Patriarchal Narratives* (Leicester, UK: InterVarsity Press, 1980), 59–92 (citation from pp. 75–76): https://biblicalstudies.org.uk/epn_3_bimson.html.

52 See "The Execration Texts," *City of David: Ancient Jerusalem*: https://www.cityofdavid.org.il/en/archeology/finds/execration-texts.

53 For this and related information about pre-Davidic Jerusalem, see "Ancient Jerusalem," israel-a-history-of.com: https://www.israel-a-history-of.com/ancient-jerusalem.html.

54 Brian Nixon, "Archaeological Evidence for Sodom: Recent Findings Shed Light on Discoveries of 'Biblical Proportions'," *Assist News Service* (December 8, 2011): https://web.archive.org/web/20120712005037/https:/www.assistnews.net/Stories/2011/s11120037.htm.

55 Steven Collins, "Tall el-Hammam Is Still Sodom: Critical Data-Sets Cast Serious Doubt on E.H. Merrill's Chronological Analysis," *Biblical Research Bulletin* Vol. 13, No. 1 (2013): https://web.archive.org/web/20130927170737/http:/www.tallelhammam.com/uploads/BRB-2013-1-Collins_Answers_Merrill.pdf.

56 Amanda Borschel-Dan, "Evidence of Sodom? Meteor blast cause of biblical destruction, say scientists," *The Times of Israel* (November 22, 2018): https://www.timesofisrael.com/evidence-of-sodom-meteor-blast-cause-of-biblical-destruction-say-scientists. See also Ted E. Bunch et al., "A Tunguska sized airburst destroyed Tall el-Hammam a Middle Bronze Age city in the Jordan Valley near the Dead Sea," *Scientific Reports* (September 20, 2021), a fantastically detailed examination, with many fascinating photographs: https://www.nature.com/articles/s41598-021-97778-3. Compare Evan Gough, "A Meteor may have Exploded in the Air 3,700 Years Ago, Obliterating Communities Near the Dead Sea," *Universe Today* (December 4, 2018): https://www.universetoday.com/140752/a-meteor-may-have-exploded-in-the-air-3700-years-ago-obliterating-communities-near-the-dead-sea.

57 Steven Collins and Phillip Silvia, "The Civilization-Ending 3.7KYrBP Event: Archaeological Data, Sample Analyses, and Biblical Implications" (November 2015): https://3182d453b68388416980-71bc4c8fd3e50b4ee0e248e517d3026f.ssl.cf2.rackcdn.com/uploaded/s/0e8156401_1544622622_sodom-and-gomorrah-archaelogical-proof.pdf.

58 *Ellicott's Commentary for English Readers* (London: 1905); comment on Genesis 37:25: https://biblehub.com/commentaries/ellicott/genesis/37.htm.

59 See, for example, "Astragalus macrocarpus DC.," *Flora of Israel and adjacent areas*: https://flora.org.il/en/plants/ASTMAC.

60 Herbert Edward Ryle, comment on Genesis 37:25, in *Cambridge Bible for Schools and Colleges* (Cambridge University Press, 1921): https://biblehub.com/commentaries/cambridge/genesis/37.htm.

61 Shimshon Ben-Yehoshua and Lumir Hanus, "Frankincense, Myrrh, and Balm of Gilead: Ancient Spices of Southern Arabia and Judea," *Horticultural Reviews* 39(1) (September 2012), 1–76: https://www.researchgate.net/publication/282748639_Frankincense_Myrrh_and_Balm_of_Gilead_Ancient_Spices_of_Southern_Arabia_and_Judea.

62 Adam Lee, "Let the Stones Speak: Part 1," *Daylight Atheism* (April 11, 2004): https://www.patheos.com/blogs/daylightatheism/essays/let-the-stones-speak-part-1.

63 Avraham Negev and Shimon Gibson, "Dothan," in Archaeological Encyclopedia of the Holy Land (New York: Continuum, revised edition of 2001), 146.

64 *Cambridge Bible for Schools and Colleges*: https://biblehub.com/commentaries/cambridge/genesis/37.htm.

65 *Ellicott's Commentary for English Readers*: https://biblehub.com/commentaries/ellicott/genesis/37.htm.

66 "Major Routes in the Land of the Bible," *Israel and You* (6-17-20): http://www.israelandyou.com/major-routes-in-the-land-of-the-bible.

67 Kenneth A. Kitchen, "The Patriarchal Age: Myth or History?," *Biblical Archaeology Review* 21:02 (March/April 1995): https://web.archive.org/web/20110718123231/http:/www.wwuheiser.com/Kitchen.pdf.

68 James K. Hoffmeier, *Israel in Egypt: The Evidence for the Authenticity of the Exodus Tradition* (New York, Oxford: Oxford University Press, 1996), 68.

69 *Id.*, 84.

70 *Id.*, 87.

71 Kenneth A. Kitchen, *On the Reliability of the Old Testament* (Grand Rapids, MI: Wm. B. Eerdmans Publishing, 2003), 346.

72 Emil G. Hirsch and J. F. McLaughlin, "Potiphar or Poti-Pherah," *Jewish Encyclopedia* (New York: Funk & Wagnalls, 1906): https://www.jewishencyclopedia.com/articles/12316-potiphar.

73 See many scores of examples of this in the RSV: https://quod.lib.umich.edu/cgi/r/rsv/rsv-idx?type=simple&format=Long&q1=pharaoh&restrict=Old+Testament&size=First+100.

74 James K. Hoffmeier, *Israel in Egypt*, 87–88.

75 Ibid., 92.

76 Kenneth A. Kitchen, *On the Reliability of the Old Testament*, 478.

77 James K. Hoffmeier, *Israel in Egypt*, 95.

78 *Ibid.*

79 "Archaeology Find: Camels In 'Bible' Are Literary Anachronisms," *National Public Radio* ("NPR") (February 14, 2014), transcript of a radio show; comment by Renee Montagne: https://www.npr.org/2014/02/14/276782474/the-genesis-of-camels.

80 Elizabeth Dias, "The Mystery of the Bible's Phantom Camels," *Time* (February 11, 2014): https://time.com/6662/the-mystery-of-the-bibles-phantom-camels/.

81 Dewayne Bryant, "Abraham's Camels," *Apologetics Press* (2014): https://apologeticspress.org/abrahams-camels-4800.

82 Joseph P. Free, "Abraham's Camels," *Journal of Near Eastern Studies* 3[3] (July 1944):187–193; citation from p. 191: https://www.jstor.org/stable/542916.

83 Kenneth A. Kitchen, *On the Reliability of the Old Testament* (Grand Rapids, MI: Wm. B. Eerdmans Publishing, 2003), 339; italics in original.

84 Joshua Berman, "Yes, Virginia, the Patriarchs really did ride on camels," *The Times of Israel* (November 12, 2020): https://blogs.timesofisrael.com/yes-virginia-the-patriarchs-really-did-ride-on-camels. Link to the *New York Times* article to which he was responding ("Camels Had No Business in Genesis"): https://www.nytimes.com/2014/02/11/science/camels-had-no-business-in-genesis.html.

85 "Horses in Ancient Egypt," University College London (2003): https://www.ucl.ac.uk/museums-static/digitalegypt/foodproduction/horse.html.

86 John E. Hartley, *The Book of Job* (Grand Rapids, MI: Wm. B. Eerdmans Publishing, 1988), 20: https://www.google.com/books/edition/The_Book_of_Job/f-m5GnRjDckC?hl=en&gbpv=1&pg=PA20&printsec=frontcover.

87 Edouard Dhorme, *A Commentary on the Book of Job* (Nashville: Thomas Nelson, 1984), clxix: https://books.google.com/books?newbks=1&newbks_redir=0&id=SrQQAQAAIAAJ&dq=book+of+job%2C+dates+from&focus=searchwithinvolume&q=date.

88 K.A. Clark, S. Ikram, and R.P. Evershed, "The significance of petroleum bitumen in ancient Egyptian mummies," *Philosophical Transactions of the Royal Society: Mathematical, Physical and Engineering Sciences* Vol. 374, Issue 2079 (10-28-16): https://royalsocietypublishing.org/doi/10.1098/rsta.2016.0229.

89 J. Connan, A. Nissenbaum, D. Dessort, "Molecular archaeology: export of

dead-sea asphalt to Canaan and Egypt in the Chalcolithic-Early Bronze Age (4th–3rd Millennium BC)," *Geochimica et Cosmochimica Acta* Vol. 56, Issue (7 July 1992), 2743-2759: https://www.sciencedirect.com/science/article/abs/pii/001670379290357O?via%3Dihub. See also A.O. Barakat et al, "Organic geochemistry indicates Gebel El Zeit, Gulf of Suez, is a source of bitumen used in some Egyptian mummies," *Geoarchaeology*, Vol. 20, Issue 3 (March 2005), 211–228: https://onlinelibrary.wiley.com/doi/epdf/10.1002/gea.20044.

90 Graham Faiella, *The Technology of Mesopotamia* (New York: Rosen Publishing Group, 2006), 27: https://books.google.com/books?id=bGMyBTS0-v0C&pg=PA27#v=onepage&q&f=false.

91 S.I. Yannopoulos, et al., "Evolution of Water Lifting Devices (Pumps) over the Centuries Worldwide," *Water* 7 (9), 5031-5060 (9-17-15), 5031-5060: https://www.mdpi.com/2073-4441/7/9/5031/htm.

92 Bart Ehrman, "Could Moses Write Hebrew & What Language Could Moses Speak" (August 25, 2017): https://ehrmanblog.org/could-moses-write-hebrew/

93 Joseph Lam is associate professor in the Department of Religious Studies at the University of North Carolina at Chapel Hill. See his *curriculum vitae*: https://religion.unc.edu/_people/full-time-faculty/lam.

94 Kenneth A. Kitchen, *On the Reliability of the Old Testament* (Grand Rapids and Cambridge: Wm. B. Eerdmans Publishing, 2003), 370–371.

95 *Id.*, 297.

96 Kenneth A. Kitchen, "Archaeology and the Hebrew Exodus," *Theology Network*, https://theologynetwork.uk/think/archaeology-and-the-hebrew-exodus.

97 Kitchen A. Kitchen, *On the Reliability of the Old Testament*, 304–305.

98 Amanda Borschel-Dan, "First written record of Semitic alphabet, from 15th century BCE, found in Egypt," *The Times of Israel* (May 22, 2018): https://www.timesofisrael.com/first-written-record-of-semitic-alphabet-from-15th-century-bce-found-in-egypt.

99 John Noble Wilford, "Discovery of Egyptian Inscriptions Indicates an Earlier Date for Origin of the Alphabet," *The New York Times* (November 13, 1999): https://webcache.googleusercontent.com/search?q=cache:2vl5qQJFA7wJ:https://archive.nytimes.com/www.nytimes.com/library/national/science/111499sci-alphabet-origin.html.

100 Amanda Borschel-Dan, "Archaeologist claims to find oldest Hebrew text in Israel, including the name of God," *The Times of Israel* (March 24, 2022): https://www.timesofisrael.com/archaeologist-claims-to-find-oldest-hebrew-text-in-israel-including-the-name-of-god/.

101 *Ibid.*

102 James K. Hoffmeier, "Rameses of the exodus narratives is the 13th B.C. Royal Ramesside Residence," *Trinity Journal* 28NS (2007), 8: https://www.academia.edu/2118891/Rameses_of_the_exodus_narratives_is_the_13th_BC_Royal_Ramessid_Residence.

103 Kenneth A. Kitchen, "Archaeology and the Hebrew Exodus.": https://web.archive.org/web/20211020101331/https://theologynetwork.uk/biblical-studies/archaeology-and-the-hebrew-exodus.

104 Jerzy Trzciński et al., "Preliminary Back-Analysis of the Height of Mud Brick Fortifications Based on Geoarchaeological Data at Tell el-Retaba Site in Egypt," *Studia Quaternaria* Vol. 34, No. 2 (2017): 99–108; citation from p. 99: http://archive.sciendo.com/SQUA/squa.2017.34.issue-2/squa-2017-0008/squa-2017-0008.pdf.

105 *Id.*, 106. Further references offered in this article: D. Arnold, *The Encyclopaedia of Ancient Egyptian Architecture* (London/New York: Emery, V.L., 2011). "Mud-Brick Architecture" in W. Wendrich (ed.), *UCLA Encyclopedia of Egyptology* (Los Angeles: Kemp, B., 2009). "Soil (including mud-brick architecture)" in Paul T. Nicholson, Ian Shaw (eds.), *Ancient Egyptian materials and technology* (Cambridge University Press, 2009), 78–103. A.J. Spencer, *Brick architecture in ancient Egypt* (Warminster, UK: Aris and Phillips Classical Texts, 1979).

106 See the Center's summary of the project here: https://pcma.uw.edu.pl/en/2019/01/12/tell-el-retaba-2.

107 Robert J. Littman, Jay Silverstein, and Marta Lorenzon, "With & without straw: How Israelite slaves made bricks," *Biblical Archaeology Review* (March 2014); citations from 60–61, 62, and 63: https://www.researchgate.net/publication/287786412_With_without_straw_How_Israelite_slaves_made_bricks.

108 Marta Lorenzon, Jessica L. Nitschke, Robert J. Littman, and Jay E. Silverstein, "Mudbricks, Construction Methods, and Stratigraphic Analysis: A Case Study at Tell Timai (Ancient Thmuis) in the Egyptian Delta," *American Journal of Archaeology* Vol. 124, No. 1 (January 2020), 105–131; citation from 116–117: https://helda.

helsinki.fi/bitstream/handle/10138/325374/mudbricks_lorenzon.pdf.

109 Virginia L. Emery, "Mud-Brick," in Willeke Wendrich et al (eds.), *UCLA Encyclopedia of Egyptology* (Los Angeles, 2016); citations from 1–2: https://escholarship.org/content/qt7v84d6rh/qt7v84d6rh.pdf.

110 Manfred Bietak and Gary A. Rendsburg, "Egypt and the Exodus," in John Merrill and Hershel Shanks (eds.), *Ancient Israel* (Washington, D. C.: Biblical Archeology Society, 4th edition, 2021), 29.

111 Miroslav Černy and Jozef Hudec "Fortifications at Tell el-Retaba," *Asian and African Studies* Vol. 25, No. 2 (2016); citations from 119, 122–123: https://orient.sav.sk/wp-content/uploads/aas/2016-2.pdf.

112 [English translation] "The Plagues of Egypt," *Zeitschrift fue die alttestamentliche Wissenschaft*, 69 (1957), 84–103 and 70 (1958), 48–59.

113 James K. Hoffmeier, *Israel in Egypt: The Evidence for the Authenticity of the Exodus Tradition* (New York, Oxford: Oxford University Press, 1996), 146–149.

114 *Live Science* Staff, "The Science of the 10 Plagues," *Live Science* (April 11, 2017): https://www.livescience.com/58638-science-of-the-10-plagues.html.

115 Benjamin Radford, "Raining Frogs & Fish: A Whirlwind of Theories," *Live Science* (April 10, 2014): https://www.livescience.com/44760-raining-frogs.html.

116 "Frogs Still Causing Traffic Jams in Greece," *CBS News/AP* (May 27, 2010): https://www.cbsnews.com/news/frogs-still-causing-traffic-jams-in-greece.

117 J.S. Marr and C.D. Malloy, "An epidemiologic analysis of the ten plagues of Egypt," *Caduceus* 12(1) (Spring 1996): 7–24: https://pubmed.ncbi.nlm.nih.gov/8673614.

118 Donald G. McNeil Jr., "Virus Deadly in Livestock Is No More, U.N. Declares," *The New York Times* (October 15, 2010): https://www.nytimes.com/2010/10/16/science/16pest.html.

119 C. Huygelen, "The Immunization of Cattle against Rinderpest in Eighteenth-Century Europe," *Medical History* 41 (1997), 182–196: https://www.ncbi.nlm.nih.gov/pmc/articles/PMC1043905/pdf/medhist00027-0064.pdf.

120 Dennis Normile, "Driven to Extinction," *Science* 319, No. 5870 (March 21, 2008): 1606–1609: https://www.science.org/doi/10.1126/science.319.5870.1606.

121 Frédéric Baldacchino et al., "Transmission of pathogens by *Stomoxys* flies (Diptera, Muscidae): a review," *Parasite* Vol. 20 (August 29, 2013): https://www.

ncbi.nlm.nih.gov/pmc/articles/PMC3756335.

122 Heba Elbasiouny et al, "Phosphorus Availability and Potential Environmental Risk Assessment in Alkaline Soils," *Agriculture 2020*, 10[5] (May 14, 2020): https://www.mdpi.com/2077-0472/10/5/172/htm.

123 Hazem Zohny, "Hail storm in Greater Cairo," *Egypt Independent* (February 26, 2010): https://egyptindependent.com/hail-storm-greater-cairo.

124 CGTN Africa, "Egypt hit by deadly storms," *YouTube* (March 13, 2020): https://www.youtube.com/watch?v=xXY4nurOYIQ.

125 Aaron Reich, "Plague of pests: Lots of locusts swarm Israel's South—watch," *The Jerusalem Post* (April 25, 2021): https://www.jpost.com/israel-news/plague-of-pests-lots-of-locusts-swarm-israels-south-watch-666251.

126 Pranav Baskar, "Locusts Are a Plague of Biblical Scope In 2020. Why? And . . . What Are They Exactly?," *National Public Radio* ("NPR") (June 14, 2020): https://www.npr.org/sections/goatsandsoda/2020/06/14/876002404/locusts-are-a-plague-of-biblical-scope-in-2020-why-and-what-are-they-exactly.

127 "The Black Sunday Dust Storm of April 14, 1935" (Norman, Oklahoma), *National Weather Service*: https://www.weather.gov/oun/events-19350414.

128 Jonathan M.S. Pearce, "Debunking the Exodus II: A Ridiculous Story with Ridiculous Claims," *OnlySky* (May 19, 2021): https://onlysky.media/jpearce/debunking-the-exodus-ii-a-ridiculous-story-with-ridiculous-claims/.

129 Colin J. Humphreys, "The Number of People in the Exodus from Egypt: Decoding Mathematically the Very Large Numbers in Numbers I and XXVI," *Vetus Testamentum* Vol. 48, Fasc. 2 (April 1998), 196–213: https://www.jstor.org/stable/1585502.

130 Ben-Zion Katz, "Recounting the Census: A Military Force of 5,500 (not 603,550) Men," *The Torah.com* (May 15, 2015): https://www.thetorah.com/article/recounting-the-census-a-military-force-of-5500.

131 Joshua J. Mark, "Pi-Ramesses," *World History Encyclopedia* (July 19, 2017): https://www.worldhistory.org/Pi-Ramesses/.

132 John Madden, "Slavery in the Roman Empire: Numbers and Origins," *Classics Ireland* 3 (1996): https://web.archive.org/web/20150622025724/http:/www.ucd.ie/cai/classics-ireland/1996/Madden96.html.

133 "Detroit, Michigan Population History 1840—2019," *BiggestUSCities.com*:

https://www.biggestuscities.com/city/detroit-michigan.

134 In Michael Slackman, "Did the Red Sea Part? No Evidence, Archaeologists Say," *The New York Times* (3 April 2007): https://www.nytimes.com/2007/04/03/world/africa/03exodus.html.

135 See a list of Carl Drews' other published, peer-reviewed articles and research in his *Curriculum Vitae*: https://acomstaff.acom.ucar.edu/drews.

136 Carl Drews and Weiqing Han, "Dynamics of Wind Setdown at Suez and the Eastern Nile Delta," *Plos One* 5(8) (August 30, 2010): https://journals.plos.org/plosone/article?id=10.1371/journal.pone.0012481.

137 "Parting of the Red Sea": https://acomstaff.acom.ucar.edu/drews/parting.shtml.

138 "Study: Wind May Have Helped Moses Part Red Sea," *National Public Radio*/"All Things Considered" (September 26, 2010): https://www.npr.org/templates/story/story.php?storyId=130112925.

139 Suzanne Goldenberg, "A miracle! Science claims it has figured out how sea was parted for Israelites," *The Guardian* (September 21, 2010): https://www.theguardian.com/environment/2010/sep/21/moses-red-sea-exodus.

140 Carl Drews, "Using Wind Setdown and Storm Surge on Lake Erie to Calibrate the Air-Sea Drag Coefficient," *Plos One* 8(8) (August 19, 2013): https://journals.plos.org/plosone/article?id=10.1371/journal.pone.0072510.

141 Mark Weiss, "Israel's nomadic Bedouins at odds with modernised state," *Irish Times* (3 January 2021): https://www.irishtimes.com/news/world/middle-east/israel-s-nomadic-bedouins-at-odds-with-modernised-state-1.4449178.

142 "The Exodus is Not Fiction," *ReformJudaism.org* (Spring 2014): https://reformjudaism.org/exodus-not-fiction.

143 Kenneth A. Kitchen, "Archaeology and the Hebrew Exodus," *Theology Network*, https://theologynetwork.uk/think/archaeology-and-the-hebrew-exodus.

144 Kenneth A. Kitchen, *On the Reliability of the Old Testament* (Grand Rapids and Cambridge: Wm. B. Eerdmans Publishing, 2003), 273.

145 Piotr Zduniak & Reuven Yosef, "Age and sex determine the phenology and biometrics of migratory Common Quail (*Coturnix coturnix*) at Eilat, Israel," *Ornis Fennica* Vol. 85 (2008): https://lintulehti.birdlife.fi:8443/pdf/artikkelit/190/tiedosto/of_85_37-45_artikkelit_190.pdf.

146 John Wilkinson, "The Quail Epidemic of Numbers 11.31–34," *The Evangelical*

Quarterly 71:3 (1999), 195–208; citation from 196–197: https://biblicalstudies.org.uk/pdf/eq/1999-3_195.pdf.

147 "Brown Quail: Basic Information," *Birds in Backyards* (February 6, 2011): https://www.birdsinbackyards.net/species/Coturnix-ypsilophora.

148 John Wilkinson, "The Quail Epidemic of Numbers 11.31–34,": https://biblicalstudies.org.uk/pdf/eq/1999-3_195.pdf. "NEB" = New English Bible. "REB" = Revised English Bible.

149 James L. Tullis, M.D., "Don't Eat the Quails," *New England Journal of Medicine* 297, No. 9 (1977), 472–475: https://www.massmed.org/about/mms-leadership/history/don-t-eat-the-quails/.

150 Adam Welz, "Jonathan Franzen: 'Egypt is the worst place to be a migratory bird,'" *The Guardian* (July 19, 2013): https://www.theguardian.com/environment/nature-up/2013/jul/19/jonathan-franzen-egypt-migratory-bird.

151 P. Eason, B. Rabia, and O. Attum, "Hunting of migratory birds in North Sinai, Egypt," *Bird Conservation International* 26 (1) (2016): 39–51 (25): https://www.researchgate.net/publication/284560515_Hunting_of_migratory_birds_in_North_Sinai_Egypt.

152 Kenneth A. Kitchen, *On the Reliability of the Old Testament*, 191–192.

153 Y. Klinger et al, "Seismic behaviour of the Dead Sea fault along Araba valley, Jordan," *Geophysical Journal International* Vol. 142, Issue 3 (September 2000): 769–782: https://academic.oup.com/gji/article/142/3/769/611025.

154 Colin Humphreys, "Science and the Miracles of Exodus," *Europhysics News* (May/June 2005): https://www.europhysicsnews.org/articles/epn/pdf/2005/03/epn05306.pdf.

155 "Sinai Peninsula: An Overview of Geology and Thermal Groundwater Potentialities": pages 25–38 of the book by Mohamed Ragaie El Tahlawi, *Thermal and Mineral Waters* (New York: Springer, 2014): https://www.researchgate.net/publication/300723080_Sinai_Peninsula_An_Overview_of_Geology_and_Thermal_Groundwater_Potentialities.

156 Arie S. Issar, *Water Shall Flow from the Rock: Hydrogeology and Climate in the Lands of the Bible*: https://link.springer.com/content/pdf/bfm:978-3-642-75028-1/1.pdf.

157 Kenneth A. Kitchen, *On the Reliability of the Old Testament* (Grand Rapids and Cambridge: Wm. B. Eerdmans Publishing, 2003), 167. For further

documentation of these three events, see J. Garstang, *Joshua Judges* (London: Constable, 1931), 126, 136–138).

158 "Earthquakes in History and Archaeology," *Israel Tours*: https://israel-tourguide.info/2011/01/10/earthquakes-history-archaeology.

159 Bart Ehrman, "Israel's Conquest of the Promised Land: Did Any of That Happen?" *The Bart Ehrman Blog* (August 25, 2021): https://ehrmanblog.org/the-conquest-of-the-promised-land-did-any-of-that-happen.

160 Jonathan MS Pearce, "The Exodus Debunked: Coming Out of Egypt," *OnlySky* (March 19, 2018): https://onlysky.media/jpearce/exodus-debunked-coming-egypt.

161 Kenneth A. Kitchen, *On the Reliability of the Old Testament*, 187.

162 "Weathering," *National Geographic*, https://www.nationalgeographic.org/encyclopedia/weathering/print.

163 Avraham Negev and Shimon Gibson, *Archaeological Encyclopedia of the Holy Land* (New York: Continuum, revised edition of 2001), "Jericho," 258–259.

164 "Climate and Average Weather Year Round in Jericho," *Weather Spark*: https://weatherspark.com/y/98833/Average-Weather-in-Jericho-Palestinian-Territories-Year-Round.

165 Adam Zertal, "Mt. Ebal," in Ephraim Stern (ed.), *The New Encyclopedia of Archaeological Excavations in the Holy Land* (Jerusalem: Carta, 1993): see pages 375–377.

166 Adam Zertal, "Mt. Ebal," in Eric M. Meyers (ed.), *The Oxford Encyclopedia of Archaeology in the Near East* (Oxford University Press, 1996), 179–180.

167 Adam Zertal, "Joshua's Altar on Mt. Ebal or Mt. Gerizim?," *Bible.ca*: https://www.bible.ca/archeology/bible-archeology-altar-of-joshua.htm.

168 Adam Zertal, "Has Joshua's Altar been Found on Mount Ebal?," *Biblical Archaeology Review* 11 (1985): 26–44: https://www.bible.ca/archeology/bible-archeology-altar-of-joshua.htm.

169 Adam Zertal, "Joshua's Altar on Mt. Ebal or Mt. Gerizim?": https://www.bible.ca/archeology/bible-archeology-altar-of-joshua.htm.

170 Adam Zertal, "Shechem and Mount Ebal in the Bible: is This Indeed Joshua's Altar?," *The Cult Site on Mt. 'Ebal*: http://ebal.haifa.ac.il/ebal06.html.

171 Richard S. Hess, in John H. Walton (ed.), *Zondervan Illustrated Bible Backgrounds Commentary: Joshua, Judges, Ruth, 1 & 2 Samuel* (Grand Rapids, MI: Zondervan, 2009), 39.

172 Kenneth A. Kitchen, *On the Reliability of the Old Testament*, 185.

173 James K. Hoffmeier, *Israel in Egypt: The Evidence for the Authenticity of the Exodus Tradition* (New York, Oxford: Oxford University Press, 1996), 35.

174 Eero Junkkaala, *Three Conquests of Canaan: A Comparative Study of Two Egyptian Military Campaigns and Joshua 10–12 in the Light of Recent Archaeological Evidence* (Turku, Finland: Abo Akademi University Press, 2006); citations from pages 230–231, 233–234: https://core.ac.uk/download/pdf/39937804.pdf.

175 *Id.*, 235–236, 238.

176 *Id.*, 238–239.

177 Kenneth A. Kitchen, *On the Reliability of the Old Testament*, 186.

178 Avraham Negev and Shimon Gibson, *Archaeological Encyclopedia of the Holy Land*, 221.

179 Bruce K. Waltke, "The Date of the Conquest," *Westminster Theological Journal* 52.2 (Fall 1990): 181–200; citation from pages 197–198: https://biblicalstudies.org.uk/article_date_waltke.html.

180 Additional source cited in Waltke's article: Israel Finkelstein, *The Archaeology of the Israelite Settlement* (Jerusalem: Israel Exploration Society, 1988), 39.

181 Kenneth A. Kitchen, *On the Reliability of the Old Testament*, 186.

182 *Id.*, 183.

183 James K. Hoffmeier, *Israel in Egypt*, 34–35.

184 *Id.*, 36.

185 *Id.*, 43–44.

186 Kenneth A. Kitchen, *On the Reliability of the Old Testament*, 189–190.

187 See Dave Armstrong, "Archaeology Verifies 13th c. BC Cities Listed in Joshua," *Biblical Evidence for Catholicism* (August 5, 2021): https://www.patheos.com/blogs/davearmstrong/2021/08/archaeology-verifies-13th-c-bc-cities-listed-in-joshua.html.

188 Kenneth A. Kitchen, *On the Reliability of the Old Testament*, 189.

189 Ruth Margalit, "In Search of King David's Lost Empire," *The New Yorker* (June 22, 2020): https://www.newyorker.com/magazine/2020/06/29/in-search-of-king-davids-lost-empire.

190 Philip R. Davies, "'House of David' Built on Sand: The Sins of the Biblical Maximizers," *Bible Archaeology Report* 20:04 (July/August 1994), 55.

191 Cited in Ruth Margalit, "In Search of King David's Lost Empire": https://www.

newyorker.com/magazine/2020/06/29/in-search-of-king-davids-lost-empire.

192 Cited in Sebastian Kettley, "Archaeology news: 'Incredible artefact testifies to the existence' of Bible's King David," *Express UK* (February 15, 2021): https://www.express.co.uk/news/science/1397280/archaeology-news-artefact-king-david-tel-dan-stele-bible-israel-evg.

193 Cited in David Keys, "Leading archaeologist says Old Testament stories are fiction," *Independent* (March 28, 1993): https://www.independent.co.uk/news/leading-archaeologist-says-old-testament-storeis-are-fiction-1500431.html.

194 Eric H. Cline, "Did David and Solomon Exist?," *The Bible and Interpretation* (October 2009): https://bibleinterp.arizona.edu/articles/cline35709.

195 Israel Finkelstein and Amihay Mazar, *The Quest for the Historical Israel: Debating Archaeology and the History of Early Israel* (Atlanta: Society of Biblical Literature, 2007), 14: https://books.google.com/books?id=jpbngoKHg8gC&q=tel+dan+stele#v=snippet&q=tel%20dan%20stele&f=false.

196 "The Mesha Stele, or Moabite Stone, a Non-Biblical Text, Confirms Some Events in the Biblical Book of Kings," *History of Information*: https://www.historyofinformation.com/detail.php?id=5053.

197 Amanda Borschel-Dan, "High-tech study of ancient stone suggests new proof of King David's dynasty," *The Times of Israel* (May 3, 2019): https://www.timesofisrael.com/high-tech-study-of-ancient-stone-keeps-davidic-dynasty-in-disputed-inscription/.

198 *Ibid.*

199 Avraham Negev and Shimon Gibson (eds.), "Bulla," in *Archaeological Encyclopedia of the Holy Land* (New York and London: Continuum, revised edition of 2001), 93–94.

200 Archaeologists Find Section of First Temple-Period Jerusalem's City Wall," *Science News* (July 15, 2021): http://www.sci-news.com/archaeology/first-temple-period-jerusalems-city-wall-09866.html.

201 Yosef Garfinkel, Saar Ganor, and Michael G. Hasel, *In the Footsteps of King David: Revelations from an Ancient Biblical City* (London: Thames & Hudson Ltd, 2018), 47, 48, 95.

202 *Id.*, 121.

203 *Id.*, 124–126.

204 Nir Hasson, "Did King David's United Monarchy Exist? Naked Mole Rats Uncover Monumental Evidence," *Haaretz* (April 19, 2018): https://www.haaretz.com/archaeology/.premium.MAGAZINE-molerat-archaeology-supports-united-monarchy-theory-says-new-study-1.6007916.

205 Amanda Borschel-Dan, "Proof of King David? Not yet. But riveting site shores up roots of Israelite era," *The Times of Israel* (May 14, 2018): https://www.timesofisrael.com/proof-of-king-david-not-yet-but-riveting-site-shores-up-roots-of-israelite-era. See also the cited lengthy scholarly report from Avraham Faust and Yair Sapir, "The 'Governor's Residency' at Tel Eton, The United Monarchy, and the Impact of the Old-House Effect on Large-Scale Archaeological Reconstructions," *Radiocarbon* (March 13, 2018), published by Cambridge University Press: https://www.cambridge.org/core/journals/radiocarbon/article/governors-residency-at-tel-eton-the-united-monarchy-and-the-impact-of-the-oldhouse-effect-on-largescale-archaeological-reconstructions/5CE54AE6CEE838CC0D076186A2FBACE5.

206 James Rogers, "Biblical city with links to King David discovered in southern Israel," *Fox News* (July 9, 2019): https://www.foxnews.com/science/biblical-city-king-david-israel.

207 James Rogers, "Ancient city gate from the time of King David discovered in Israel," *Fox News* (June 21, 2019): https://www.foxnews.com/science/city-gate-from-time-of-king-david-discovered-israel.

208 Zachary Keyser, "Archaeologists identify city gate from time of King David," *Jerusalem Post* (July 8, 2019): https://www.jpost.com/Israel-News/Archaeologists-discover-city-gate-from-time-of-King-David-591653.

209 Avraham Negev and Shimon Gibson (eds.), *Archaeological Encyclopedia of the Holy Land* (New York and London: Continuum, revised edition of 2001), "Bethsaida," 81.

210 Josephus, *Antiquities of the Jews*, Book XII, ch. 8, sec. 6: https://www.gutenberg.org/files/2848/2848-h/2848-h.htm#link122HCH0008.

211 Leibel Reznick, "Did Hebron Disappear?," *Aish* (May 8, 2009): https://aish.com/48964966.

212 Steven Austin, G.W. Franz, and Eric Frost, "Amos's earthquake: An extraordinary Middle East seismic event of 750 BC," *International Geology*

Review 42(7) (July 2000): 657–671; citation from Abstract, 657: https://www.researchgate.net/publication/298846141_Amos%27s_earthquake_An_extraordinary_Middle_East_seismic_event_of_750_BC.

213 Ruth Schuster, "Fact-checking the Book of Amos: There Was a Huge Quake in Eighth Century B.C.E.," *Haaretz* (January 3, 2019): https://www.haaretz.com/archaeology/.premium.MAGAZINE-fact-checking-the-book-of-amos-there-was-a-huge-quake-in-eighth-century-b-c-e-1.6807298.

214 Shmuel Marco and Amotz Agnon, "High-resolution stratigraphy reveals repeated earthquake faulting in the Masada Fault Zone, Dead Sea Transform," *Tectonophysics* 408 (2005) 101–112: https://www.tau.ac.il/~shmulikm/Publications/Masada_ms.pdf.

215 Rossella Tercatin, "Evidence of 2,800-year-old biblical earthquake found in Jerusalem," *The Jerusalem Post* (August 4, 2021): https://www.jpost.com/archaeology/evidence-of-2800-year-old-biblical-earthquake-found-in-jerusalem-675809.

216 Amanda Borschel-Dan, "Archaeologists unearth 1st Jerusalem evidence of quake from Bible's Book of Amos," *The Times of Israel* (August 4, 2021): https://www.timesofisrael.com/archaeologists-unearth-1st-jerusalem-evidence-of-quake-from-bibles-book-of-amos.

217 Livia Gershon, "Researchers Find Physical Evidence of Earthquake Described in Old Testament," *Smithsonian Magazine* (August 6, 2021): https://www.smithsonianmag.com/smart-news/scientists-find-evidence-8th-century-bc-earthquake-described-old-testament-180978385.

218 "Isaiah," *Jewish Virtual Library*: https://www.jewishvirtuallibrary.org/isaiah.

219 Will Heilpern, "Biblical King's seal discovered in dump site," *CNN* (December 4, 2015): https://edition.cnn.com/2015/12/03/middleeast/king-hezekiah-royal-seal/index.html.

220 Eilat Mazar, "Is This the Prophet Isaiah's Signature?," *Biblical Archaeology Review* 44:2 (March-June 2018): https://www.baslibrary.org/biblical-archaeology-review/44/2/7.

221 Terrence McCoy, "More reasons why the Greek poet Homer may never have existed," *The Washington Post* (January 6, 2015): https://www.washingtonpost.com/news/morning-mix/wp/2015/01/06/more-reasons-why-the-greek-poet-

homer-may-never-have-existed.

222 Leibel Reznick, "Biblical Archeology: Bringing the Bible to Life: Independent sources confirm many of the major and minor characters of the Bible," *Aish* (July 12, 2015): https://aish.com/48969466.

223 See Hayim Tadmor, *The Inscriptions of Tiglath-pileser III King of Assyria* (Jerusalem: Israel Academy of Sciences and Humanities, 1994), 170–171, and James B. Pritchard, *Ancient Near Eastern Texts* (Princeton University Press, 1950), 282, as well as several seals and bullae. See also *Biblical Archaeology Review* 24:03 (May/ June 1998) and Oded Bustanay, *Ahaz's appeal to Tiglath-Pileser III in the Context of the Assyrian Policy of Expansion* (vol. 3, University of Haifa, 1993), 63–71.

224 See Anthony J. Spalinger, "Esarhaddon and Egypt: An analysis of the First Invasion of Egypt," *Orientalia* Vol. 43 (1974), 295–326 and Donald J. Wiseman, "An Esarhaddon cylinder from Nimrud," *Iraq* Vol.14 (1952), 54–60 and Albrecht Goetze, "Esarhaddon's Inscription from the Inanna Temple in Nippur," *Journal of Cuneiform Studies* Vol. 17 (1963), 119–131.

225 See Nahman Avigad, "The Jotham Seal from Elath," *Bulletin of the American Schools of Oriental Research* Vol. 163 (1961), 8–22 and *Biblical Archaeology Review* 24:03 (May/June 1998). Jotham reigned as King of Judah from c. 750–735 B.C.

226 See James B. Pritchard, *Ancient Near Eastern Texts* (Princeton University Press: 1950), 284, and Hayim Tadmor, *The inscriptions of Tiglath-pileser III King of Assyria* (Jerusalem: Israel Academy of Sciences and Humanities, 1994), 140–141.

227 See Kenneth A. Kitchen, *On the Reliability of the Old Testament* (Grand Rapids, MI: Wm. B. Eerdmans Publishing, 2003), 503, note 13.

228 See Robert D. Biggs and John A. Brinkman, *From the Workshop of the Chicago Assyrian Dictionary: Studies Presented to A. Leo Oppenheim* (Chicago University Press, 1964), 50–53.

229 Kenneth A. Kitchen, *The Third Intermediate Period in Egypt (1100–650 BC)* (Oxford: Aris & Phillips Ltd., 1996), 380–391; 161.

230 Laura Sexton, "Book of Jeremiah Confirmed?," *Archaeological Institute of America* (July 23, 2007): https://archive.archaeology.org/online/features/jeremiah.See also Hillel Fendel, "Babylonian King's Eunuch Really Existed!," *Israel National News* (November 7, 2007): https://www.israelnationalnews.com/news/123041.

As to Samgar-nebo (Jer. 39:3), an official in Nebuchadnezzar's court, a cuneiform tablet discovered in 1920 near Baghdad confirmed his existence. See Fendel, *id.*

231 Sebastian Kettley, "Archaeology news: Ancient seals unearthed in Israel prove Biblical prophet existed - claim," *The Express* (March 1, 2021): https://www.express.co.uk/news/science/1402594/archaeology-news-ancient-seals-jerusalem-israel-prove-bible-prophet-jeremiah-existed-evg.

232 John Oakes, "Is there any historical or archaeological evidence outside the Bible for the prophets of Israel such as Daniel and Jeremiah?," *Evidence for Christianity* (July 13, 2020): https://evidenceforchristianity.org/is-there-any-historical-or-archaeological-evidence-outside-the-bible-for-the-prophets-of-israel-such-as-daniel-and-jeremiah.

233 Leibel Reznick, "Biblical Archeology: Bringing the Bible to Life: Independent sources confirm many of the major and minor characters of the Bible": https://aish.com/48969466.

234 See Nachum Avigad and Binyamin Sass, *Corpus of West Semitic Stamp Seals* (Jerusalem: Israel Academy, Israel Exploration Society, Israel Institute of Archaeology, Hebrew University: 1997), 181–182.

235 Leibel Reznick, "Biblical Archeology: Bringing the Bible to Life: Independent sources confirm many of the major and minor characters of the Bible": https://aish.com/48969466. See *Biblical Archaeology Review* (Mar/Apr 1999).

236 *Ibid.*

237 Etgar Lefkovits, "Seal of King Zedekiah's minister found in J'lem dig," *The Jerusalem Post* (July 31, 2008): https://www.jpost.com/Local-Israel/In-Jerusalem/Seal-of-King-Zedekiahs-minister-found-in-Jlem-dig.

238 Leibel Reznick, "Biblical Archeology: Bringing the Bible to Life: Independent sources confirm many of the major and minor characters of the Bible": https://aish.com/48969466. See *Biblical Archaeology Review* 13:05 (Sept/Oct 1987).

239 See Nadav Naaman, "Hezekiah's Fortified Cities and the LMLK Stamps," *Bulletin of the American Schools of Oriental Research* Vol. 261 (1986), 5–2, and *Biblical Archaeology Review* 01:04 (1975).

240 See *Biblical Archaeology Review* 13:05 (Sept/Oct 1987).

241 See James B. Pritchard, *Ancient Near Eastern Texts* (Princeton University Press, 1950), 308. Ration Tablets or Tables: http://helpmewithbiblestudy.

org/17Archeology/InscriptionBabylonianRationTablets.aspx.

242 Leibel Reznick, "Biblical Archeology: Bringing the Bible to Life: Independent sources confirm many of the major and minor characters of the Bible": https://aish.com/48969466. See Rena Rossner, "The once and future city," *The Jerusalem Post* (January 26, 2006): https://www.jpost.com/Local-Israel/In-Jerusalem/The-once-and-future-city.

243 See *Biblical Archaeology Review* 13:05 (Sept/Oct 1987).

244 James B. Pritchard, *Ancient Near Eastern Texts*, 291.

245 See *Biblical Archaeology Review* 17:04 (Jul/Aug 1991).

246 Leibel Reznick, "Biblical Archeology: Bringing the Bible to Life: Independent sources confirm many of the major and minor characters of the Bible": https://aish.com/48969466.

247 Jim Davila, "Archaeology, history, and the Book of Daniel," *PaleoJudaica.com* (September 6, 2022): https://paleojudaica.blogspot.com/2022/09/archaeology-history-and-book-of-daniel.html.

248 "The Cyrus Cylinder," *British Museum*: https://www.britishmuseum.org/collection/object/W_1880-0617-1941.

249 Josephus, *Antiquities of the Jews*, Book XI: https://penelope.uchicago.edu/josephus/ant-11.html.

250 "The Nabonidus Cylinder from Sippar," *Livius*: https://web.archive.org/web/20070207104255/http://www.livius.org/na-nd/nabonidus/cylinder.html.

251 Donald J. Wiseman, "Babylonia 605–539 B.C.," in John Boardman et al (eds.), *The Cambridge Ancient History: III Part 2: The Assyrian and Babylonian Empires and Other States of the Near East, from the Eighth to the Sixth Centuries B.C.*, second edition (Cambridge University Press, 1991), 247–248: https://books.google.com/books?id=OGBGauNBK8kC&q=Neriglissar#v=snippet&q=tema&f=false.

252 Clyde E. Fant and Mitchell G. Reddish, *Lost Treasures of the Bible: Understanding the Bible Through Archaeological Artifacts in World Museums* (Grand Rapids, MI: Wm. B. Eerdmans Publishing, 2008), 228.

253 Translation (possibly by Michael Jursa) found in Nigel Reynolds, "Tiny Tablet provides proof for Old Testament," *Telegraph* (July 13, 2007): https://web.archive.org/web/20070914043526/http://www.telegraph.co.uk/news/main.jht

ml?xml=%2Fnews%2F2007%2F07%2F11%2Fntablet111.xml.

254 "Nebo-Sarsekim Tablet," *Help Me With Bible Study*: http://helpmewithbiblestudy.org/17Archeology/InscriptionNeboSarsekim.aspx.

255 "15 Scariest Mental Disorders of All Time," *Online Psychology Degree Guide*: https://www.onlinepsychologydegree.info/terrifying-mental-disorders.

256 James A. Montgomery, *A Critical and Exegetical Commentary on the Book of Daniel* (Edinburgh: T. & T. Clark, 1927): https://biblicalstudies.org.uk/pdf/e-books/montgomery_james-a/daniel_montgomery.pdf.

257 Tawny L. Holm, "The fiery furnace in the book of Daniel and the ancient Near East," *Journal of the American Oriental Society* (January 1, 2008): https://www.thefreelibrary.com/The+fiery+furnace+in+the+book+of+Daniel+and+the+ancient+Near+East.-a0201100572.

258 "Lion hunting: The sport of kings," *British Museum*: https://www.britishmuseum.org/blog/lion-hunting-sport-kings.

259 "Lion Hunting Scene—750 BC," *Joy of Museums*: https://joyofmuseums.com/museums/europe/germany-museums/berlin-museums/the-pergamon-museum/lion-hunting-scene-750-bc.

260 Eran Almagor, "The Horse and the Lion in Achaemenid Persia: Representations of a Duality," *Arts 10*(3), 41 (June 23, 2021); special issue, "Animals in Ancient Material Cultures (vol. 1)": https://www.mdpi.com/2076-0752/10/3/41/htm.

261 See Frederick M. Fales, "Old Aramaic," in Stefan Weninger et al (eds.), *The Semitic Languages: An International Handbook.* (Berlin-Boston: Walter de Gruyter, 2012), 555–73. See also Klaus Beyer, *The Aramaic Language: Its Distribution and Subdivisions* (Göttingen: Vandenhoeck & Ruprecht: 1986), 14.

262 Zdravko Stefanovic, doctoral dissertation: *Correlations between Old Aramaic Inscriptions and the Aramaic Section of Daniel*: https://digitalcommons.andrews.edu/cgi/viewcontent.cgi?article=1145&context=dissertations.

263 S.R. Driver, *An Introduction to the Literature of the Old Testament* (New York: Meridian Books, 1957; originally published in 1891), 508.

264 E.B. Pusey, *Daniel the Prophet* (Oxford: James Parker & Co. / London: Rivingtons): https://archive.org/details/a604991500puseuoft/page/648/mode/2up.

265 Kenneth A. Kitchen, "The Aramaic of Daniel," in *Notes on Some Problems in the*

Book of Daniel (London: Tyndale, 1970), 43; italics in original.

266 Prods Oktor Skjærvø, *An Introduction to Old Persian* (Cambridge, Harvard: 2nd ed., 2005): https://web.archive.org/web/20170402172708/http://www.fas.harvard.edu/~iranian/OldPersian/opcomplete.pdf.

267 "Magi," in William Smith; revised by Charles Anthon, *A New Classical Dictionary of Greek and Roman Biography Mythology and Geography Partly Based Upon the Dictionary of Greek and Roman Biography and Mythology* (New York: Harper & Brothers, 1878), 469: https://books.google.com/books?id=6noOAAAAYAAJ&newbks=1&newbks_redir=0&source=gbs_navlinks_s.

268 Walter Drum, "Magi," *Catholic Encyclopedia* (1910): https://www.newadvent.org/cathen/09527a.htm.

269 *Ibid.*

270 "Camel Fact Sheet," *PBS* (September 17, 2020): https://www.pbs.org/wnet/nature/blog/camel-fact-sheet.

271 Bryant G. Wood, "The Israelites and The Kings Highway," *Bible and Spade* Vol. 07:4 (Autumn 1978): https://www.biblia.work/sermons/theisraelites-and-the-kings-highway-2.

272 "Desert Survival: Water," *PBS / Lawrence of Arabia*: https://www.pbs.org/lawrenceofarabia/revolt/water.html.

273 John Mosley, "Common Errors in 'Star of Bethlehem' Planetarium Shows," *Planetarian* (Third Quarter 1981): https://www.ips-planetarium.org/page/a_mosley1981.

274 John A. Cramer, "Herod's Death, Jesus' Birth and a Lunar Eclipse: Letters to the Editor debate dates of Herod's death and Jesus' birth," *Bible History Daily /* Biblical Archaeology Society (November 30, 2020; originally January 7, 2015): https://www.biblicalarchaeology.org/daily/people-cultures-in-the-bible/jesus-historical-jesus/herods-death-jesus-birth-and-a-lunar-eclipse.

275 Josephus, *Antiquities of the Jews,* Book XVII, ch. 9, sec. 3: https://penelope.uchicago.edu/josephus/ant-17.html; *The Jewish War* II. 1.3: http://penelope.uchicago.edu/josephus/war-2.html.

276 John A. Cramer, "Herod's Death, Jesus' Birth and a Lunar Eclipse: Letters to the Editor debate dates of Herod's death and Jesus' birth": https://www.biblicalarchaeology.org/daily/people-cultures-in-the-bible/jesus-historical-

jesus/herods-death-jesus-birth-and-a-lunar-eclipse.

277 Jack Finegan, *Handbook of Biblical Chronology* (Grand Rapids, MI: Hendrickson, 1998), 298–299.

278 See "Phenomenological language in Scripture," *CathInfo.com* (February 13, 2018): https://www.cathinfo.com/the-earth-god-made-flat-earth-geocentrism/phenomenological-language-in-scripture.

279 Dag Kihlman, *The Star of Bethlehem and Babylonian Astrology: Astronomy and Revelation Reveal What the Magi Saw* (self-published, 2017), 97–98.

280 Christopher Crockett, "What is retrograde motion?," *EarthSky* (February 6, 2017): https://web.archive.org/web/20220418193828/https://earthsky.org/astronomy-essentials/what-is-retrograde-motion/. See also (with fun moving diagrams!): "Retrograde motion can be real or illusory," *EarthSky* (May 10, 2022): https://earthsky.org/astronomy-essentials/what-is-retrograde-motion/.

281 Ernest L. Martin, *The Star That Astonished the World* (1991), available online at *Associates for Scriptural Knowledge*: https://www.askelm.com/star/index.asp.

282 R.T. France, *The Gospel According to Matthew: An Introduction and Commentary* (Grand Rapids, MI: Wm. B. Eerdmans Publishing, 1985), 84: https://www.amazon.com/Matthew-Introduction-Commentary-Testament-Commentaries/dp/0830842314.

283 D.A. Carson, *Matthew*; part of *The Expositor's Bible Commentary* (Grand Rapids, MI: Zondervan Academic, revised ed., 2017), page undetermined at the Google Books page: https://www.amazon.com/Matthew-Expositors-Bible-Commentary-Carson-ebook/dp/B01N2BKWIG.

284 Peter Pett, *Pett's Commentary on the Bible* (2013): https://www.studylight.org/commentaries/eng/pet/matthew-2.html#verse-9.

285 Ivor Bulmer-Thomas, "Star of Bethlehem," *Quarterly Journal of the Royal Astronomical Society* Vol. 33 (December 1992), 371: https://articles.adsabs.harvard.edu/full/1992QJRAS..33..363B/0000370.000.html.

286 See my own articles: "Was Christ Actually Born Dec. 25?," *National Catholic Register* (December 18, 2018): http://www.ncregister.com/blog/darmstrong/was-christ-actually-born-dec.-25; "Christmas & Dec. 25th: *Not* Derived from Saturnalia (Nor from *Sol Invictus* . . .)," *Biblical Evidence for Catholicism* (December 8, 2021): https://www.patheos.com/blogs/davearmstrong/2021/12/

christmas-dec-25th-not-derived-from-saturnalia.html; "Hippolytus (early 3rd c.) & a December 25th Christmas," *Biblical Evidence for Catholicism* (December 10, 2021): https://www.patheos.com/blogs/davearmstrong/2021/12/hippolytus-early-3rd-c-a-december-25th-christmas.html.

287 For extensive argumentation regarding a date for the death of Herod and the birth of Jesus, see James A. Nollet, "Astronomical and Historical Evidence for Dating the Nativity in 2 B.C.," *Perspectives on Science and Christian Faith* Vol. 64, No. 4 (December 2012): 211–219: https://www.asa3.org/ASA/PSCF/2012/PSCF12-12Nollet.pdf. I opt for 3 B.C. rather than 2 B.C., based on the wise men's visit a year or two *after* Jesus' birth (not the night he was born) and the astronomical data. But Nollet allows for the plausible possibility of "between 3 B.C. and 1 B.C." Another helpful article on the same topics, as well as the "Quirinius controversy" and the census or enrollment called by Caesar Augustus, is Jimmy Akin, "The Enrollment of Jesus' Birth," JimmyAkin.com (March 9, 2022): http://jimmyakin.com/2022/03/the-enrollment-of-jesus-birth.html.

288 Amanda Borschel-Dan, "What do we know about Nazareth in Jesus' time? An archaeologist explains," *The Times of Israel* (July 22, 2020): https://www.timesofisrael.com/listen-what-do-we-know-about-nazareth-in-jesus-time-an-archaeologist-explains. See also my own article, "Archaeology & 1st Century Nazareth," *Biblical Evidence for Catholicism* (February 25, 2022): https://www.patheos.com/blogs/davearmstrong/2022/02/pearces-potshots-64-archaeology-1st-century-nazareth.html.

289 John Hogg, "On the City of Abila, and the District Called Abilene near Mount Lebanon, and on a Latin Inscription at the River Lycus, in the North of Syria," *Journal of the Royal Geographical Society of London* Vol. 20 (1850), 43: https://archive.org/details/jstor-1798016/mode/2up.

290 Josephus, *Antiquities of the Jews*, Book XIX, ch. 5, sec. 1: https://penelope.uchicago.edu/josephus/ant-19.html.

291 *Id.*, Book XVII, ch. 8, sec. 1: https://penelope.uchicago.edu/josephus/ant-17.html.

292 Jerry Vardaman, "A New Inscription Which Mentions Pilate as 'Prefect,'" *Journal of Biblical Literature* Vol. 81 (1962): 70-71.

293 Josephus, *Antiquities of the Jews*, Book XVIII, ch. 2, sec. 2: https://penelope.uchicago.edu/josephus/ant-18.html.

294 *Bible Archaeology Review* 18:05 (Sep/Oct 1992): https://www.baslibrary.org/biblical-archaeology-review/18/5/7.

295 "Israeli authorities: 2,000-year-old burial box is the real deal," *CNN*, (June 30, 2011): http://www.cnn.com/2011/WORLD/meast/06/29/israel.ancient.burial/index.html.

296 Abraham Rabinovich, "'Jesus Boat' Causes Ripples," *Jerusalem Post* (1999): https://web.archive.org/web/20091229182509/http://christianactionforisrael.org/isreport/jboat.html.

297 "Capernaum-City of Jesus and its Jewish Synagogue," *Israel Ministry of Foreign Affairs* (November 26, 2003). See also my article: "St. Peter's House in Capernaum and Recent Archaeology," *Biblical Evidence for Catholicism* (October 2, 2015): https://www.patheos.com/blogs/davearmstrong/2015/10/archaeology-st-peters-house-in-capernaum.html.

298 Leen Ritmeyer, "The Synagogue of Capernaum in which Jesus taught," *Ritmeyer Archaeological Design* (March 15, 2018): https://www.ritmeyer.com/2018/03/15/the-synagogue-of-capernaum-in-which-jesus-taught.

299 Avraham Negev and Shimon Gibson, *Archaeological Encyclopedia of the Holy Land* (New York and London: Continuum, 2003), "Chorazin," 118–119.

300 Aryeh Kindler, "The Coins of the Tetrarch Philip and Bethsaida," *Cathedra* 53 (September 1989), 26–24 (Hebrew).

301 Stephen Weizman, "Ancient Galilee church unearthed, said to be home to apostles Peter and Andrew," *The Times of Israel* (July 19, 2019): https://www.timesofisrael.com/ancient-galilee-church-unearthed-said-to-be-home-to-apostles-peter-and-andrew.

302 See David W. Chapman, *Ancient Jewish and Christian Perceptions of Crucifixion* (Tübingen: Mohr Siebeck Verlag, 2008), 86-89; David Ingham & Corinne Duhig, "Crucifixion in the Fens: Life and Death in Roman Fenstanton," *British Archaeology* (Jan.-Feb. 2022): https://www.archaeologyuk.org/resource/free-access-to-crucifixion-in-the-fens-life-and-death-in-roman-fenstanton.html.

303 Robert M. Grant, *A Historical Introduction to the New Testament* (Harper and Row, 1963), 149: https://archive.org/details/historicalintrod0000gran/page/144/mode/2up?q=five+thousand.

304 "The Historicity of the book of Acts (3/5)," *Bible Apologetics*, first section:

https://bibleapologetics.wordpress.com/the-historicity-of-the-book-of-acts-35.

305 "How many people heard the Sermon on the Mount? Or the Gettysburg Address?," *Inside Science*/Fox News Channel (October 21, 2015): https://www.foxnews.com/science/how-many-people-heard-the-sermon-on-the-mount-or-the-gettysburg-address.

306 Thomas Kidd, "The Science of Sound: Whitefield's Massive Crowds," *The Gospel Coalition* (January 8, 2014): https://www.thegospelcoalition.org/article/the-science-of-sound-whitefields-massive-crowds.

307 B. Cobbey Crisler, "The Acoustics and Crowd Capacity of Natural Theaters in Palestine," *The Biblical Archaeologist* 39.4 (December 1976), 128–141: https://www.jstor.org/stable/3209424.

308 Rabbi Daniel Cohn, "What Are Pilgrimage Festivals?," *My Jewish Learning*: https://www.myjewishlearning.com/article/pilgrimage-festivals.

309 "The Historicity of the book of Acts (3/5)": https://bibleapologetics.wordpress.com/the-historicity-of-the-book-of-acts-35.

310 Craig S. Hawkins, "The Book of Acts and Archaeology," *Apologetics Information Ministry*: http://bibleinfobrokers.com/wp-content/Resources/Book_of_Acts_and_Archaeology.htm.

311 Josephus, *Antiquities of the Jews*, Book XIX, ch. 8, sec. 2: https://penelope.uchicago.edu/josephus/ant-19.html.

312 "Ascariasis," *Mayo Clinic*: https://www.mayoclinic.org/diseases-conditions/ascariasis/symptoms-causes/syc-20369593.

313 Quan-yue Li et al., "Life-threatening complications of ascariasis in trauma patients: a review of the literature," *World Journal of Emergency Medicine* 5(3) (2014), 165-170: https://www.ncbi.nlm.nih.gov/pmc/articles/PMC4163807.

314 "Parasites—Myiasis," *Centers for Disease Control and Prevention*: https://www.cdc.gov/parasites/myiasis/index.html.

315 A.T. Sandison, "The last illness of Herod the Great, king of Judaea," *Medical History* Oct; 11(4) (1967), 381-388: https://www.cambridge.org/core/services/aop-cambridge-core/content/view/7256FC6EF96AFD96D23AF97FE4E8A2A7/S0025727300012527a.pdf/the-last-illness-of-herod-the-great-king-of-judaea.pdf.

316 "Sergius Paulus, *Easton's Bible Dictionary* (Edinburgh: Thomas Nelson, 3rd ed., 1897): https://www.biblestudytools.com/dictionaries/eastons-bible-dictionary/

sergius-paulus.html.

317 Luigi Palma di Cesnola, *Cyprus: Its Ancient Cities, Tombs, and Temples* (London: John Murray, 1878), 229: https://books.google.com/books?id=Um_PAAAAMAAJ&q=sergius+paulus#v=snippet&q=sergius%20paulus&f=false.

318 Bryan Windle, "Top Ten Discoveries Related to Paul," *Bible Archaeology Report* (May 14, 2021): https://biblearchaeologyreport.com/2021/05/14/top-ten-discoveries-related-to-paul.

319 "Lystra," in James Orr (ed.), *International Standard Bible Encyclopedia* (Grand Rapids, MI: Wm. B. Eerdmans Publishing, 1939): https://www.internationalstandardbible.com/L/lystra.html.

320 Merrill F. Unger, "Archaeology and Paul's Campaign at Philippi," *Bibliotheca Sacra* (April 1962), 153-154: https://biblicalstudies.org.uk/pdf/bsac/1962_150_unger.pdf.

321 Clyde E. Fant and Mitchell G. Reddish, *A Guide to Biblical Sites in Greece and Turkey* (Oxford University Press, 2003), 328-329.

322 David E. Graves, "What is the Madder with Lydia's Purple? A Reexamination of the Purpurarii in Thyatira and Philippi," *Near East Archaeological Society Bulletin* Vol. 62 (January 1, 2017): 3-29: https://www.researchgate.net/publication/321241274_What_is_the_Madder_with_Lydia%27s_Purple_A_Reexamination_of_the_Purpurarii_in_Thyatira_and_Philippi.

323 "Politarch," in Merrill C. Tenney (ed.), *Zondervan Pictorial Encyclopedia of the Bible* (Grand Rapids, MI: Zondervan, 1975).

324 Kyle Butt, "Archaeology and the New Testament," *Apologetics Press*: https://apologeticspress.org/archaeology-and-the-new-testament-1420. See also John McRay, *Archaeology and the New Testament* (Grand Rapids, MI: Baker: 1991), 295.

325 *Ellicott's Commentary for English Readers* (London, 1905): on Acts 17:18: https://biblehub.com/commentaries/ellicott/acts/17.htm.

326 Edwin Yamauchi, *The Stones and the Scriptures: An Introduction to Biblical Archaeology* (Grand Rapids, MI: Baker Book House, 1981), 116.

327 Seneca, *Epistulae Morales ad Lucilium* ("Moral Letters to Lucilius"), also known as the *Moral Epistles* and *Letters from a Stoic*, a collection of 124 letters. The quotation comes from Letter #104 ("On Care of Health and Peace of Mind"—see p. 191): https://archive.org/details/adluciliumepistu03sene/page/190/

mode/2up?view=theater.

328 "The Judgement Seat," in Walter C. Kaiser Jr. and Duane Garrett (eds.), *NIV Archaeological Study Bible* (Grand Rapids, MI: Zondervan, 2005), 1891.

329 Bryan Windle, "Top Ten Discoveries Related to Paul": https://biblearchaeologyreport.com/2021/05/14/top-ten-discoveries-related-to-paul.

330 F.F. Bruce, *Commentary on the Book of Acts* (Grand Rapids, MI: Wm. B. Eerdmans Publishing, 1979), 391–392.

331 Bryan Windle, "Top Ten Discoveries Related to Paul": https://biblearchaeologyreport.com/2021/05/14/top-ten-discoveries-related-to-paul. See also John McRay, "Archaeology and the Book of Acts," *Criswell Theological Review* 5.1 (1990), 77: https://www.scribd.com/document/369669488/Archaeology-the-Book-of-Acts.

332 "Townclerk," in *McClintock and Strong Biblical Cyclopedia* (New York: Harper and Brothers, 1880): https://www.biblicalcyclopedia.com/T/townclerk.html.

333 Clyde E. Fant and Mitchell G. Reddish, *Lost Treasures of the Bible* (Grand Rapids, MI: Wm. B. Eerdmans Publishing, 2008), 328.

334 See Fred Drogula, "The Lex Porcia and the Development of Legal Restraints on Roman Governors," *Chiron* 41 (January 2011), 91-124: https://www.researchgate.net/publication/259592675_The_Lex_Porcia_and_the_Development_of_Legal_Restraints_on_Roman_Governors.

335 Adrian Nicholas Sherwin-White, *The Roman Citizenship* (Oxford: Clarendon Press, 1973), 237-250): https://www.amazon.com/Roman-Citizenship-N-Sherwin-White-dp-019814847X/dp/019814847X/ref=mt_other.

336 Josephus, *Antiquities of the Jews*, Book XX, ch. 5, sec. 2: https://penelope.uchicago.edu/josephus/ant-20.html.

337 *Id.*, ch. 7, sec. 2: https://penelope.uchicago.edu/josephus/ant-20.html.

338 *Id.*, ch. 8, sections 9, 11: https://penelope.uchicago.edu/josephus/ant-20.html.

339 Harry W. Tajra, *The Trial of St. Paul: A Juridical Exegesis of the Second Half of the Acts of the Apostles* (Eugene, OR: Wipf and Stock, 2010), 146; see Chapter VII: "IV. Excursus: The Appeal under the early Emperors" (page 146 is viewable by means of the Amazon "Look Inside" feature): https://www.amazon.com/Trial-St-Paul-Juridical-Exegesis/dp/1610970055/ref=sr_1_1.

340 Josephus, *Antiquities of the Jews*, Book XX, ch. 7, sec. 1: http://penelope.

uchicago.edu/josephus/ant-20.html; *Wars of the Jews*, Book II, ch.12, sec. 8: https://www.gutenberg.org/files/2850/2850-h/2850-h.htm#link22HCH0013. See in particular (as to the title "king") Harold H. Hoehner, *Herod Antipas* (Cambridge University Press, 1972), 108: https://books.google.com/books?id=Aw00tXpMSpIC&pg=PA108#v=onepage&q&f=false.

341 Harold H. Hoehner, *id.*, 108.

342 Baruch Kanael, "Ancient Jewish Coins and Their Historical Importance," *The Biblical Archaeologist* Vol. 26, No. 2 (May 1963), 52: https://www.jstor.org/stable/3210995.

343 Craig S. Hawkins, "The Book of Acts and Archaeology": http://bibleinfobrokers.com/wp-content/Resources/Book_of_Acts_and_Archaeology.htm. He cites Adolf Deissmann, *Light from the Ancient East* (Grand Rapids, MI: Baker Book House, 1980, from the 1978 German edition, translated by Lionel Strachan).

344 F.F. Bruce, *The New Testament Documents: Are They Reliable?*, fifth revised edition (Grand Rapids, MI: Wm. B. Eerdmans Publishing, 1978), 82.

345 "Roman Prisons," *United Nations of Roma Victrix*: https://www.unrv.com/government/roman-prisons.php.

346 Adolf Harnack, *The Acts of the Apostles* (New York: Putnam's Sons, 1909), 299: https://archive.org/details/theactsoftheapos00harnuoft.

347 Rami Arav, "Bethsaida Biblical Archaeology," *University of Nebraska Omaha* (2013): https://web.archive.org/web/20130129204907/http:/world.unomaha.edu/Bethsaida.

348 R.H. Charles, *The Jewish Book of Jubilees* (London: A. and C. Black, 1902), 200: https://archive.org/details/bookofjubileesor00char/page/200/mode/2up.

349 Mishna; Menahot ("the plain of Ein Soker"): http://www.emishnah.com/kadshim_vol_1/Menahot-10.pdf.

350 Urban C. von Wahlde, "Archaeology and John's Gospel," in James H. Charlesworth (ed.), *Jesus and Archaeology* (Grand Rapids, MI: Wm. B. Eerdmans Publishing, 2006), 523-586.

351 "Jacob's Well (2)," in *McClintock and Strong Biblical Cyclopedia* (New York: 1880): https://www.biblicalcyclopedia.com/J/jacobs-well-(2).html.

352 "Jacob's Well," in Merrill C. Tenney (ed.), *Zondervan Pictorial Encyclopedia of the Bible*:

https://www.biblegateway.com/resources/encyclopedia-of-the-bible/Jacobs-Well.

353 J.M. Allegro, *The Treasure of the Copper Scroll* (Garden City, NY: Doubleday, 2nd ed., 1964), 84.

354 Benjamin Mazar, *The Mountain of the Lord* (Garden City, NY: Doubleday, 1975), 202.

355 Urban C. von Wahlde, "The Puzzling Pool of Bethesda," *Biblical Archaeology Review* 37.5 (2011), 40-47, 65: https://webcache.googleusercontent.com/search?q=cache:sbB0ooQK9P8J:https://www.baslibrary.org/biblical-archaeology-review/37/5/4+&cd=18&hl=en&ct=clnk&gl=us.

356 "Archaeologists identify traces of 'miracle' pool" (*NBC News / Associated Press* (December 23, 2004): https://www.nbcnews.com/id/wbna6750670.

357 Hershel Shanks, "The Siloam Pool Where Jesus Cured the Blind Man," *Biblical Archaeology Review* 31 (5) (Sep.-Oct. 2005), 16-23: https://web.archive.org/web/20050917114323/http:/www.bib-arch.org/siloam.pdf.

358 Josephus, *The Wars of the Jews*, Book V, ch. 5, sec. 1: https://www.gutenberg.org/files/2850/2850-h/2850-h.htm#link52HCH0005.

359 Josephus, *Antiquities of the Jews*, Book XX, ch. 9, sec. 7: https://penelope.uchicago.edu/josephus/ant-20.html.

360 *Id.*, Book XVIII, ch. 2, sec. 2: https://penelope.uchicago.edu/josephus/ant-18.html.

361 Kenneth A. Kitchen, *On the Reliability of the Old Testament* (Grand Rapids and Cambridge: Wm. B. Eerdmans Publishing, 2003), 183.

362 *Ibid.*

363 Avraham Negev and Shimon Gibson, *Archaeological Encyclopedia of the Holy Land* (New York and London: Continuum, 2003), 299.

364 Kenneth A. Kitchen, *On the Reliability of the Old Testament*, 184.

365 *Ibid.*, 184.

366 Ilan Ben Zion, "Archaeologists to break ground at biblical site where Ark of the Covenant stood," *The Times of Israel* (11 March 2022): https://www.timesofisrael.com/archaeologists-to-break-ground-at-biblical-site-where-ark-of-the-covenant-stood/.

367 Kenneth A. Kitchen, *On the Reliability of the Old Testament*, 184.

368 Avraham Negev and Shimon Gibson, *Archaeological Encyclopedia of the Holy Land*, "Yarmut," 545.

369 Kenneth A. Kitchen, *On the Reliability of the Old Testament*, 183.

370 Avraham Negev and Shimon Gibson, *Archaeological Encyclopedia of the Holy Land*, "Erani," 166.

371 Kenneth A. Kitchen, *On the Reliability of the Old Testament*, 184.

372 Avraham Negev and Shimon Gibson, *Archaeological Encyclopedia of the Holy Land*, 196-199.

373 *Id.*, "Gaza," 191.

374 *Id.*, "Shimron," 464.

375 *Id.*, "Achshaph," 16.

376 *Id.*, "Kinneret," 285.

377 *Id.*, "Merom," 332.

378 *Id.*, "Sidon," 470.

379 *Id.*, "Misrepoth Maim," 340.

380 *Id.*, "Aroer (a)," 53.

381 Kenneth A. Kitchen, *On the Reliability of the Old Testament*, 185.

382 Avraham Negev and Shimon Gibson, *Archaeological Encyclopedia of the Holy Land*, "Aphek (a)," 38.

383 Kenneth A. Kitchen, *On the Reliability of the Old Testament*, 185.

384 Avraham Negev and Shimon Gibson, *Archaeological Encyclopedia of the Holy Land*, "Taanach," 487.

385 Kenneth A. Kitchen, *On the Reliability of the Old Testament*, 185.

386 *Id.*, 186.

387 Avraham Negev and Shimon Gibson, *Archaeological Encyclopedia of the Holy Land*, "Kedesh (b)," 278.

388 Kenneth A. Kitchen, *On the Reliability of the Old Testament*, 185.

389 Avraham Negev and Shimon Gibson, *Archaeological Encyclopedia of the Holy Land*, "Yoqneam (Tel)," 550.

390 Kenneth A. Kitchen, *On the Reliability of the Old Testament*, 185.

391 Avraham Negev and Shimon Gibson, *Archaeological Encyclopedia of the Holy Land*, "Dor (Tel)," 144.

392 Kenneth A. Kitchen, *On the Reliability of the Old Testament*, 185.

393 Avraham Negev and Shimon Gibson, *Archaeological Encyclopedia of the Holy Land*, "Farah, Tell-El- (North)", 171.